Oscar Burton

Any Porth in a Storm

The Long-Distance Walk that Goes South

S   A Gone South book

First published 2021 by Gone South books
www.anyporthinastorm.com
Text, maps, cover art and design © Oscar Burton 2021
All rights reserved.
ISBN 978-1-8384307-0-2
Typeset in Baskerville
A small number of names, and exact locations, have been changed or omitted to avoid mortification.

001

Dedicated to Sultan,
in search of a safe haven

for FS!

'Any port in a storm. Said when one is in difficulty and has to take whatever refuge, literal or metaphorical, offers itself.'
Ayto, John. *Brewer's Dictionary of Phrase & Fable. Seventeenth Edition*. London: Weidenfeld & Nicolson. 2005

'The great majority of Cornish names are composed of epithets suffixed to certain nouns, such as ... *porth*, a creek or harbour ... There are, however, certain considerations, grammatical and topographical, which should be kept carefully in mind in attempting to discover the meanings of these names, and it is a disregard of these considerations that has made most of the published works on the subject so singularly valueless.'
Jenner, Henry. *Cornish Language Chiefly in its Latest Stages with some Account of its History and Literature*. London: David Nutt, at the Sign of the Phoenix. 1904

'Go south (v.) Deteriorate or decline, as in *The stock market is headed south again*. This expression is generally thought to allude to compasses and two-dimensional maps where north is up and south is down. However, among some Native Americans, the term was a euphemism for dying, and possibly this sense led to the present usage. [Slang: first half of 1900s] Also see GO WEST.'
Ammer, Christine. *The American Heritage Dictionary of Idioms: American English Idiomatic Expressions & Phrases*. 2nd Edition. Boston: Mifflin Houghton. 2013

A short list of misjudgments

N

W · E

S

Eden

Deadman's
Cove

Hell's
Mouth

Also
German Coast

50% Off Point
(no returns)

End of
the Earth

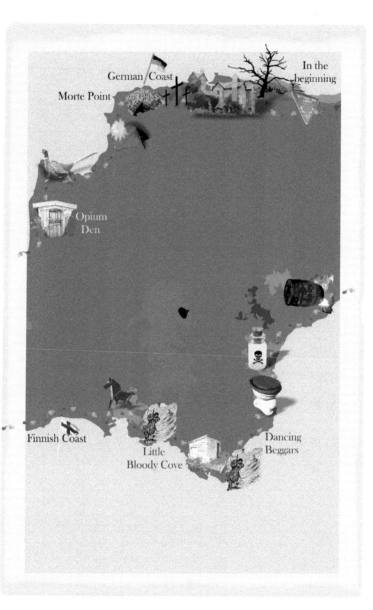

Perrin Beach

In the End

Danger Area

N
W E
S

Prologue

A t the top of the hill I made out a light below. On the descent into the village could be seen what resembled a pub but as I approached, it was clear the sea was encroaching. Waves pounded the windows of the inn, the road covered in rocks and weed. I stood, waiting and timing the backwash between the crashing waves. As the wave hit I bolted through the retreating water, pulling at the door and squeezing myself and backpack between it and the frame.

The wave thudded the windows, like a barking dog reaching the limits of its chain, as I slid into the bar. I was met by the cold stare of its regulars and their chatter stopped with the impact. Facing my audience I dripped methodically, steaming slightly. The waterproof gloves I had bought, clearly from charlatans, in Plymouth hung ridiculously; sodden flippers on the end of my raincoat which clung to my bony limbs. Balloons of water gathered around the ankles of my waterproof trousers, choosing this opportune moment to spill onto the floor.

The bar was full and the customers clearly knew one another, a community wary of strangers. With the whole house focused on me I stood framed in the doorway. I had entered a lock-in. A wake. A West Country republican arms deal.

Three people were seated at the bar, two men and a woman who showed signs of having been drinking throughout the storm (it was only six o'clock). The older man - sideburns, slicked back hair and thick eyebrows - rotated his body from the waist towards the crowd, demanding their attention. This was *Key Largo* and he its Edward G Robinson. He spoke loudly with a Devon accent while looking directly at me.

'We've got another one!' The whole bar broke into laughter. I desperately needed to go to the toilet.

ONE: The Beginning

Germs of sanity

I'd like to say that my main motivation for walking was something philanthropic. I intended to raise money for the homeless and while that played a role, I can't say it was the main reason. Or, that I had an overwhelming need to discover something about myself by taking a long journey. Or even that I just wanted to *get hench* (a colloquial British youth term which I had to look up - it means to have developed musculature). My favourite reason for walking was suggested by Richard, a Buddhist friend - that walking is a primeval urge, a catharsis from the stresses of life. We should call that urge what it really is, obsessive compulsiveness, though lacking any direction offered by a map. I wasn't motivated by any of these things. I was motivated by something else, I just didn't know what it was.

This wasn't the first time I'd been on a journey of discovery. I had travelled extensively in Asia and what I discovered was that I was really not the best person to embark on a quest to find myself. To paraphrase Mick Hucknall of the 80s band *Simply Red,* if you don't know you by now, you're never going to know you. Besides, the idea of spending months by myself would be more tolerable if only the company were better. There was more of misanthropy than philanthropy in me.

It was only when I'd been walking for two weeks and I ran into a stranger that it occurred to me what the real reason might be. He was 49, my age. He was walking for a charity and was covering the whole length of the Path with his own shelter. He even had a similar backpack and rain cover and wore a black merino wool sweater that matched mine. It suddenly occurred to me when I met him in Tintagel, in that pub with Arthurian pretensions, what we were both bent upon and it wasn't necessarily a good thing.

Of course, as I set off from London and then Minehead I wasn't thinking about my motivation, at least not with this level of clarity. I was just someone whose job had ceased to be and who had always wanted to walk the Path - to experience its landscape, art and literature. Well, *always* being since acquiring Paddy Dillon's Cicerone guide to the South West Coast Path in 2004.

The South West Coast Path, I was to find, was littered with people staring at the sea, who had escaped cities - exchanging hedge funds for hedges. They nurtured the germ of sanity, which told them that they could change, that there was more to life than this.

A recent event explains at least the timing of the journey. I worked in the international division of a humanitarian organisation and my days were numbered. I had worked in Afghanistan, northern Balochistan, Mongolia, Kosovo, Kyrgyzstan. These locations may, in part, explain my decision to walk the coast; they all had rubbish beaches.

In my place of work public health was no longer in high demand. A series of casual remarks and our removal from plans indicated that we had become the unwelcome guest at dinner. My redundancy was announced 12 years to the day from my start date, July 2nd, 2007 – this day also being the midpoint of the year – with as many days in front of it as behind it. July 2nd is the Gregorian calendar limbo.

Exactly 12 years earlier I had moved to London. That first working day, July 2nd, was one I remember clearly because it was the morning my motorcycle was set on fire. I had been in London, my bike in Oxford. I missed the display because I was lying on the slightly waxy floor of a massage therapist, a friend who had offered me temporary residence when I was unable to find somewhere to live. A beautiful Roman candle burned over the rooftops of Oxford. It was arson on a housing estate, fuelled by misspent youth and jealousy. *If I can't have you, even by burglary, nobody else will have you.* The bike had eventually burned itself out but not before falling onto the neighbours' car and writing that off too. Relations with the neighbours had never been the same again, but thankfully I didn't live there. They were my girlfriend's neighbours. Relations with my girlfriend were never the same again either. Apologising to me years later for the smouldering end to our romance, she explained that she had been looking for a knight in shining armour and instead got an absent one with a burning mule.

I didn't see the burning bike with my own eyes, but I received her eyewitness account live from the scene. It was described to me by phone at two in the morning with cries of 'ooooh,' and 'ahhh' like an audience with children at a fireworks display, only slightly more shocked and with a tinge of accusation (I had chosen to burden her with my inflammable transportation). She occasionally offered technical details like 'I think that was the sound of the petrol tank catching'. This had been my welcome to London, homeless and without my steed.

A sole survivor of the immolation was an air freshener in the form of Zippy, the loquacious character from the 1970s children's television series *Rainbow*. He had sat on the handlebars of my bike, attached to the ignition key, staring wildly at me with huge blue eyes, his mouth uncharacteristically closed as he vibrated in the wind. He had been with me on the road trip I took to the West Country with my closest friend Rodney, and would be returning.

When I left my place of work for the last time, I took Zippy with me as my constant companion on the Path, tied securely onto my pack with string and the keyring from the late bike. Zippy's body, and his yellow, oval head still smelled faintly of lemon. Nobody else seemed to notice, but I knew it was there.

I walked out of my office carrying a black box full of my public health books, covering the stimulating topics of health in conflict, dead bodies in disasters and faecal waste management.

This image may seem bleak, but things would get much, much better before they got worse.

With me I also took a miniature latrine, which my friend Kenny had fashioned from steel and covered in tiny posters from my favourite films. 'Let me know where you'll be in a couple of weeks,' Kenny said on our leaving drinks night in the pub, 'and I'll join you. As long as there are no Rangers' matches.' Though coming from Glasgow, Kenny struggled with the sectarian associations of the team but couldn't help himself. He was religious about the game. I gave him a few stops on my itinerary and he said 'count me in'. His offer was echoed by other slurred voices around the bar. Had I believed everyone on that drunken evening who had volunteered to accompany me, I would have stayed in London. I just wanted to be alone.

Afterwards, with my black box of treasures, I walked dreamlike through the City of London. I was numb, anaesthetised by the feeling of betrayal, of being cast away. For the last time I passed the three cheap Eurohike tents (the new face of homelessness) next to my former office, camped under the scaffolding of a vacant commercial property. It was the end of August, still summer, 2019. There had been a 50 per cent increase in the daily number made homeless or sleeping rough compared to the previous year and this was to become much worse.

As I approached these tents did I stop by to say hello? Did I bring food? Did I offer some information on shelters available? I did none of these things. I floated past like any other commuter (apart from my black box, the cliché of the recently redundant), discomfited by the sight of these unlucky few – or of the unlucky many. I silently wished them well and hoped a little of what I raised, or the awareness generated, would help some of them or people like them.

The backdrop to this was recession, and the UK's exit from the European Union was a symptom of this. Although the majority of Londoners had voted to remain, leaving the capital felt like the right thing to do. Greater London was a city outside the walls of England and I needed to know what was on the inside.

Say goodbye
Day 1. 10ᵗʰ September 2019

The South West Coast Path begins in Minehead, Somerset. This was not the first time I had been to this forgotten seaside town. I had photographic evidence of a family trip to Butlin's holiday camp in 1972. I was three years old. I have no recollection of it, though we were there in black-and-white on the monorail, I on my father's knee and my sister, brother and mother beside. My older sister, Julie, must have been taking the picture.

Now it was 2019, and this time I was with my wife Mags, as she prepared to wave me off. As I edged between breakfast tables in our Minehead bed and breakfast I was asked, 'How much does that pack weigh?' I honestly didn't know but I guessed 15 kilos. It wasn't until South Devon that I weighed myself with it. 'What training have you done?' I was further interrogated. I had been walking since I was able to; it had never occurred to me to train. And my overseas trips always included an over-packed backpack.

I have always insisted on carrying a backpack for security reasons. My logic goes as follows. If I were in Afghanistan and there was shooting, I would be able to run. With slight probing this argument falls apart. 'Wouldn't you just leave your pack if you were under fire? Isn't it just as easy to run with a wheelie trolley?' Possibly. But I did test this theory in a race with my Canadian friend, Steve, in Italy. He pulled his Gatwick trolley (his would be a Vancouver valise) and I strapped on my old Karrimor Global backpack over one-hundred metres. Though we were both almost crippled from the ordeal one thing was certain. With his suitcase lurching and airborne for most of the distance, then on its side and scraping over the designer Italian concrete, I looked cooler than he did. He just looked silly. Though I suffered temporary paralysis I looked fairly normal, like a man racing to an airport gate or dodging a bullet. Steve was a man possessed being chased by a loud suitcase. And, if I had taken a bullet that day in Genoa, it would have lodged in the totally unnecessary steel I was carrying around on my back to the Cinque Terre. If there was someone who knew how to comprehensively overpack, it was me.

I had become what my Finnish friend Kristiina (who was determined to join me) would call 'equipment sport'. This loosely translates as a nerd with kit worship. My gear included the improbably named Pocket Rocket® and Hubba Hubba®, plus a golden trowel. My sleeping bag, also golden, was light but suitable for a blizzard. Kristiina liked to tease, but I rationalised my behaviour as a practical response to having to carry in excess of 20 kilograms (I still hadn't checked but I'm adding water) over 1015 kilometres with ascents of 35,000 metres (or four Everests, as the Coast Path promotion likes to say, though clearly not all at the same time). Becoming a person with the most efficient lightweight gear was a completely practical response to circumstances. Wasn't it?

The concerned breakfasters in the Minehead B&B, John and Heather, were my first route sponsors. Their questions unsettled me somewhat, but I reasoned that this was a series of short walks in the West Country. I wasn't climbing Annapurna.

Admittedly, this suggests a lack of planning, but I did have a practice run earlier that year. Dan, a friend and sanitation engineer, had joined me for a walk and camp in Wales during a cold snap. Though it had been icy, my gear had worked well and had kept me warm and dry. Dan's tent was a Saunders' Jetpacker Plus from the 1980s. He explained with pride how it had sheltered him on Mount Kilimanjaro, Mount Kenya and Mount Cameroon. However, by the time it reached that hill in Wales the tent had perished. The cotton was largely held together with PVA glue so was now very waterproof, making it difficult to breathe once inside. Dan's sleeping bag was of a similar vintage and it chose that night to inopportunely malfunction by exploding. In the morning he emerged from the green tube looking not unlike Lawrence Oates, wearing a balaclava helmet and a shocked expression. Dan was frozen, breathless and heavily feathered. He had offered to join me on the coast if he could, but I wouldn't blame him if he urgently had to build a dry-stone wall or de-sludge a latrine with a bucket instead.

On Minehead's western edge is a large steel sculpture of hands holding a map of the South West Coast Path. Here, walkers - if they are lucky enough to have someone who might miss them - exchange goodbyes, or else simply register their departure with a photograph. I was fortunate that Mags was there to say goodbye, although I wasn't expecting an emotional farewell.

Perhaps it is her Irish heritage that means she finds open displays of affection more difficult than some. Perhaps it's just her. A story better illustrates Mags. One day I was interviewed for a job that I had reluctantly applied for and did not get. Rejection from an unwanted relationship can still hurt. So my confidence slumped and I moped. The following afternoon I returned from work to find a gift. It was a small spaceperson with a visor and umbilical cable. When the visor was lifted their eyes lit up. That sums up Mags. She might not express herself emotionally, but when you need her there is a small person which lights up. A little white knight. Everybody loves Mags. If this were her story there would be people behind her all the way.

So we approached my point of departure, optimistically late in the day. Another couple hovered nearby. They carried a tent and a large camera, as laden as I was. They were a young German couple, a good omen. Germans, efficient and good planners, were in the same situation; I'd be fine. We took their photograph and then they set off down the coast. In the wrong direction.

Strangely, the first official Coast Path journey was not along the coast but between two houses across the road. We realised this when Mags and I had checked the Guide, by which time the Germans were out of earshot. Running after them with the Elgin Marbles strapped to my back was out of the question. The confidence the European couple had instilled quickly dissipated.

'Use the joint fund if it rains, don't rough it every night,' Mags insisted.

'Have you been to the West Country?' The question was, of course, redundant. 'If it doesn't rain every day, I'll be very happy. Besides, I don't mind rain, it's the wind I can't stand.' My words were two fingers to fate, but I wasn't superstitious.

We said our goodbyes, there was a little tearfulness (one of us was crying), and I went off in the right direction, up the hill. I peeked to see that she was still there until she was obscured by trees. It was simply a series of flights of steep steps but already I was out of breath and too flustered to consult the Guide. Manageable on the flat, when I ascended, it was like trying to move an upright piano up a flight of steps. There was no way I could complete the remaining 1014.5km with this albatross.

At a stone marker for Exmoor National Park the path levelled, I immediately forgot the pain, ridiculed my immediately former self for his negativity and rationalised the load as the bare minimum I could take. What was I expecting? It was all essential and, in any case, after a few days I wouldn't even feel the load.

At this point I should introduce the Guide properly. The cover featured a photograph of rocky outcrops broken by an idyllic turquoise sea beneath a pale blue sky. The title in screaming capitals read THE SOUTH WEST COAST PATH *FROM MINEHEAD TO SOUTH HAVEN POINT.*[1] Inside, Paddy Dillon was pictured in a pristine white hat and red fleece, with a beard and glasses. Apart from Zippy, Paddy would be my only other constant companion for the next 2-3 months. I was sure we would become friends. My copy was dated 2003; I'd resisted buying the updated and slightly heavier 2016 edition. What could have changed? 'If in doubt, keep the sea to your right,' I had been advised.

The Guide would also serve as a record of the trip. A series of post-it notes would ensure that at least my memories of *when, where* and *who* would approximate to reality.

I walked on above Minehead Bluff then rested to consult the oracle. Paddy explained that the route the Germans had taken was the Alternative Rugged Coast Path. I made a mental note not to become embroiled in anything alternative or rugged.

One thing makes the South West Coast Path more challenging than other long-distance routes. Unlike many others, it was not created to serve a typical human need to travel from one place to another. Generally, humans and other mammals follow land contours. The coast paths were not created to go between one town and another or even for leisurely strolls. They were created in the 1800s, paths connecting coastguard stations to watch for smugglers. Whereas the Pennine Way and Appalachian Trail were created by ramblers and foresters, this was a route devised by arseholes.

As cliffs are formed by coastal erosion and landslips, they eat into the contours of the land rather than follow them, creating an undulating cross-section. If the Coast Path had followed contours it would lose view of the sea, defeating its purpose, so instead it follows the path of most resistance. The endless changes in elevation make it one of the most challenging for walkers, and intrinsically dangerous. Undoubtedly to some, the Coast Path conjures up images of walks along beaches and planks over dunes. Day hikers might convince themselves that the particular hill they are on is the exception.

As I now thought myself, as I descended a very steep slope. Were there equivalently steep climbs? Surely not. There were no steps, just treacherously loose earth straight down towards the sea from the top of Bossington Hill. Having had two-hundred years to improve on this potential calamity the Coastguard were clearly sloppy on health and safety. In the Guide, Paddy mentioned the Germans' alternative rugged route coming in from the right at the bottom. Perhaps travelling from Poole to Minehead you could take that alternative on confronting this terrifying incline. One thing was certain, if anyone says they prefer going up rather than down, then either: a) their knees are shot; or b) they are lying.

At sea level was a dead forest. Bare, white wood without bark or leaves, protruded like frozen ground-to-cloud lightning. Porlock's ancient shingle dyke had been breached and the sea had intruded, killing whatever trees were growing.

As I seemed to be ahead of schedule I loitered and took pictures. I was grateful for my camera and telephoto lens. For all its additional weight it was worth it. I watched as people passed by the trees, hardly noticing them, missing the beauty of their decay. These would be unique photographs, I thought. After I'd put my camera away and opened my flask of tea, a woman in her sixties in tweeds, and with a dog, stopped beside me.

'I come here most days. They're striking, aren't they? They must be the most photographed trees in Somerset'. I tried looking nonchalant. 'Are you travelling far?'

'To Poole,' I said with the confidence that I would complete it.

'In one go? Quite a distance. That looks heavy.' It was a statement rather than a question. She was looking at my pack which, for once, behaved itself by sitting upright on the grass.

'It doesn't feel as heavy when you're wearing it.'

'Oh, heavy enough I'd imagine.' The pack then fell to the ground with an air-dispersing *whumpf.* She nodded sagely, wished me luck, then wandered off. Turning to Zippy I ran silently through all my possible retorts as I maintained a forced smile. She made her way past the other walkers who all chose that moment to photograph the trees.

The camera recorded the location, altitude and time of every shot. The camera may lie but there will be a record of where and when it told its tale. It was heavy, but indispensable. An indication of how late I was, early on in the walk was that I took my last picture there at 18:22.

On this first day, sunrise was at 6:30 and sunset was 19:30. There were thirteen hours of daylight. One month later the day would be two hours shorter. I was losing four minutes of light every day, an hour a fortnight, and the decay was linear from the end of August until the beginning of November when it would slow. I was oblivious to the fact that I had chosen to take a 1000 kilometre walk at the time of year with the fastest decay in daylight hours. Today, though, as far as I was concerned, I could afford to stroll. The sun was high, the day long and I was blind to the rapidly compressing days ahead. If there was a storm approaching it was far away, beyond my horizons.

Near the dead forest I came across a simple concrete monument to a wartime air crash. The inscription described how 'due to heavy rain and poor visibility, the aircraft clipped the top of Bossington Hill and crashed into the marsh at Porlock not far from this memorial'. Eleven in the Liberator bomber had been killed, with one lone survivor.

Zippy and I traversed the shingle bank to Porlock Weir then sat at a picnic table near the seafront to finish our flask of tea. The phone signal disappeared with the sun. There were two pubs and a green, a nice place. Still, I felt too conspicuous, so found drinking water in a public toilet and headed up through woods. The track passed a toll house-cum-lodge bearing an old warning: 'No responsibility attaches to the owner of this road for any carnage or injury suffered by any person ... due to the said owners negligence, non-feasance or misfeasance ...' and so on. Unable to distinguish between nonfeasance and misfeasance, I decided against the toll road. Carnage or injury – what sort of calamity were they protecting themselves against?

The Path led beneath a tunnel with a small castellated turret, another tunnel, and then onto forest tracks where there were remnants of an additional tunnel. My first pitch was by a tree with a bench and a sea view. An idyll.

Upwards seemed the most likely direction to find a phone signal so I walked through a dark passage created by overhanging trees. My torch picked up a flash of red in a recess. It was a memorial stone with fresh wreaths and a Canadian flag. The track was an odd place for a memorial; who would ever come across this unsettling place? The stone was dedicated to four airmen, Gardner, Schultz, Hansen and Stokes who, in 1943 crashed their Handley Page Halifax bomber into the woodland in thick fog. Local men from Worthy Combe sawmill helped in the rescue of two survivors from the burning wreck but the fuel exploded and one of the rescuers was also badly burned.[2] The bomber had narrowly missed the north wing of Ashley Combe House,[3] an Italianate mansion which housed evacuated children during the war. I had skirted the ruins earlier. The tunnels ensured that workers and their vehicles could use the trade entrance unobserved. This was the second of many memorials I would see on the Path. They represented death, destruction and dangerous weather, but also everyday heroism.

Finding no phone signal, and unnerved by the memorial in the darkness of the wood, I returned to my camp only to discover that all the books I had loaded onto my Nook e-reader had been erased. Perhaps it had been the tight compression of my pack triggering a factory reset. I had nothing to read for the next 1000km. This realisation wiped the pleasure from my little woodland idyll.

No such thing as a coincidence. Probably
Day 2. 11th *September*

I t was a long time since I had woken up in the open air of a forest. The last time I did so was with my old school gang.

The gang I grew up with in Australia would have been politely termed 'miscellaneous'. To our contemporaries we were dweebs or dorks (a *dweeb* is 'a boring, studious, or socially inept person' whereas the more clearly defined *dork* is 'a *contemptible*, socially inept person'[4]). My code of camping derives from those bushwalking days. Being uncool, we had rules. Rule #1: carry only essential equipment.

Fossil, our navigator, applied this rule sparingly. His own maxim was *safety first*. Older than us, he drove a large station wagon. Were any of us to remove our seatbelts prematurely, he liked to brake sharply, causing us to involuntarily headbutt the dashboard. Health and safety were priorities for Fossil. He loved to give illustrative community service messages, even if he killed us in delivering them.

Safety was important, so safety became essential luggage. If packing light is a challenge for me today, I owe it to the training I had on those 1980s lost weekends. A trainee paramedic, Fossil brought a large trunk marked 'St John Ambulance'. We took turns hauling the medicine chest over the terrifying terrain. At some point when we were overheating and finding everything too stressful, we insisted on inspecting it. Within were the entire contents of an ambulance - sutures, syringes and, inexplicably, enema bulbs. Fossil insisted it was all essential. We all secretly

15

harboured the hope that one of us would suffer at least one compound fracture so that the carrying would not have been in vain. We also hoped that the victim wouldn't be Fossil, as he was the only one remotely qualified to use the kit. The most likely way we would create such an accident, of course, was by carrying Fossil's first aid kit so we took turns, as though passing a hot potato.

It was, though, inevitable that I would inherit *some* of the packing habits of those days. Some of the gang were concerned about open defaecation. This wasn't a preoccupation normally – they weren't weird. At least, they weren't weird in *that* way; this preoccupation stemmed from either a general concern for the environment or fear of rats. Hence Rule #2 of camping (leave it in the ground). We brought a portable, folding shovel. It was a shovel that folded. In all other respects - weight, size, function - it was a shovel. I made a point of not carrying it as it weighed two kilograms. I honestly cannot explain why we didn't just use a rock or a frightened rodent to dig us a hole.

At Porlock Weir, Fossil would have been dismayed to learn, I was carrying nothing heavier than a sticking plaster with which to stem the flow from a severed artery. The three suggestively named objects I carried with me on *this* journey were a Pocket Rocket® (a tiny Mountain Safety Research or MSR folding gas stove), a Hubba Hubba® (the MSR tent large enough for two if you employ the annexes for kit), and a golden trowel (the Deuce® #3 latrine trowel, 27.6g of aluminium to the folding shovel's two kilos but it had the same function).

This third item was the main reason for rising early, and 6:30am quickly became what French photographer Henri Cartier-Bresson would define as the *decisive moment*. I won't go into details, but I aimed (if you will excuse the unfortunate past participle) to make use of it off the beaten track where I could not be easily observed.

A friend had once remarked 'toilet paper is the scourge of the countryside'. I disagree. Tissue is simply biodegradable paper, but it *is* an indicator that the waste itself is not buried. That is the public health risk and it's also disgusting. More than once on the Path I would find squished remains peering from beneath a rock or presented shrine-like in a hollow of bushes decorated with leaves. Toilet paper might, at least, serve as an early warning.

Whatever I left of myself, it would not contaminate fresh water, offer food for flies or risk contact with human skin. Hence the trowel.

Later, while I was sitting on my tree bench inspecting the Guide a couple of walkers stopped to chat. Retired Germans, they were walking for a fortnight, exploring the coast and its history. Despite being in their 70s they set a faster steadier pace than I did; the inertia created by my pack was becoming a liability. We met again in the tiny old Culbone Church which had belonged to Ashley Combe House. It was dedicated to St Beuno. The latin is Bonus, and it is often anglicised as Bono, though the name Beuno refers to 'knowing cattle'. Presumably not in the Biblical sense, but this *was* the West Country.

The couple looked at me with concern, probably registering the weight and contemplating the distance. 'Go at your own pace,' the man said, seeming to grant me permission to be slow. It was a passing comment, but I was to hold onto those words throughout my journey. They promised to look me up and then wished me well.

Leaving the woods, I crossed a stream and, according to Paddy Dillon, we were now in North Devon.

In a novel, in the fading light a car crosses this border from Somerset into Devon along the coast. It turns onto a driveway, three miles long, which ends at a retreat, a house being used for bomb disposal training. The book was Canadian author Michael Ondaatje's *The English Patient* (1992).[5]

Hidden from view below the path, and on the county border, is Glenthorne, once belonging to Ondaatje's older brother Christopher, where he is said to have written much of that novel. The manor house was built by the Rev Walter Stevenson Halliday in around 1831. Halliday had used smugglers' paths to transport materials for its construction from the pebble beach. A map the Reverend commissioned of the Countisbury Estate is mentioned in *The English Patient*. The novel tells of a burnt airman being cared for by a Canadian nurse among the ruins of Italian villas as he reflects on his adventures and doomed love before the war. I wondered, had Ondaatje been aware of the burnt airmen (including a Canadian) and their rescuers in the nearby woods on the Somerset side? It would be quite a coincidence if not, as the location and circumstances - the Italianate mansion, the cause as the aircraft fuel and the injuries – are so similar.

On the subject of coincidence, I had begun to ponder the strangeness of a chance meeting with someone I knew on the Path. Many people knew I was here, and some had arranged to meet me, and even those who had not so agreed might decide to come on a whim perhaps because I had planted the seed. What if I encountered someone I knew, who did not know I was walking the Path? That surely would be a coincidence. How likely would it be?

The thing about rare events depending on multiple factors is, the probability is very difficult to predict *a priori*. There are an infinite number of permutations of individual behaviour. Unless we assumed that the people I know (who are unaware of my walk – say, 250) are planning a holiday to one of the 49,000 towns and villages in the UK. I pass through five settlements daily and I assume if they are in one of those that they will also be on the coast. That gives two chances in one if they are walking against me, one chance in one if they walk in the same direction or one chance in thirteen if they are crossing my path. I had a fighting chance of meeting somebody I knew during those weeks.

Deep down I knew, of course, that I had inflated the odds. Most people I knew were not walkers, they may have been in a town I was in but not on the Path and the chances are that I would meet nobody. Probably. The thought depressed me, like the possibility that there is no life outside our solar system, or that I would never meet John Irving. Zippy simply stared, numbed into silence by the thought. *So, it's just you and me?*

I met the older Germans again in a light drizzle beside the Sisters Fountain where a heavily laden Australian had also stopped. Walking for a week, he carried everything he came to the country with, and it was a lot. I ensured I was the last to leave, mostly as I knew I would be overtaken, and it embarrassed me.

The Sisters Fountain belongs to the Glenthorne Estate and the sisters who played there as children were nieces of the Reverend Halliday who built the house. It's said to be a holy well: Joseph of Arimathea struck the ground with his staff and from there the spring came. I'm no more certain whether he came here than I'm certain that Jesus visited Glastonbury or 'Che' Guevara visited Kilkee in Ireland. But, as Maxwell Scott said to *The Man Who Shot Liberty Valance*, 'This is the west sir. When the legend becomes fact, print the legend'.[6] So, being short of water I drank from Joseph's spring, a dark pool with a mossy cross atop a stone roof (but not before mixing chlorine, waiting 10 minutes and carrying the sterilized water for a further 30 minutes - I was taking no chances however holy its provenance).

At a path approaching a forest road I encountered another German. It was beginning to feel like a benign occupation. His leg was bandaged at the knee and supported by two sticks but otherwise he appeared fit.

'I was confused with the days and booked accommodation for Porlock Weir for today by mistake,' he explained, laughing. 'Last night I paid £150 for a suite at the inn.'

It was bad luck. 'Do your sticks help?' I asked to distract him from his losses.

'Oh yes, I couldn't walk without them.' To me, though, they seemed just more to carry. He went on ahead cheerfully and at a pace.

After a gate bearing two stone boars' heads I came to a road where a group of women gathered around the Walkers Honesty Café. They were the first of many all-female rambling groups who were completing the Coast Path over years, though not necessarily the same women all of the time, but all of the sections just not in any particular order. I assume they nominated a secretary to keep tally. I let them go ahead, keeping them in sight to regulate my pace.

19

All was well until the path to Foreland Point Lighthouse, where the wind began to blow. There had been barely a breeze in the valley. The climb was excruciating with the wind at my face and the pack dragging behind, so I was glad when Lynmouth was in sight. *I must do something about the pack when I'm in town.* To know what you should let go of, first carry it all on your back.

The road descending to town was familiar; I was here with my closest friend, Rodney, after I returned from Cambodia.

Rodney was the worst pillion passenger in the world. He and I had taken a motorcycle road trip in 2005, and Zippy was with us. We collected Rodney in Bristol and rode down to Lynmouth and Lynton before heading south across Exmoor to meet Tony at the arts college where I had once worked. Rodney was an incompetent passenger, never having owned a licence for any vehicle (he almost mastered a bicycle). He would lean around me to speak or down to adjust his foot pegs during motion, destabilizing the bike at inopportune times, causing us to weave. We survived the road trip as we'd survived the ones in Cambodia, but barely.

To his huge credit, Rodney was the 1990s equivalent of Wikipedia, which then, of course, didn't exist. Though mechanically and spatially incompetent, he had a mind like a records store. In fact, he *was* a records store manager and archivist, which is how I met him - as assistant to the archivist. If there was a pub argument on history, politics or entertainment Rodney could be called from the payphone to give a correct answer, or at least a convincing one, and the debate would be settled.

They were uncertain times for me, living in a bedsit off the Peckham Road in South East London with heroin users shooting up in the garden. I was rapidly running out of money. It was a strange house. An Iranian chemistry student lived above, his experiments leaving my drying laundry full of chemical burn holes. He removed all traces of messages from Tehran including the underlying sheets from the telephone notepad.

Another tenant, Julian, rode a motorcycle. He wore his dressing gown like a smoking jacket, permanently, and I never saw him clothed. Though it couldn't be so, in my imagination he left each day, throttling his Yamaha along the Walworth Road in the striped gown. Julian received an eviction notice and took revenge by cutting up his floor with a jigsaw before riding off. Needless to say, this madhouse was unsettling for a young immigrant like myself.

When first I met him, Rodney was on the telephone to an insurance seller who had asked him if it was a bad day to call. He responded with, 'No, not at all, it's a bad year,' and hung up. We were both recently separated, he from a tiny, beautiful singer, who despite her size had the voice of Billie Holliday. I had been married by accident to an Australian after a misunderstanding with passport control, rapidly divorced, and then left marooned and alone in the city. Perhaps it was the similarity of our circumstances at that time that formed our solid bond.

When I married Mags in 2011, Rodney was my best man. His speech to our guests warned them about the rural short-cuts I might suggest which would mean walking through boggy fields in the dark while wearing moccasins. I could hardly be blamed for his choice of footwear. My confessor and advisor, he shadowed me from my first work in England, my public health study in Scotland, exploring eastern Europe, working in Asia and more recently to the west coast of Ireland.

Rodney is one of those people who will seek you out at the ends of the earth – from Edinburgh to Kompong Som and places in between. I hoped to see him on the Path but schedules can be unpredictable.

So, Zippy and I walked down the same scarily steep road we'd taken fifteen years earlier. I didn't feel the need to seek our B&B, nor the road we had taken to it. I didn't want to think about anything at all. It was in a melancholy mood that I arrived at a sign for the funicular railway, the cable train scaling the cliff from Lynmouth to Lynton. A town of two halves, it's more suited to goats than pedestrians, and don't mention the goats, as they divide people too (The Lynton Feral Goat Preservation Society opposes the regular cull).

'One please,' I said to the man in the kiosk. I desperately wanted to put the pack down but I feared I wouldn't be able to pick it up, and the train looked ready to depart.

He told me the price and I fumbled with my zip-lock plastic bag that had become my wallet. 'Wait! You,' he said, staring at me. Which misdemeanour had I been reported for? Open defaecation? Trespass? A blend of the two? I had crossed the county line. 'Are you doing the Coast Path – the whole thing?' I nodded. 'Sorry, I didn't notice. You're doing it for charity.' He pointed at the bright orange t-shirt beneath my rain jacket.

'For St Mungo's, a homeless charity.'

'You go free.' He said it matter-of-factly like there was nothing unusual about it and there was to be no argument. All I could say was thank you; I said it three times before climbing over a dog and finding a seat. The train ascended and I felt my mood lift. It was a rare feeling - I'm just not the type that people help. For the first time I thought, perhaps, I would be able to finish this thing.

Still smiling when I reached the post office, I pulled out a collection of things I could neither afford to lose nor afford to keep. My SLR camera, lens, teleconverter, batteries and charger, and cable release went into a box. What had I been thinking? My compass. If the sea is on my left, I'm going in the wrong direction. Besides, I had Paddy. I included my wristwatch with the broken catch which was letting in water. My phone had Leica lenses and a clock.[7] My fleece and a spare merino sweater could go. How cold could it get? All this I sent special delivery and I was 3.5kg lighter – the difference meaning I no longer had to lean forward to gather momentum from a resting position, and I had the reassurance that my knees would not suddenly bend backwards, a constant though irrational fear.

I met the German with the knee bandage on the main street who had found a decent hotel, Lee House, more castle than house. He asked me my plans and I pretended to have found somewhere to stay. 'At least today is over, that was difficult,' I said.

'The worst is to come,' he corrected me, laughing. 'The next stage is over the highest point on the whole Coast Path.' He had been planning while I had been drifting. When he entered his castle, I noticed that my bag was open and the small padlock from my side pocket was gone. I walked up and down the road but there was nothing. It was gone, so I told myself it was just unnecessary additional weight.

The Crown in Lynton offered food and a warm atmosphere so I found a table, then began searching for camp sites. The camp was on the edge of town and had instructions on the reception door to camp and pay in the morning. I camped beside the river Lyn, showered and inspected the damage. My hips were bloodied love handles, gripped too hard by the pack waistband. I cleaned the sores, covered them in blister tape and made plans for emergency repairs to my reading material in the morning.

Rule #3 of camping: leave nothing of value and everything else in a mess. A thief will have to spend time packing it up (they won't) or just take what appeals.

Travel in the twenty-first century is lighter than at any time in history. Your music collection fits on a device weighing 90 grams. Your library fits on an e-reader of 175 grams.

Heavier though they might be, there was little to go wrong with a C90 cassette or a book that couldn't easily be fixed with a pencil and some sticky tape. With an e-reader all your eggs are in one basket. As I walked the Lyn Way, a back road into Lynton, I acknowledged that my chances of success were remote. To avoid months of empty evenings I needed a computer connected to the internet, books without encryption and possibly the e-reader software.

After the bus journey I temporarily registered with Barnstaple library. Mags had emailed a selection of books I had bought before setting off. Despite the library machine being protected against viral contamination, it recognised my Nook's USB cable and allowed me to save directly to its hard drive. I had my books back.

As I made repairs to my e-reader outside the library, homeless people gathered beneath the awning. Libraries are some of the very few places people can use at no charge. It was good to be without my gear, to have somewhere to leave it with a semblance of security, to use a toilet and shower. These are the daily challenges of rough living, having to carry what you own around with the fear that someone could take it all from you or set fire to your tent, or urinate on you. One rough sleeper I spoke to had described his tent being doused in fuel and set alight. It reached such a temperature that his cans of dog food exploded. His terrified dog was found running in circles in a park. These are not irrational fears, but a reality for many thousands of people with no other choices. I could walk away from this at any time.

Lynton post office was open so I returned to post some more deadweight, a mini tripod. 'Did you drop something when you came last night?' the owner asked.

'My padlock! I thought I must have dropped it. Thank you.' The piece of metal returned to being essential unnecessary baggage. I returned to camp.

My cooking pot had a transparent plastic grey-tinted bowl designed to fit over it when stored. I kept this risk in mind each time I cooked and yet I took no action. I made a mental note to put some red electrical tape on the bowl as a warning, then had some rum. A grey cooking pot and a practically invisible plastic bowl seemed to me an accident waiting to happen. So, naturally, I waited.

It felt good to crawl into my tent and the cocoon of my gold sleeping bag to read Washington Irving's *The Legend of Sleepy Hollow*[9] for which I'd never made the time before. It was an appropriate choice given that the woods were full of ghosts. I fell asleep to the sound of the river.

Playing with fire
Day 4. 13ᵗʰ September

I t's possible to make an art form of dawdling. Rum and nightmares of headless Hessians hadn't helped. Pausing and chatting on the way to the Valley of Rocks, the spectacular rock formations west of Lynmouth, I loitered when I should have been pacing. People were curious about the solar panel on my pack, which they assumed powered the pack, so providing me with an excuse not to walk. The weight felt more manageable, but it was hot and there were few clouds. A woman with a small dog intended to walk the whole Path and seemed very relaxed about her pace; the dog's legs were short. I noted privately the folly of her relaxed approach and strolled on with renewed self-delusion.

Goats loitered on the rocks waiting to unleash anti-social behaviour on the townspeople while eyeing three as yet unoccupied crucifixes, which had been erected on the hillside. A banner near Lee Abbey proclaimed, in screaming capitals, 'TRY PRAYING'. Perhaps an eerie prophecy, I evicted it from my mind and wandered, soon forgetting the low budget Calvary.

Constant enquiries from generous walkers provided me with a steady flow of cash donations. I was able to transfer these digitally so there was no need to hunt for cash machines. Blackberries were ubiquitous; they were free so became my main source of fruit. The world was one big fruit machine.

The heat meant I was drinking a lot of water. At Hollow Brook I filled from a waterfall, then set off towards the valley at Heddon's Mouth. By three o'clock I was again low on water with the direct sun and the weight of the pack. At Holdstone Down I was out of water and tea, and all the streams ran dry.

A cluster of bungalows sat on the ridge near a carpark, so I hid my pack in a gorse bush at a fork in the path, then walked with my bottles. The second house had two excited little dogs. Newton stated, in his first law of motion, 'Every body perseveres in its state of being at rest ... except insofar as it is compelled to change its state by forces impressed'. These dogs were not compelled to go anywhere so I concluded that there must be water present. Knocking at the door of this remote spot I was reassured that the owner of toy dogs is unlikely to be a homicidal loner. An assumption, true, but one that had never let me down.

The man who came to the door was friendly and regaled me with a tale of young German campers who were washed out by flash floods, so he let them camp in his garden. It was hard to imagine in this brown and parched landscape.

I have learnt since that Moors murderers Mira Hindley and Ian Brady, serial killers Dennis Nilsen and John Wayne Gacy and even Adolf Hitler loved little dogs. Those German campers may lie there still ...

The valley of Sherrycombe was the beginning of the ascent of the Great Hangman. It was already five o'clock and it would soon be dark. I found a heart-shaped stone and placed it in the crown of a tree, above head height. My intention was that this would cheer fellow walkers before their own ascent, though on reflection there was a risk that it would concuss them should it come loose.

Hangman derives from the Germanic and Celtic words for hillside and slope, hang mynnedd. Essentially *big sloping hill*. Nothing to do with nooses, but it felt like a slow execution. The sun was already low in the sky when I reached the cairn at the top, so I crossed Little Hangman and descended, in the waning light, the treacherous earthen steps to Combe Martin.

The nearest camping place was in darkness but the reception had a contact number for late arrivals. A stern female voice answered my call.

'I'm sorry, we don't take new arrivals after eight o'clock as it disturbs other residents.' The time was five minutes past.

I explained that I'd walked over 30 kilometres. Silence. 'I could set up the tent blindfold.' I heard some discussion.

'Can you pay cash?' Her tone, reluctant and suggestive of a gross breach of rules, inferred she was doing me a great favour. The cash from generous walkers meant I could respond in the affirmative. 'Okay, someone will meet you at the gate.' Combe

Martin did have a reputation for being open half the year - when they could be bothered.

A friendly elderly man met me by torchlight and gently pointed me to a pitch that had a working lamp. By the time I had camped and returned from town with food, the air was chilled. No longer having a fleece I layered my remaining clothes, quietly cooked and settled down to sleep. My last recollection was of indignance at the receptionist suggesting I would disturb other residents.

My old Aussie gang had a rule on fires. Rule #4: no unprotected fires. We wouldn't camp if there was a drought or if the ground was very dry. Fires would be protected with rocks and all the scrub removed from nearby. It would be in a sheltered place away from the wind. We kept an eye on embers and covered the remnants in ash before departing. Gas stoves existed but were beyond our means, but now in 2019 I had my tiny Pocket Rocket® stove.

If there was to be an explosion my preference was for a quiet one. Only a fool cooks with gas when half asleep. I had relatives who had burned down buildings or ignited themselves through the accidental application of fuel while being tired or distracted. My mother had set fire to a kitchen with a pan of spilling hot oil, and had then taken a desperate rugby slide on the fat-lubricated tiles, crying out - in a confused state - for a scone cutter to extinguish the flames. I came from a long line of accidental arsonists.

Although I had kept the risk in mind, I still had not put any markers on my invisible plastic bowl which fitted the pot snugly. So snugly, in fact, that it appeared as a slightly larger identical pot. Tired, and distracted by having to dry my sleeping bag and tent from the condensation of the cool air of Combe Martin valley, I put the water on for morning tea and proceeded to set fire to my plastic bowl.

Although groggy, I was immediately sensible of the calamity that morning. As someone with personal experience of arson involving combustible fuels it was obvious how this could end (though admittedly it was second-hand experience, relayed by phone by a girlfriend watching my bike explode).

It was important that I did not lose my tent to the inevitable inferno, but the gas canister being smothered in molten bowl made an explosion not unlikely and in that instant I was certain my walking days were at an end. More importantly, it would play into the hands of the officious camp manager whom I'd made a point of telling I would not disturb other campers. As I juggled my flaming equipment I looked for her out of the corner of my watering eyes.

The dripping plastic base drooped over the gas flame like molten mozzarella. Before any rational plan formed, I had pulled the stringy plastic from the flame with my fingers, and only then extinguished the stove. The bowl was lost, pieces sticking to my fingers and the gas canister but, judging by the vapour hanging about me, much of it had sublimed. There was no explosion.

Miraculously, other campers remained oblivious to my fireball, hanging out washing or drinking coffee like any other morning, while I stamped out the remaining incendiaries on the grass.

I made a mental note to contact the manufacturer to report this intrinsic hazard so that they might send me another free bowl with the same propensity for self-immolation. Some months later they did just this, for which I am grateful.

Until a replacement silicone bowl presented itself I would have to eat from the cooking pot. Joining the Path, I naïvely assuming that this would be my only brush with explosives for the day.

At Hele Bay I left my solar backpack in the sunlight to collect charge and sat down to discharge. In Ilfracombe I would find supplies and possibly a physiotherapist or counsellor.

The path from Ilfracombe ascended a series of hairpin bends. At one of the bends we stopped for tea and I immediately put my hand in faeces; unless the dog had used toilet paper, it was human. There had been an attempt, in shame or malice, to disguise it with leaves like a premature yule log.

'Hello.' An athletic woman hopped up the steps like a deer and stood smiling before me, her ponytail bobbing in the sun. It was an unforgettable, striking face. I had passed her earlier in Ilfracombe when I harassed the theatre bar tender for water. The recognition hit me at the same time as the odour. I moved the offending hand behind my back casually so as not to draw attention. She fixed me in a stare, and said slowly, 'Horrible, isn't it!'

'Pardon?' I felt myself reddening. Then it occurred to me that perhaps she had weirdly left it there for me to find.

'It's a bit too hot to climb such a steep slope, I mean. Are you walking the Coast Path?' she asked.

'Yes. You?'

'Just doing a circular from Ilfracombe. Anyway, enjoy the day.' She paused for a moment and sniffed the air, frowned, then smiled as though finally recognising the wild odours of Devon. She sprung off up the hill, her hair swinging with each leap and I wanted to leap after her. Alas, I was covered in someone else's poo and I was in no condition to leap.

Zippy's innocent but absorbent face stared at me, accusingly, as I sought cloth. *I don't know what you're looking at.* Moss, coated in alcohol hand gel, removed the veneer of excrement.

We passed over grassy slopes, below us Brandy Cove and Shag Point (one surely leads to the other). The Path descended into Lee Bay, which had facilities. I took water for the remainder of the journey, including two litres in a backpack bladder as I doubted that we would reach Woolacombe. Taking water from handwashing/drying machines involves a split-second operation, failure resulting in a bottle of soap-scented air-warmed water - eau de toilette. It was almost four o'clock.

We passed Damage Cliffs, not damaged cliffs although I suspect they were. Names in the vicinity included Mortehoe and Morte Point, and a local pub with the name Ship Aground. The references to mayhem and death were not wasted on me. Paddy Dillon's next description was similarly revealing: 'The route becomes like a roller-coaster, with flights of steps leading into and out of a couple of little valleys'. The term 'roller-coaster', I soon realised, didn't describe the exhilaration in the groin of a downward descent. It was a roller-coaster, but not in a good way. I have only two photographs from the journey between Lee Bay and Bull Head and these are from a bridge at the bottom of one valley where I had paused as the blood throbbed in my head.

The now discontinued but energy-efficient iPod helped on hills. The Cranberries' *Zombie* offered me the aggression to climb steep slopes which were increasingly problematic. I had begun doing something which should have been a warning sign: to count steps on ascents. Ten, or fifteen and then a rest. I was drinking too much water though carrying four litres; it was both an aid and a limitation. I just didn't have the energy to lift my weight without regularly stopping. Music was not enough, not even Dolores O'Riordan.

At Bull Head the lights of Woolacombe flickered on. I had no desire to be among families and their dogs interchangeably licking fallen ice cream and gonads. Nearby was a lighthouse and some strange lines of toadstools reaching to the cliff. The land was flat and grassy. *This must be the place.*

While waiting for darkness, and the remaining walkers to disperse, I met a woman approaching the cliff. She was watching for porpoises. Strictly speaking, she was watching for signs that there may be porpoises, such as feeding birds, cormorants and such like. She asked where I was walking and why. I could see she was curious about where I was going to sleep, though in that very British way, too polite to ask directly. She pointed out a camp far inland near Morthoe and I lied that I might go there. Once she had left, I watched the sunset behind the lighthouse and then camped. Soon after, the full moon rose on the opposite horizon. The air grew cold, so I layered and cooked dinner on a bench near the cliffs beneath moon and stars. In the tent I was the luckiest person alive in an idyllic setting, without a worry.

There followed a loud explosion and a bright flash nearby. Was it a firework or distress flare from a boat? A military training exercise? A second explosion closer to the tent lit up the inside. Someone was trying to scare me. They were going to burn the tent. How could I be so stupid as to camp here? What had I been thinking?

I sat in fear in the darkness, not breathing. How could they even see me, being so well-hidden? It was difficult to position my legs, which were using my hips painfully as fulcrums. If only I had the fleece to place between my knees. After a while the discomfort displaced my anxiety and I fell asleep.

Die endlose Fahrt
Day 6. 13th September

As I struck camp, the woman returned to the cliffs for porpoise watch. She again reported none of the mysterious signs of their presence. She was, as they say, without porpoise. 'Perhaps they were frightened off by those explosions,' she suggested, catching my eye knowingly. The implication was that the pyrotechnics were my doing, and despite being no wiser than her on the cause I felt my skin reddening. I made my excuses and left before I felt compelled to confess.

Woolacombe was, unsurprisingly, filled with children, screaming parents and dogs licking fallen ice cream and sniffing each other's genitals to an accompaniment of fine drizzle.

Beyond the grassed promontory of Downend Point was a grey ruined tower. I discovered that it was new, incomplete rather than ruined, and belonged to Edward Short. Called *The Lighthouse*, it was his dream of escape from London but had already cost two million pounds, mainly due to the driveway, which resembled a motorway slip road. The cost would rise to four million.

Holes covered in ugly aluminium frames gave it the appearance of a derelict tower and a local's graffiti shouted, 'Finish it'. Short's project was featured in an episode of Channel 4's *Grand Designs,* showing the proposed design in 3D render, minimalist and spectacular. It was suggested, however, that Short would never complete it. 'Beware that siren call,' concluded presenter Kevin McCloud, 'because if a lighthouse has a single message that it shouts out it is this: "stay away or risk destruction"'.[9] It had cost the man financial solvency, marriage and peace of mind. A small price to pay for architectural immortality, I would have thought.

Beyond the construction site I crossed a huge expanse of a field before casually glancing back at the gate, on which I noticed the sign: 'Bull in field'. Large backpacks, I already knew, sent dogs into a frenzy. Imagine what they could do to an animal that is ordinarily provoked by a flapping cape and a man in knee length skin-tight trousers. A woman weeding outside a gentrified farmhouse gave a surprised, 'Oh, hello!' and looked about me as though searching for the trail of blood, but I was miraculously unimpaled. *Farmers Weekly* would be hearing from me.

The only campsite open was in a village outside Braunton which was recorded in the Domesday book as having 13 villagers, six smallholders, three slaves and three miscellaneous. It wasn't much larger in 2019. The young German couple from the starting line were busy erecting their tent. Their names were Christian and Lisa. They, too, had encountered a field warning of a bull.

'Today was very boring,' said Christian with German dourness. 'The sign promised a bull but there were no bulls. Disappointing.' While mildly offended for my country, at the same time I had to agree; it had been dull. Even the hazards were uneventful.

One other thing we agreed on was how difficult this was. 'We were at Annapurna base camp this year,' Christian said, where I had also been years before. 'Compared to this, Annapurna was a walk in the park.' I'm paraphrasing. I can't be sure if he used this expression. Was it a *walk in the park*, a *short walk in the Hindu Kush* or a *piece of piss*? It wasn't as though I made notes as he spoke – that would have been weird. The gist of what he said, though, was that he really didn't think Annapurna was that difficult compared to this back-breaking series of marathons. Lisa was nodding and repeating affirmations.

Lisa still had her heavy SLR camera. She had developed leg problems due to the weight and so had also posted some things back home.

Christian and Lisa used Paddy 2.0, but their GPS measurements convinced them that some – but not all - of the distances were underestimations.

Since we are on the subject of Germans and guidebooks, I recall visiting East Germany in the 1980s. A backpacker in East Berlin showed me his copy of *Let's Go Europe* circa 1985. Of St Thomas's church in Leipzig it claimed that, 'Mozart and Mendelssohn also performed in this church, and Richard Wagner (of *Hart to Hart* fame) was confirmed here'. Alas, it was corrected in subsequent editions. The day I arrived in the city I was refused a train ticket and was instead driven to Leipzig police station, not due to trespass – though trespass and theft I had indeed committed - but because of a failure to meet daily security police checks compounded by a rapidly expiring visa. A failure. My failure.

A portrait of Chancellor Erich Honecker stared down at me. My uniformed interviewer spoke to me in accented, Home Counties English. Very polite, he fed me my responses which excused all my crimes before I had even been accused of them. 'You were unable to find the police station in Wurzen. It's an easy oversight and understandable. But you're here now.' After thirty minutes beneath Erich's glare (which felt like an hour), he returned my passport and stamped it. An international incident averted, I was free to go, and on leaving the station came face-to-face with that landmark I had studied in the guidebook in Berlin. There was Wagner's St Thomas's Church, framed by communist drabness. This story serves to illustrate the Wagnerian fallibility of all guidebooks and the importance of the disclaimer: *correct* [or otherwise] *at the time of publication.*

Paddy was simply repeating distances he had been given. The South West Coast Path Association was probably reluctant to update official estimates given its investments in timber signage. Trackside errata would be both expensive and annoying.

Lisa and Christian had only two weeks so would take buses to skip the long *boring parts.* Like tomorrow's estuaries.

'Do you know if there is a campsite at Clover Lea?' asked Christian. I wasn't entirely sure where Clover Lea was, though it sounded familiar. Camp anywhere, I suggested, as long as there are no farmers, guns or bulls.

The camp café was little more than an awning outside a hut. Christian asked the woman at the counter if they might cook under the shelter because it had begun to rain. Her prickly response was of the order that only food bought from the shack could be consumed under the shack awning. He explained that he only wanted to cook it, not to consume it, there. It was a precise German distinction. There followed rumblings about making a living. Lisa asked if she could make an exception if they were to also purchase coffee or hot chocolate. They must have sensed it was a losing battle and so fell silent. Her posture and rapid jagged wiping of the countertop with a cloth that could easily have been a serrated blade, suggested an impending explosion. My head was down as I scanned the Guide for references to Clover Lea and made inappropriate notes on my yellow stickers. Her business partner made himself busy unnecessarily rearranging sauce sachets, actively deaf to this exchange and the distant roll of metaphorical thunder. In the end Lisa and Christian abandoned their own cuisine and bought food, unsettled by this very British form of hospitality.

The male business partner came out of the kitchen and made small talk to clear the air, directed only at me. He seemed to instinctively sense that he shouldn't be seen to make friends with these Euro-freeloaders. It was the freeloading of the Brit that he was oblivious to.

At sunrise, Lisa and Christian said farewell and sought a bus somewhere less boring while I headed off in search of the railway track bed that formed the route towards Barnstaple. The pack seemed heavier, and my body suffered the cumulative effect of carrying too much mass for too long. As rain threatened, I felt safe to empty a kilo of water.

Paddy Dillon commented on this section: 'Some walkers skip it entirely, even catching a bus all the way from Saunton to Westward Ho! – but if you start doing things like this, the chances

are that you will keep doing it, leaving your long walk in tatters!'
He then drew attention to ferries between Instow and Appledore,
leaving me unsure whose side he was on.

We passed a concrete shelter resembling a train with the
destination *Nowhere* and a woman and fox as drivers. The spirit
of the Tarka Trail, a fox driving a concrete train. The rain
became torrential, so I rested in an arty shelter made from old
railway materials. An oncoming cyclist met me inside. Rain is one
of the few situations forcing strangers together in cities, as poorly
prepared urbanites reluctantly huddle under awnings and in
station entrances. It was odd to do the same in the countryside,
but this was rare weather. The man happened to be a friend of
the British Road Championship rider Gary Crewe, whose winning
race happened to be emblazoned onto my restored 1970s
Holdsworth (it's a beautiful steel-framed bicycle which gained cult
status among those who prefer a heavier and less comfortable
ride). I recalled Spanish cyclists looking at it like it was a piece of
history, stroking it and reading the list of awards on the seat tube.
That was when it was all beaten up, before I recognised its
importance. That bike had ridden into Santiago de Compostela at
the end of the Camino. It had been raining that day too. Gary
Crewe – what are the chances? He had won it the year I was in
Minehead, 1972, the holiday I couldn't remember. The rain was
growing less intense, so we said goodbye; the dryness pushed us
apart.

The distance, the weight and the hard ground made my body
ache and it was difficult to stand again. For a while I had
considered sleeping but there were forty kilometres to cover.

On the far side of the old Long Bridge in Bideford was a
monument to Tarka the otter who swam here in Henry
Williamson's unsentimental book.[10] Nobody seemed to notice,
beneath the bronze otter, a miniature statue of Jesus, a fanatical
expression, like Zippy's own, staring from behind a Perspex brick.
What was that all about?

Bideford's suburbs led to a winding woodland track. My bottle
and flask were empty, and I regretted the saving in weight I had
made. A stream clogged with litter and black ooze was the only
fresh water and I briefly considered it. Soon we passed through a

graveyard of ships, rusting and rotten rib cages protruding from mud. One occupied boat warned: 'For the sad 1%. Merchant's [sic] Shipping Act 1995 Section 104, Unless you are police ... with a warrant ... you cannot board this vessel'. Actually, Customs and Excise could. And police with reasonable grounds (suspicious hand-written sign). And pirates.

An enormous shipyard incongruously shadowed the fields surrounding little Appledore. There were no viable camping spots. It was either boat industry or else quaint residential. However, a public toilet was open, offering water and an outdoor shower – both good news. Despite a lack of sleeping places at least it wasn't raining.

It started to rain. There was only one option, and that was to leave the village before dark. It was then that I received a message from my Canadian sponsor. Barbara was a very old friend from the days I lived in Cambodia. I had done some work for her recently, not a great deal but some statistical work enough to make it easier for her to get a contract. 'Would you accept me paying for you to stay somewhere decent? As a donation.'

I thought about this for a while, looked at the rain-filled sky and replied that I would. She made the booking through an online agency. Unfortunately, there was no reply. After some standing in the shelter of the toilet, a message from Barbara explained that the owner had gone to their daughter's birthday party in Bideford, but that if I was prepared to wait until 9:30 they would be back.

So, I found a fish and chip café, The Royal Plaice, and decided to encamp there for a couple of hours. The owner-manager asked 'What can I get you?'

'Anything unbattered will do.

'You're going for a walk?'

'I'm doing the Coast Path.'

'Any particular reason?' He began preparing some fish.

I told him that I had worked in London and over the years had seen more and more people sleeping rough. Then, I decided to do this as a rough sleeping walk. With the exception of Appledore, I hoped.

There was something else that made me more conscious of the problem. I used to see mainly eastern Europeans, Irish and predominantly white people sleeping rough. Mike, a friend who had worked in homeless shelters through the 1980s,[11] recalled meeting virtually no black residents – in part through their choice but also there were far fewer of them. Over a long period there were noticeably more black people sleeping rough. Perhaps naïvely, I had assumed that black communities looked after their own; I just didn't see them on the streets when I first arrived[12] – and it wasn't because of prosperity. In 2019 black people comprised 14 per cent of homeless and rough sleepers (yet they comprise only 3.3 per cent of the England and Wales population). A black person is six times more likely than a white person to become homeless in Britain today.

The café owner nodded as though it was familiar, though it was difficult to imagine a homeless crisis in Appledore. 'I used to work in London,' he said, fish preparation over. 'Used to see a whole city of people in underpasses like Waterloo. It was a revelation, I had no idea there were people living like that, like a secret world of cardboard boxes. Especially with the ice in winter. It was sobering.' This reminded me of Ralph McTell's song *Streets of London.* McTell first recorded it in 1969, perhaps no coincidence that it was the same year St Mungo's formed.[13] The song contrasts the petty problems of people with the existential problems of rough sleepers. It is, perhaps, apt that it was beaten to Number 1 in the charts by Mud's *Lonely This Christmas.*

As Zippy and I left the café with our bundle of pain, he called me back and handed me ten pounds. 'This is for the charity,' he said.

'This is probably the same one I gave you for the food.'

'Ah, there'll be others. It's a good thing.' Although still raining and now much colder, sitting under a lamp by the river mouth I felt warmed inside. He had given a free meal to his only customer. I separated his donation from my money as a reminder and watched the lights from Instow melting into the sea.

'Hello, Oscar. I'm Colin. From the B&B.' A man with two large fluffy dogs was standing over me.

'How did you know it was me?'

'Your Canadian friend told me to look for someone who looked like they'd been sleeping around a bit. You look the part. Anna is inside - just knock and she'll let you in. I have to take the dogs for a walk.'

The house was a very tall terrace filled with old trinkets. I was in the attic, but before retiring Colin and Anna shared rum with me in their lounge and talked about their plans of restoration, antiques and meeting strangers. 'We don't want it to be just a B&B though, we want to make people welcome. If you like, I'll show you around the area tomorrow.'

Robert Harris was in town in a few days for the Appledore Literary Festival. He'd written a book about nearby Exmoor, *The Second Sleep*. Alas, I would be on the road by then, and tickets were sold out. According to the publisher's blurb *The Second Sleep* is a tale of the church and the death of a priest in the Middle Ages.[14] The title refers to that period of wakefulness that was believed to have been common, something that still exists in my own house. Something else, though, connected me to this book, but which I discovered only much later. It won't make much sense right now as it didn't to me. After all, it had just been published.

As promised, in the morning Colin showed me the beach and Westward Ho! Returning to Appledore, I found the Beaver Inn on the lane leading to the Lifeboat Station. As it was our wedding anniversary, I called Mags from the seafront. It was strange to be apart, but relationships need times of separation to realise their importance.

This was advice I could have passed on to Colin, but under the circumstances I didn't. Additional to the parking on the cliff, several things Colin had done were apparently proscribed or seriously discouraged for health reasons, and that night I was to inadvertently drop him in it with Anna. While I regaled her with our adventure, Colin would suddenly grimace and make cutting gestures across his throat behind her. By the time I realised my confessions by proxy the damage was done, several times over. In bed I told myself that these are the tests that keep a relationship alive. That, or extinguish it forever.

The pied piper of Hamlyn
Day 9. 18ᵗʰ September

A large sand spit beyond Appledore – the Burrows - meant beach walking. RNLI lifeguards sat talking on the top of the beach by their hut, framed by the blue sky. Their dreadlocks were bleached and wiry bodies browned like inverted *Fantasia* mops.

Westward Ho! is a traditional seaside holiday town with a row of beach huts displayed on the promenade. Some were open and occupied by tea drinkers. The pavement beside the huts recorded the words of Kipling's poem *If* in cobbles set into the tar. Kipling had been here as a boy in United Services College (now apartments); his placement had more to do with his mother knowing the headmaster than with her aspirations for Kipling as a soldier. He wrote a collection of stories based on his experiences here, collected as *Stalky & Co.*[15]

I had read enough of Kipling's *Stalky & Co.* to know that I didn't want to delve further into the world of Arthur and Reggie. Public schoolboys smoking pipes and speaking of *jolly good subtle japes* and their *beastly strict* consequences failed to stir anything in me. But the poem *If,* that was something else and one part in particular resonated as I shuffled over its cobbled words:

> *If you can force your heart and nerve and sinew*
> *To serve your turn long after they are gone,*
> *And so hold on when there is nothing in you*
> *Except the Will which says to them: 'Hold on!'*[16]

This verse wasn't included in the tar; the council had run out of space. Kipling probably never walked the South West Coast Path, but he spoke to me in that stanza as my spine was in compression. As Bridget Jones once said, 'Poem is good. Very good, almost like self-help book.'[17]

An overgrown half-timber house, like an abandoned set from a Hammer Horror film, stood at the beginning of the former Bideford to Appledore rail bed. The invisible railway turned inland but the Path continued along the coast. It passed the old kiln and shingle beach below it, where Colin and I had taken the dogs.

An Irishman stopped me and pointed to the beach. 'You see, down there, that hut?' I saw it. 'A man built that months ago. At first it was just a tarpaulin. He's been improving on it since with driftwood and anything he can find. I saw him bring what looked like his whole family down there one day. Nobody bothers him.' He laughed, like it was the most improbable thing. When we parted I looked back at the hut, pressed up against the cliff. To live so close to the sea was freedom, but at a price – there was no means of escape.

Once alone I consulted the Guide. My destination, according to Paddy, was Clovelly, pronounced Cla-vel-li with an emphasis on the middle syllable. Hence, I had always assumed Clovelly was either a village in Wales or an Indian townhouse. Then I realised – Clover Lea had been Christian and Lisa's destination without a place to camp and this must be the same.

Pheasants gathered on the road ahead of me. It was more of a track really, with a rocky surface. You could drive a coach and horses through the Hobby Drive to Clovelly; that's all it was designed for. The pheasants were growing in number simply because there was nowhere for them to go, the woodland being steep on either side, to our left up, to our right down to the sea. Essentially dinner with feathers, they walked. Pheasants' flight served only two functions: to scare people during eerie quiet moments or in order to be shot.

There were now several hundred of the birds on the Hobby Drive in front of me. They didn't want to make friends with me but neither did they seem capable of leaving. For an hour or more I was the pied piper, pushing these birds to Clovelly rather than pulling them away. As a walker there is one thing only mildly less irritating than having someone walk directly behind you, and that's having someone, or something, walking directly in front of you. Though for no discernible reason, it is exhausting.

In the darkening forest I caught glimpses of brightly coloured metallic mushrooms. The mushrooms worried me in the same way that a gingerbread house deep in a forest would. Daylight was dissolving so I made haste, though by this time I was quite tired, nerve and sinew long gone.

It occurred to me that I should avoid pitching the tent in a steep wood if I was to avoid the need to repeatedly climb to the top of the tent during the night.

Climbing from the road using tree roots for foot holds, then scrambling to the top using trees as leverage, I located a site. My place rested beneath a farmer's field (always to be avoided as they scream *PRIVATE* and *SHOTGUN* in equal volume). On leaf-covered ground and far from the road, I was invisible in my 1.5 metre square of flat earth. It was dark when I unpacked so used the torch to find my way back to the track with my valuables. On the Hobby Drive I impaled a receipt on a stick, planting it in the ground in order to find my climbing point in the dark, then headed for the pub to steal its electricity.

Entering the New Inn, I removed a leafed branch from inside my collar and threw it out the door, then checked to see if anyone had noticed. A young woman in goth garb eyed me suspiciously, a glare I was equal to and returned. The bartender was oblivious, so I ordered.

'I'm afraid we're not doing food tonight, sir. Off season, you see. We have snacks.' I ordered a drink and crisps then found a quiet corner to siphon electricity and secretly eat my leftovers.

According to the pub, the Estate was run by descendants of the Hamlyn family (after being passed on by the Carys). The pied piper of Hamlyn; I considered taking the pheasants with me when I left.

There would be little time in the morning, so I explored the village by night while eating my remaining sandwiches. Sleds and containers for transporting goods lay at the top of the main road, and the cobbles were smoothed by repeated runs down to the harbour. Diners sat inside the Red Lion Hotel and a few walkers strolled along the breakwater under a waning gibbous moon.

Back at the Hobby Drive, my paper impaled on a stick had either blown away or been eaten by a pheasant. Over-confident from booze, I estimated the spot and began to climb. There was as much sliding backwards as climbing, then I had to follow the wire fence until falling onto the tent. All was as I had left it except for a few creatures crawling. Strange sounds emanated from the woods. I sent a message to Rodney. 'There are strange sounds in these woods.'

'Oscar,' he replied, 'all woods have strange sounds'. Something between a squawk and a howl emanated from nearby. There was no way I could sleep with unknown wild animals, a shotgun-bearing farmer and unnaturally coloured mushrooms. At some point I drifted off.

In the pale morning light I decamped then, for safety, lowered the pack ahead so that I could climb down the cliff of roots unencumbered. In the process of being careful I slipped, the pack fell with a thud and I was left dangling from the roots by a leg and arm. After checking that my undignified descent had been unobserved (the drive was deserted), I fell to the ground.

My first task was to locate water. Only in daylight did I realise that there was an entrance fee to Clovelly which appeared to be a private estate with a complex of ticket office and shop separating it from the car park. No toilets were open, so I approached a ground keeper who shuffled and mumbled to himself. He saw my bottle and nodded for me to follow. His clothes were worn and dirty, and the room in which he put his sack was little more than an outhouse. Unlocking one side of a bollard he revealed a tap. 'Everything is secured and private here,' I said as he filled my bottle and flask. He nodded.

In our brief exchange he revealed that the green, blue and red steel mushrooms were tube feeders full of seed. So they *were* a witch's lure after all. Each year people were invited to shoot the birds, fattened for slaughter in the darkened forest.

'It's eighty-five pound a bird.' He shuffled uncomfortably.

'For one? But there are thousands.' I imagined all those bodies and wondered what happened to the carcasses.

I was about to leave when he held out an arm, directing his stare at me for the first time. 'I won't beat, you know. I'll do anything else, but they can't make me do that.' I wasn't sure why he was telling me this, but I could see it was important to him. I nodded in understanding and thanked him for the water.

The hill from the village peaked at a wooden shelter, a perfect place to sleep - a view with a room. Hindsight is a cruel thing. Had I known, though, I would never have experienced that night in the forest with my screeching pheasant friends with whom I now felt a kinship.

Ahead stood the Bronze Age burial mound of Gallantry Bower. Three-thousand years ago the dead were interred here overlooking the sea. Perhaps there was no sea then. Beyond this, the four-sided Angel Wings shelter and further into the forest a junction.

At the sign I turned right as directed and walked towards a clearing only to stop dead, swaying with my inertia. Below me was nothing for 100 metres until the sea and rocks. I must have lost concentration; it could have ended very badly. Backing away from the edge I looked again at the sign and there it was – a Coast Path marker pointing towards the edge but someone, in a comical hand, had made a small felt-tip ink arrow curving away from the cliff. *Reminder not to walk in darkness.* An estate quad bike sent up a cloud of dirt and leaves as it headed back towards the village. The rider made no sign of acknowledgment. Rude. Zippy and I were covered in a thin film of red dust.

The path descended beneath a private chapel to coastal ruins and again up to the level of the church, by now hidden by trees.

Between two fields I stopped by a small monument to unfold the solar panel. The crew of a Wellington Bomber had perished there in 1942. It had flown from the airfield in Braunton in poor visibility. Five were lost, aged twenty-one to thirty.[18] It was difficult to imagine those conditions now, the sky a deep blue and crane flies scattering across dry fields. It's unhealthy to dwell on this destruction.

A radar mushroom guided us to a headland with a green wooden corrugated roofed shack selling ice cream. Convinced that I was expending more energy than I was consuming I bought chocolate and an ice cream. Walkers and labourers, from the nearby Hartland Point lighthouse restoration, sat in the sun. A family with a baby I had seen earlier laughed, their red hair radiant in the sun like a Discover Ireland promotion. All thoughts of premature death and foul weather evaporated from my mind, if only for a moment.

Beyond the lighthouse, a memorial to the crew of the hospital ship *Glenart Castle*, described its torpedoing in 1918. Though 162 were killed, there was something much worse. The ship had come from South Wales, bound for France to serve the young men from the trenches suffering festering wounds and makeshift amputations.

The rocks became dramatic shards as we made our way up the steep hill, where the couple with the baby overtook us. I pretended to admire the view, struggling to regulate my breathing, straightening my back and making hand gestures and smiling at them rather than trying to speak. In the next valley was Blackpool Mill which had stood in for the cottage near Land's End in the BBC adaptation of John le Carré's *The Night Manager.*

Hartland Quay was reached by way of a ruined tower and a field of mushrooms. A version of Daphne du Maurier's *Rebecca*[19] had been filmed there that summer, also displaced from Cornwall. Ben Wheatley claimed the space where Hitchcock had stood in 1940. Replacing Joan Fontaine was Lily James who had been here the year before in the adaptation of *The Guernsey Literary and Potato Peel Pie Society* (2018), Clovelly standing in for Guernsey. James was a good choice for du Maurier's narrator, but few women could raise their eyebrow quite like Joan Fontaine.

From the Quay the Path headed behind a hill and I diverted inland to Elmscott bunkhouse, being in need of a fixed address for a luggage transfer. The next stage was challenging, the Guide describing it as 'one of the toughest'; I needed to temporarily lighten my load.

John, the bunkhouse warden, greeted me, and soon Thursa, the owner, brought me eggs - refusing payment. John had walked the Path himself and he explained that the route to Bude had relentless ascents. 'Even without luggage it's a challenge. If you pace yourself it will be fine.' He worked at various hostels. I assumed he had retired, and this lifestyle provided beautiful surroundings, accommodation and company. 'I'm sorry the shop is a little bare,' he apologised. 'It's late in the season. I'll come along later and bring you something.'

I had the sensation that I was walking into a dormant period; that the deeper I travelled down the Path, the more boarded up would be the landscape until it would be impossible for me to go on.

From the lounge, the sun appeared to melt into the fields. I shared the view with a contractor working on the Hartland Point Lighthouse. 'Never buy a property close to the sea,' he warned. The coastal erosion around the now privately owned tower was catastrophic. 'We pulled back the earth and grass and that's all that held the land together. When the weight becomes too much it falls. In rain, it takes some of the rock with it.'

'Can it be saved?'

'Oh, we'll save it, but it will cost. People buy properties in beautiful locations, and the views are great, but the sea is just waiting to take them back.' He told me of a house belonging to a woman where there had been a coastal erosion project many kilometres away. Despite the distance, the work changed the usual pattern of tides where the woman lived, and the sea began to consume her large garden. After some months there were only metres left before her house was devoured. I thought about the halted 'Lighthouse' construction near Braunton. Coastal property is Steinbeck's pearl, desired for its beauty and what it promises but instead it causes poverty and conflict and, like the pearl, is ultimately reclaimed by the ocean.

'I would never buy a house within 500 metres of the sea,' he repeated. 'I like this, though, staying at bunkhouses and hostels. You can just bring your own food and do your own thing. And you never have to own it. What brings you here?'

I told him of my plans, and that I was now ten days into the journey. He asked if I had read a book about a couple's journey on the Coast Path.

'No, I haven't but everyone I meet has.'

'Then I won't give too much away, wouldn't want to put you off the walk. There are difficulties. Wash-outs, that sort of thing. Some wrong decisions. You've heard something of it then?'

'A little.'

'They don't make it, you know. They find a place and come back the next year when it's warmer. You think you'll make it?'

'So far it's been good. And I've told everyone I'm doing it, so I have to finish it now.' Yet, now I was no longer sure.

'That's a plan of sorts. Your reputation is at stake.'

'If I fail I can always stage my own death, or get new friends.'

He laughed. 'Tea?' We shared a drink, talked a while and then I prepared my bag for transportation.

Zippy looked up at me. *Don't worry, you're coming with me.* When you have very little the little becomes so much more important. He was a link with my past, what I had lost and what might be again. I emptied the bag and tied together my tent and sleeping bag and a few other things in the day pack ready to be transported. The large pack, Zippy atop, had the essentials for the journey to Bude - an important milestone.

Before sleeping I phoned Mags and described the night. 'Can it really be ten days already?' she asked. I hoped I was missed a little. After the call I sat outside and watched the stars in a black sky. The air was motionless and chilled but not cold. This was just how I imagined the trip should be. I wished I could capture it and share it with someone, but there was nobody. If it is true, as William Nicholson would have us believe, that 'we read to know we are not alone,'[20] then we wander to confirm that we *are* alone. Not simply to be reminded of our aloneness, in those prickling moments of neglect when we recognise the indifference of trusted acquaintances. No, to wander alone is to be completely immersed in the feeling - to be separate and accepting of isolation, to step in from light rain to the deluge beneath broken guttering.

My thoughts were broken by John, the warden, who came by as I was sitting outside the bunkhouse. He explained that the shop had no cheese but that I could have some of his own which he gave me, wrapped in aluminium foil. 'You'll need it tomorrow,' he said. 'Good luck.' A kind offering.

Zippy
Day 11. 20ᵗʰ September

Nervously, I left my odd assortment of precious materials
for collection in the porch of the main building. We
headed seaward, Zippy on lookout for cows over my
shoulder. Having spent over ten years as a vegan in the last
century I have no doubt that the final battle will be fought not
over animal welfare or the environment but over cheese.

A sign unapologetically pointed towards Welcombe Mouth, a
series of small falls and circular giraffe-paved stepping-stones.
There was a cool breeze but I was without my ballast, carrying
only the half-empty pack. Despite the distance and Paddy's
promise of a path which 'sometimes climbs steeply and descends
steeply over and over again,' I felt relaxed.

Nevertheless, the stillness of yesterday had been replaced by
strong wind especially on the peaks, Zippy grimacing atop the
pack. We climbed steeply and, on the descent, visited poet and
writer Ronald Duncan's writing hut. The interior was warm and
quiet with great views of Marsland Mouth below. I confess to
knowing nothing of Duncan apart from what I saw in the hut,
although I had seen the film of his screenplay *Girl on a
Motorcycle* (1968). It starred Marianne Faithfull and Alain Delon
and I was unmoved. Delon I will always associate with the
eponymous brand of cigarettes marketed in Cambodia in 1992,
which arrived at the same time as the French troops who smoked
something more expensive.

Duncan wrote four autobiographies – make of that what you
will. In his second autobiography he wrote, 'An accurate
autobiography would never find a publisher, if it did, it would
never hold a reader'[21] (his last found neither). Anna Claire
Trussler explained his method:

> *For example, one of Duncan's mistresses is written into one brief episode of the first autobiography with her proper name, but this is retained only up until their second meeting. Here, the protagonist suddenly shifts his passions to her (fictional) best friend who is later killed off in a car crash. The crash is shortly after the original woman's engagement to another well-known person is announced.*[22]

Clearly, he knew a great number of writers but the overall impression the little hut left was of an egocentric dabbling with being *one of the people*. Despite being enamoured with the working class and farm practices, he liked to claim that his father had been the great-grandson of the last crown prince of Bavaria. It was something the House of Wittelsbach (the Royal Bavarian Dynasty) chose not to comment on at the risk that it might 'stir up dust'.[23]

Steep steps led down to Marsland Mouth where we crossed a footbridge marked by a pile of white rope. 'Look at that, Zippy, we've reached the border.' On the far side was a simple wooden sign 'Cornwall Kernow' and the coat of arms – an inverted triangle of 15 coins on a shield. Atop the sign someone had placed a stone painted with the likeness of a girl in a red dress smiling with arms in the air. A welcome.

The next cliff gave views of an islet with the ubiquitous name Gull Rock. More steps downhill and up the other side, and again, the wind all this time growing stronger.

In the next valley was the sheltered Hawker's Hut. Hawker was its maker, the antiquarian and parson Robert Stephen Hawker. His hut was embedded in the cliff and was composed of driftwood and material from shipwrecks. He is described across the internet as having used the hut for smoking opium and writing poetry. Like all stories designed to shock (his fictional contemporary Sherlock Holmes smoked opium and injected cocaine) there is a reasonable explanation. First, he didn't smoke it, he ate it. He was an opium eater.[24] Second, his wife had recently died, he was depressed, and he suffered severe sciatica.[25]

This last I could empathise with. Reason enough, I would have thought, to find solace in Chinese molasses.

After the next steep valley we were severely blown about as the path remained high along grass-topped cliffs. The wind whistled through fences.

A rectangular roofing slate stood against a post and proclaimed: 'I'm worried that I am makeing the <u>wrong</u> desitions' [sic]. I was reminded of what the lighthouse construction worker had hinted at, the likelihood of failure. This seemed to me a premonition, so I tried to put it out of my mind. It was after leaving Stanbury Mouth, exhausted from the climb, and still dwelling on the message on that slate that I noticed the sinister GCHQ radar station once outed by Edward Snowden. It was the one that siphoned British and European internet traffic and emails. Legal on face value, it was justified by 'applying old law to new technology ... an obscure clause which allows the foreign secretary to sign a certificate for the interception of broad categories of material, as long as one end of the monitored communications was abroad. The nature of modern fibre-optic communications means that a portion of internal UK traffic is relayed abroad and then returns through the cables.'[26]

The parts visible to us are the *listeners*, the dishes, but the invisible parts are the data-dredging cables connecting it with the USA and Europe, arriving in Bude and elsewhere. 'Do you think they're listening to us?' I casually asked Zippy.

Naturally I didn't expect a response. I'm not a complete lunatic. But I did sense that something wasn't quite right. I strained my neck but saw no flash of yellow. In seconds I had the pack off. Where Zippy had been was now an unadorned key ring flapping in the wind. I looked frantically about. *Zippy!* The field was flat and empty, so I focused on the area downwind, leaving the pack in the centre and walking through the longer grass. When was the last time that we had spoken? Perhaps it was Hawker's hut. That was two valleys ago. I walked back a kilometre, oblivious to the security of my pack, scanning the blackberry bushes and gorse for snagged yellow. After some time I realised the futility of my search. The chance of finding him in this wind and over so many kilometres, was tiny, so I retraced my steps back to the pack, and sat down beside it.

Once more I checked my pack on the remote chance that he had lodged between the straps. Perhaps someone would find him and give him a home. He could be blown into the Atlantic. I couldn't understand how this had happened; I had triple-tied his string, though it was an old piece of string. Everything had been going so well, and now I felt hollow. Zippy, my one companion - gone. He had been with me for 16 years, had crossed Exmoor with Rodney and survived a malicious arson, only to be blown away. I was a bad guardian. Worst of all, whenever I thought of him I would be reminded of GCHQ.[27] The radar dishes stood at different angles, a pretentious tableau vivant. I hated them. I stood, grabbed my pack and trudged on.

After Duckpool, a steep-sided valley, the terrain became easier but I was too self-absorbed to make much of the views. I took no more photographs, my last - like a hex - being that piece of misspelled slate. I fear I may be 'makeing the wrong desitions'. The wind gave my face a taunting slap.

Apart from the physical effect of wind, it gnaws at the nerves. Wind can influence the mental health of people living in windy places. Ill winds. In the short story *The Man Who Planted Trees*[28] (recommended to me by a friend when she knew I was taking this journey) the narrator describes an area of France where the Alps meet Provence. 'I was crossing this country at its widest part, and after walking for three days, I found myself in the most complete desolation. I was camped next to the skeleton of an abandoned village. I had used the last of my water the day before and I needed to find more.' He goes on, 'the equally ceaseless wind irritates the nerves. There are epidemics of suicides and numerous cases of insanity, almost always murderous.' The physical discomfort of fierce wind can force you indoors, if you have an indoors, but there is also the mental impact of the relentless sound. A breeze through leaves can be relaxing, but sustained high velocity wind through artificial objects - houses, fences, electrical pylons – taxes the nerves. Stand next to a wire fence in high wind and you will understand.[29]

Wind screamed along the Path and as its strength grew, it became intolerable. I was relieved when I found myself in the shelter of Bude.

My gear had arrived in the camp south of the town, so I pitched as best I could in the wind, then walked into Bude to find food. I sat with my back against a dune and watched the sunset. 'Kenny,' I wrote into my phone, 'Zippy is gone.'

'What do you mean "gone"?'

'He blew away.'

'Did you not tie him on? What are you playing at? Did you not keep him in the wee latrine I made him?'

'Naturally, I carry a steel latrine with me.'

'Oscar, 4th to 6th November - will you still be walking and will you be near Bristol? As in - short train journey from Bristol? Appreciate it will be a rough estimate at this stage.'

'I'll be walking forever. I'll keep the dates free. I should be in Dorset.'

'No idea where Dorset is, but will have a look on my map of my colonial masters.'

I drank rum and toasted Zippy until it became too cold to sit and I walked back to cook.

The man who met Paddy Dillon
Day 12. 21ˢᵗ September

Now that Zippy had disappeared I had only one companion - Paddy Dillon. His bearded face squinted at me from beneath that glowing white hat.

I captured the sun with my solar panel in the morning. The route was flat to begin, but the heat meant I had to casually strip by a main road near the Chough Hotel. This was relatively simple to do inconspicuously – I rationalised – since nobody in their right mind would get naked so publicly, so nobody would suspect it. Mooning in plain sight. This was the last time I would wear trousers when walking. From now on I would wear swimming shorts with, or without, rain gear. It was simply easier to move and, especially, to climb.

The wind was tolerable but there was a light drizzle as I descended into Dizzard[30] woods. It was sufficient to make using the panel a problem. I had already noticed some of the USB ports had signs of rust and had failed. Should they all fail, the panel would be useless. Without power - no phone, photographs or record of distance.

Steep valleys, with only horses for company, lay ahead. These finished me off, so the sight of a place with Haven in the name appealed. Who wouldn't like a place called Crackington Haven? In a café I ordered coffee and special cake and immediately someone engaged me in conversation. Steve Crummay shared his card. He was described as an independent ecological & environmental consultant, outdoor instructor & environmental guide. He was guiding two women around the coast.

'I just met someone with exactly the same gear as you.' It was an unusual introduction.

'Really?' I thought perhaps it *had* been me. I had recently passed a few walkers, one a guide and my memory of faces was unreliable.

'Same backpack, same rain cover, same clothes. Same mission. I assume you're doing the whole thing?' I hadn't felt I had a mission, quite the opposite. 'He's walking the whole Path, but he's flying. He plans to do it in thirty days.'

'That's madness.' Perhaps it had been me. It was not beyond me to make up such a story out of sheer boredom. 'When did he start?'

'About a week ago.' This gave me a sinking feeling; I was no longer unique except in my general tardiness.

'Have you got the Guide there?' Steve picked up my copy. 'They're good. This is the old copy. Hasn't changed much I suppose.'

'I hope not. The distances are a bit enthusiastic,' I said, hoping for a confirmation.

'Yes, well Paddy's a driven man.' He said it with authority.

'You say it like you know him.' Steve's credentials showed that he had worked with Sir Ranulph Fiennes, but I was more interested in Dillon than the English Patient's distant cousin.

'I have *met* him. We did some work together. He's driven – completely focused on walking. I won't say he's not interested in what's off the beaten track, but he's more focused on what's directly in front of him. Totally focused on getting from one place to the next and the detail in between. He walks in trainers and shorts. Takes lots of notes.'

'That makes sense. These distances are okay if you're carrying nothing. He seems to know all the food stops.' I had a better impression of my remaining literary companion now.

'We're sitting in a café now.' He smiled and explained that eating places would be more difficult to find this time of year, which might make things harder. 'Where are you staying tonight?'

'I haven't decided.'

He suspected the rain was coming in but that there used to be a camping field nearby and it might still be open. He pointed at the map in the book and shouted a question to the woman behind the counter who shrugged a *maybe*. Steve described the route to the farm and then the three departed to find their accommodation.

Paddy Dillon, I have since discovered, doesn't wear trainers but a type of rugged walking shoe. On longer, more remote trips he carries camping gear and other lightweight equipment. He probably just makes it look easy. Neither Irish nor Welsh, he's actually from East Lancashire. The adjective most commonly used to describe Dillon in publishers' blurbs and online biographies is *indefatigable*. That which cannot be wearied or worn out.

I *defatigably* climbed the road to a field gate bearing the sign 'CAMPSITE CLOSED'. The surrounding land had the tell-tale signs of residents with something to protect – closed-circuit television cameras and high gate posts with ball finials – so I took a track back to the cliffs and found flat ground on the edge of a copse. It was hidden from the grand houses in a dip. While I was apprehensive at first, as it grew dark and the rain continued there was little chance of walkers finding me, and the dark green of the tent was soon invisible against the trees. A trail took me through the long grass to the cliff.

Cornwall. It sounded good. Cornwall was proper walking, rugged and remote. Another country. It occurred to me, as I stood at the cliff edge, that I would never meet my mysterious twin, the walker Steve had mentioned. He was already ahead of me and travelling at twice my speed. The thought made me a little sad. How had we missed each other? The rhythmic sighs of an owl led me back to the tent.

Folie à deux
Day 13. 22ᵈ September

I awoke, blinked and made out the shadows of small leaves, perhaps beech, on the inside shell of the tent. They felt firmer than leaves and tighter, more rigid, and there were tens of them. I prodded another and it slowly moved upwards away from my finger, to borrow a phrase, in much the same way that leaves don't. It was a slug.

I flicked the bodies, which simply adhered to the tent lower down. Those that reached the outer fly only began their slimy ascent anew. Before breakfast those that had somehow migrated inside had to be evicted. I carefully checked my food for hitchhikers and the thought of them made me gag. Some were black, others the colour of baby poo, and all had to be removed from the tent before packing. There could be no possibility of squished remains in the evening.

The sky was deep blue, streaked with white cloud, like jet tail streams. Another Gull Rock and the islands of the Beeny Sisters were spectacular against the blueness. It is the loneliest sensation to be in the most beautiful of places and to be unable to share it; to hold a precious secret and have no other soul with whom to betray it.

Soon I was in Boscastle in a tourist trap café where I did what tourists do. This involved an unexpected and memorable conversation with the man behind the counter.

'Do you do anything gluten free?'

'We do. What did you have in mind?'

'Something cakey?'

'We can do a cream tea sans gluten.'

'With a scone and cream?'

'Indeed, with a *scone*,' he emphasised the local preference of scone like cone, 'and cream *with jam*'.

'I'll have that.'

'Would you like it with tea?' Now, I thought this was a trick question.

'I think so, yes. Doesn't it come with tea?'

'You *could*,' he leaned across the counter and looked slyly sideways as though checking for eavesdroppers while he broke a house rule, 'have it with *coffee* or ... *nothing at all!*' This last came out quickly as though whipping a towel from his waist to surprise.

I wanted to do this properly. If a cream tea came with coffee surely it was a cream coffee, and that sounded like a biscuit. If it came with nothing at all, it was a scone. 'I'll have mine with tea,' I said firmly.

'A good choice.' What a relief. 'Would you like that hot?'

'The tea?'

'The scone.'

'Is it normally hot?'

'Normally? Warm.'

'I think I'd like mine to be normal.'

'I know *exactly* what you mean.' I didn't know what *he* meant, but I gave him the benefit of the doubt. He was being very cosy. Did he put this much effort into his other customers? It was exhausting. It wasn't as though there was much repeat trade in this cavernous cul-de-sac. Still, I appreciated the individual touch and chuckled to myself as I took my seat to relax and check my compass position, so to speak.

A whisper of 'Hhhhello,' close to my ear made me jump. 'Here you are. We heated the scone. Hot tea, warm scone, *ambient* cream and jam.' He placed the tray on the table, and I noticed that an elderly couple were watching.

'That looks good,' the woman said.

'It's my first cream tea.' And I wasn't sharing it.

Above us was a sign showing the height of the flood waters in August 2004. The Guide hadn't mentioned it because it hadn't happened yet.

'You've noticed the flood marker. Hard to imagine all that water coming down in a matter of minutes,' she said.

'Yes, it is. It was tragic. So much water. Today's such a contrast,' I said, tempting fate but leaving worrying to the superstitious – of which there were many, the place being full of witches.

After tea I sought drinking water from a public toilet, walking nervously past the Museum of Witchcraft. I need not have bothered. As I climbed out of the harbour valley the skies opened, not for a shower but a Biblical deluge and it continued for the next three hours. I imagined the couple in the café hanging onto the table and tray as the torrent flowed under them - the owner hanging onto the espresso machine and asking if they wanted their scones reheated. *No trouble at all.*

Rain means that everything is a little heavier. The ground was jagged and I was conscious of the sharp rocks against my ankles as I slid down their surfaces. One group of walkers heading to Boscastle approached me, but we were all so overwhelmed with the deluge and the noise that we simply nodded in sympathy beneath our hoods and moved on. The rain had lessened by the time the castellated Camelot Hotel came into view. Out to sea stood a rock resembling a crumpled witch's hat. The hotel, aptly, had been a set for Nicolas Roeg's 1990 film of Roald Dahl's *The Witches*, the story of a child and his grandmother fighting a coven of witches masquerading as ordinary people. Roeg had another connection to Cornwall, having filmed an adaptation of Daphne du Maurier's long story about grief, *Don't Look Now,*[31] which has been highly influential in film and music, its editing disjointed and time-disorienting. Roeg had died exactly ten months earlier, in London.

The final kissing gate was a narrow triangular atrium clearly designed by an intellectual giant who believed sheep could walk upright. In the squeeze I heard my tent tear on the wood, and I cursed the gifted carpenter. On the edge of town, in the shadow of the creepy hotel, was a campsite. As the only tent dweller, I chose a drier pitch under a pine tree. By the time I had finished mine it was no longer the lone tent. He had the same gear as me, a black merino sweater, black trousers and beside his half-erected tent stood an Osprey backpack and green rain cover. I knew him; the man was clearly unhinged.

'Shouldn't you be further ahead?' I asked.

'Sorry?'

'You're walking the Path in thirty days, aren't you?'

'I am. Paul.' He put out his hand politely, though he was clearly confused.

'Oscar. A guide called Steve mentioned you and told me to look for you. I thought you'd be long gone.'

'That makes sense now. I spent last night at a spa hotel, a treat with my partner. Fancy a beer?'

Like all places in the area the pub claimed Arthurian heritage. Paul wasn't eating so I got him a beer while I finished my food. He was surprised that I wasn't cooking, but I had been so wet and it gave me the opportunity to sample the local cuisine.

Paul was raising funds for a hospice. His brother had lost his daughter and this was for him in her memory. It was a thoughtful gesture. The speed he was moving was simply because he had to get back to work, a problem I no longer had to deal with, at least not in the short-term. Paul was my age, had started five days after me, and his body was similarly taped up to stop the abrasion of the pack.

The similarities struck me and I fell into a silence, staring at my drink. That's when it occurred to me that perhaps I had a reason for this after all. As I thought aloud, Paul's pint froze halfway to his face, his mouth agape.

We were both forty-nine, doing the walk in a fairly extreme way at the tail end of the year, and for similar reasons - on the surface. Of course, I didn't mean to suggest an ulterior motive, just an alternative one. The alternative was not quite a breakdown but stalling, confronting our demons, denying our mortality.

There would be no sports car, relationship with a younger person or tattoo of a phoenix. Even that trade-off is forced if you don't own a car driving licence, are attracted more by experience than youth and are hirsute meaning a tattoo of anything but a tarsier is a risky proposition. A quest was the default option. I paused in my reflection.

He laughed and drank some beer. 'I never thought of it like that. Do you think we're trying to prove something? Like, we can still do it?'

That might have been part of it. Neither of us was being particularly quiet about the quest. There was something darker though, something more self-destructive. Cervantes' *Don Quixote*,[32] remember, was also nearing 50 years when he embarked on his imagined chivalric quest. With a troubled mind induced by reading too many romances, his wild imaginings were to create problems for both he and his companion and he was driven quickly to anger. If he was delusional to think himself a knight errant, consider the adjective itself – to travel in search of adventure, and to err or stray from the accepted course. Quixote did both, so was perhaps not completely delusional. But, delusional enough.

Paul was rising early and walking until dark. When passing through somewhere interesting, he would take out his phone, take a shot and then keep walking. It was relentless. He had met the woman with the dog who still wasn't making much progress.

He offered me a donation of sleeping bags for the charity. A generous gesture.

'We better get some rest,' I suggested

'Yes, and I have to finish drying some gear.' We walked out. 'Do you suppose King Arthur was really here?'

I looked about at the tourist shop windows and the King Arthur's Arms. 'He was as much here as anywhere else,' I said, knowing this was probably the truth.

As I lay in my tent I reflected on behaving like someone much younger. Isn't that the whole point of a mid-like crisis? After all, it was important that I did this properly.

In the low morning light we chatted as Paul dismantled his tent.

'Look, Oscar, you've got my number. I live near Exmouth. When I get there, friends will ferry me around the estuaries and take me back home to rest, and carry my gear to the next stop. I'll be travelling as light and as fast as I can. When *you* get to the Star Cross Ferry it won't be operating, guaranteed. Call me and I'll come and get you, show you a good time and take your bag on to the next place. We could even walk together for a while.'

'That's decent of you, Paul.'

'It's a difficult thing that we're doing, and I don't see anyone else doing it. It would be an honour.' He meant it. We embraced and he walked off for the Path, his head hunched into the wind. Suddenly he paused, turned and shouted back, 'Drink milk shakes', and then turned the corner.

I no longer felt completely alone even though I was being left behind. It was a little hope to hang onto. Besides, I was in a romantic place. Tintagel was the legendary home of King Arthur's Camelot. More precisely, Tintagel is one of around twenty locations believed to be the site of Camelot. He was a romantic figure of the fifth century but only appears in writing from the late Middle Ages. Arthur was recorded as subduing or slaughtering Britain's neighbours from Ireland to Gaul and Norway, often by his own sword.[33] From the perspective of this century, he comes across as a bit of a thug. What there is written of him has little, if any, source material and there is nothing of him in archaeology. Recent consensus among historians is that Arthur is an invention or a blend of other historical figures, a fiction to hold back our enemies who would otherwise come here for the promise of afternoon tea in pleasant weather.

The wind grew, slapping at the tent as I threw my possessions around to frustrate would-be thieves, and drew it closed. My grail quest was to find a vessel to replace the invisible bowl that I had set ablaze. It had to be lightweight, preferably flexible, and collapsible would be ideal. At the door to one tourist shop was a metal garbage bin filled with hundreds of plastic swords bearing the sign 'Excalibur. £1.99'. Unique, mysterious, and without a doubt a bargain. If this were a film, one would already be strapped to my pack.

Though I found material to patch my tent, there was no bowl and after several shops I began to despair, so I treated myself to another cream tea. This seemed to be the centre of alternative cream teas. The young waiter took my order and repeated it slowly.

'You don't want to know if I want tea with it?'

'It comes with tea. It's a cream *tea*.'

'Oh, thanks.' My skin flushed and people in the café stared as though at an imbecile. To give myself something to focus on I watched the rain streak the windows and read about the journey ahead until my very normal cream tea arrived.

The final shop at the edge of town sold camping gear, pots and pans and various household items. 'I don't suppose you have something like a silicon bowl for camping?'

'I don't think we do. You mean the collapsible ones, right?' He knew.

'That's it. But nothing, eh?' I resigned myself to eating from the hot pot for the next couple of months.

'We have *one* thing, but it's not really supposed to be for you to eat from.' He ducked beneath the counter and then reappeared with something orange. He flicked it and it opened out.

'I'll take it. It's perfect.' *The cup of a king*, and a bargain.

Content with my purchase I headed back to the camp and checked the tent. The wind was growing in strength, but everything seemed intact. I placed my new bowl in the centre of the tent. Orange silicon, collapsible and with a hot-hold edge it was just what I had been looking for. The two bone-shaped holes on either side of the grey rim added style that was wasted on dogs.

After lunch I walked the lanes to the church of St Materiana near the cliffs. Inside the porch was a sign 'ADDERS!!!' in hysterical yellow capitals on black. It was unclear if the warning was for inside or out. I lit two votive candles, for Mags' father and my mother. These were not tealights but proper candles that can melt, lean over and set fire to the pews and lectern.

The castle ruins could be seen from the Path but, in any case, they were closed due to high wind. The ghostly statue of Arthur was visible on the island, joined to the coast by a new bridge.

'This *is* impressive.' His American accent indicated that the couple next to me may be tourists. With their perfect teeth, hair and matching leisure gear they were 1970s tv.

'Are you walking?' his partner asked.

My journey seemed to be novel to them. Perhaps it wasn't something done so much for charity in the USA, more for health or a personal challenge or in order to provide Bill Bryson with writing material.

I took their photograph looking towards the castle and suggested they check out the twelfth century church. 'Watch out for snakes,' I shouted as they moved off.

'Oh, we have them in our churches too,' he said, smiling and waving goodbye.

'No, dear, I think he means real snakes,' her voice trailed off as they approached the nest of vipers.

A storm was whipping up, so dinner was in the camp laundry. It was the usual, with a flask of tea first then the messier rice and whatever protein I had found in Camelot, this time eaten out of a fluorescent dog bowl.

Being in the laundry area meant a series of visitors came in from the gale. We made introductions. Lindsay and Enda were from County Mayo in Ireland.

'You're walking in this?' Enda's glasses were steamed up, so he took them off to wipe them. They immediately steamed up again.

'There have been a couple of days of rain, mostly it's been like summer.'

'But this, Umberto! Are you in a tent?' Lindsay asked.

'No, I'm Oscar. Yes, that green one under the tree.' I pointed to the far side of the field.

Enda clarified: 'This is tropical storm Humberto. It's going to be gale force. It will eat your tent'. I wasn't sure what it was already if not gale force. Every so often the window would thud as though from a distant explosion. 'It *was* a hurricane, downgraded to a tropical storm - the tail end, but it will cause some damage.'

This seemed a communication oversight from my friends tucked up in their Hackney wine bars, especially as many had worked in emergency response. As a hurricane downgraded to a tropical storm it was entitled to a temporary entry visa so I should have been warned.

Before they left Lindsay said, 'Look, we're in the camper near you if things get really hairy. Here's a tenner for the charity'.

Dinner over, back at the tent two heads peered in. The couple introduced themselves as Christine and George. 'Look, if things get bad give us a knock. We're in the second van. And in the morning, knock on the door and we'll make you breakfast.' It was very kind and I told them that I intended to leave at around eight thirty. 'No problem. Please knock.'

The tent shook, flapped and strained at the guys which I had pegged deeply and at ninety degrees. The vibrations sent the miniature lantern into a spin, exaggerating the movement. It made me more nervous, so I switched it off and used the light from the e-reader.

With a little power remaining in my phone, I sent a brief insincere mailshot to thank everyone for the forewarning of the storm and there followed a volley of responses, some of concern and one offering a structural assessment of my tent. An Icelandic friend in Mongolia, aptly called Thor, said: 'With all due respect ... how much do I have to contribute to have you stop this?' It was generous and I believed him. He had once asked me to write a commitment for $5000 in red wine on a serviette when his office was in financial crisis. I suspected he might return the favour. The tent walls made a sharp cracking sound.

Morning arrived and the weather was calmer. Christine and George were as good as their word and made me coffee and scrambled eggs in a microwave, which takes some skill. They were concerned for me, and we shared our phone numbers so I could update them on progress. It was almost like having parents around, and I had to remind myself that my residual self-image of a teenager was outdated.

The Guide promised little between Tintagel and Port Isaac and sure enough, there was little civilisation and most was closed for business.

Seas were dramatic despite the calm weather, but I concentrated on counting the steps ascending valleys and taking regular rests. The route beyond Dannonchapel was to be the hardest part of the walk. There, the ground became an oily, slippery shale and there were signs warning that the path was unsafe. Two men in the valley ahead struggled, though with the aid of poles. Perhaps walking poles were the answer and I should dispense with my vanity. I slid for a while down the treacherous, steep path. There was nothing to grip but sharp bushes and the ground had the temperament of black ice. If I fell forward my top-heavy mass would have me plummeting onto the rocks below, but I found myself instinctively leaning forward for balance due to the pack. Inevitably I took an undignified slide, leaning back then forward from the hips to balance in the way that novice skaters appear comical; I was more conscious about how I might look to the two below than concerned about my survival.

In the event, I found myself face down in muddy shale looking over the edge at the crashing waves, a career-limiting distance below me. My blood didn't bother circulating, it just slept in pools in my belly. Down in the valley the two men were oblivious to my peril. From now on I would fall on my backpack.

At the bottom of one of these valleys I caught up with the two, an easy exercise as I was sliding most of the way. 'It looks like a storm's coming,' one said. I had noticed it too.

'Where are you heading?' I asked.

'We left the car in Port Isaac. You?' The rain started. They were wearing shorts.

'I'm hoping for Port Gaverne or Port Isaac.'

'Good luck, let's hope we stay ahead of this weather.' And they started up the hillside. The rain became a deluge.

In Port Gaverne I squelched behind the beachfront where there were some old fishery buildings and, miraculously, a public toilet. My waterproofs were wet and muddy, my boots the same both inside and out. I was ridiculous. There was no way of drying myself now if I camped and I was starting to chill. Reluctantly I left the shelter of the toilet and followed the road up to Port Isaac.

Halfway down towards the port I found a café open. I dripped conspicuously on the flooring so put my pack near the door, out of the way, and discreetly found a seat at the rear. My shoulders steamed while I waited for someone to serve me.

'Do you serve milkshakes?'

'Hang on a second.' She picked up her writing pad and squinted at me. 'You're the second person to come in with that backpack and ask for a milkshake.'

'It's my own pack. I've been trying to lose it, to be honest. Was this other person walking the Coast Path, dark hair?'

'That's right. For a hospice.'

'Yesterday? Yes, I know him. I'll have what he had. And a latte. Thank you. There will be another twenty of us, but we're ahead of the group.' There was no sensible reason to have said this, but it was said. I had to warm up, but the heating wasn't on.

There was only so much small talk I could make to delay going back into the rain, so I used the bathroom and headed in search of somewhere flat and secluded. The church had an area at the rear, but sheltering was a risk in an urban area. This struck me as a community with a civic society firmly grasping the edge of its curtains. Other than carparks, the land was at an impractical gradient right down to the little harbour. Shivering, I set off up the hill where I thought I might find a shop in which to think, but on the road out of town was a sign advertising rooms. I rang, but with no response to my call I left a message. Seconds later the phone rang and someone called Nilsa was inviting me to stay.

'I'm really sorry, I'm very wet,' I said as she opened the door.

'You *are* very wet. Take them off and I'll hang them in the bathroom. Get clean then come upstairs and I'll make coffee.'

I showered with my gear on and stayed there until I was warm. The sodden clothes (which in my head were still called *waterproofs*) and the tent, I positioned around the room on hooks and over open wardrobe doors so as to make them lighter to carry in the morning.

The muffled sound of a Brexit debate, until so recently the eternal subject of radio discussions, led me to the dining room where I found Nilsa, glued to her radio. She let out regular squeals of outrage, and while we talked, most of her side of the conversation had interruptions of imaginative expletives aimed at Boris, Gove, Cummings and Farage.

An interesting woman, Nilsa told me she had studied art and was involved in local affairs including ensuring there remained a public toilet, something I appreciated. Residents may complain about the cost of amenities, she explained, but they miss them when they're gone. At times I felt I was outside the conversation as she cursed at the radio, but I was tired, and happy to be an observer. In due course the subject of the Coast Path came up.

'Let me know if there are any parts that have problems and I can deal with them.'

'There was one stretch before Port Gaverne which was a shale and mudstone slide.' I wasn't sure if it was Gaverne as in *Gavin and Stacey* but I opted for *Laverne and Shirley*. 'I suspect it would be a good fracking site. Certainly, it was not much use for walking on.'

'Really? Was it raining?'

'Not when I slid down it, no. Later, yes. I imagine it's lethal now, but there was already a warning sign which practically read *You will injure yourself. Good luck.* Rope would have been more helpful.'

She considered this and nodded. 'Stay clear of the edge.'

'Don't worry, I stay well clear of edges. I'm terrified of edges.' That was the truth; edges are so final.

We called it a night and I slept like a person who had walked in a storm on treacherous terrain with porous waterproofs - trying not to fill my dreams with existential angst.

Lie of the land
Day 16. 25ᵗʰ September

I shouted goodbye but there was no response so I left the keys in a bowl and closed the door gently. Picking up the Path where I had left it near the people's palace that was the public toilet, I passed the milkshake café when a voice came from a side street.

'Hey, Oscar!' Nilsa was walking her dog to the beach. 'So, you'll go to Padstow? It's a nice walk. The weather should be good and the worst is behind you. Be careful.'

'I will, thanks.' I liked her. She had both essential qualities for a humanitarian - genuine concern for the welfare of others and passion about council lavatories. Once she was out of sight I relaxed, slouched and limped as normal.

Journeys are misleading, not in any philosophical sense but in how we perceive them. Imperial measurements don't help, and the British stubborn grip on these, despite the process of metrication having started in 1965, is juvenile. Metric has 10 millimetres in a centimetre, 100 centimetres in a metre and 1000 metres in a kilometre. Imperial distance measurement is inconsistent: inches have binary subunits (2, 4, 8, 16, 32, 64); there are twelve inches in a foot; 3 feet make a yard; and 1760 yards reach a mile. What evidence is there that the Age of Enlightenment ever reached our shores? With wet-eyed nostalgia we cling to these pointless notions as we do to airing cupboards and original old-style Agas (technically Swedish, but production has been in the UK since 1947 as we truly appreciate inefficiency).

My friend and neighbour once rejected metric with: 'But I can *picture* a mile. I used to ride ponies as a child, and I knew what a mile was. It's half a mile to Highgate.' But this was a fantasy. It was not half a mile to Highgate, it was double that. We're terrible at estimating distances, even with the aid of daymarks like church spires and towers. When the landscape is featureless, with no trees, people, animals or houses, it is harder still.

Imagine, in the middle distance is a headland. You can visualise yourself walking there and you mentally allocate a time to the journey. After a while you have exceeded that time and you are perhaps only a third of the distance there. Tiny undulations in the far-off smooth hillsides, as they come into the near distance become mountains. The slight lateral displacement of the way, as seen from afar, is a huge arc up close. But, you are not dismayed. Your powers of underestimation are without limit.

I don't think I'm an entire imbecile, but I do repeatedly make the same misjudgements. Even when I know it to be wrong, and even when I say this aloud to myself (frequently) I still harbour the illusion that the headland is just around the next bend. Even the next bend isn't around the next bend. Perhaps it is just hope. As I said, journeys mislead – it's the lie of the land. The trail felt longer, the pack heavier, the hope unbearably greater.

I came up to a group of women who were resting by a rock long enough for me to overhear that they had been walking the Path in sections for years. They were together, talking the way men don't. They were sharing. One held an SLR, on the outside of the group like a stranger, pointing it at the rest while they were unaware, laughing together. She was serious, unsmiling, capturing, bottling the atmosphere – seeing girls, not women in her viewfinder. *That would be me*, I reflected, dispassionately recording events. If the school gang was walking again, that is; if they weren't married, or stuck in a rut, or drunk at noon. We exchanged a few words and then I watched them go on ahead with an envious heart.

The next village was Port Quin, and featured only one facility for walkers, a water point - a *tourist tap*. One of the group's stragglers filled her bottle and then hurried to catch up with the others. She looked frail, as though she might easily snap, but the group would look after her.

Forgive me, for I have sinned. I have failed to mention this before as it doesn't paint me in a particularly good light. On the Path, as I approached someone, I would do something. Before I explain, I'd like to offer an apologia.

Many years ago, I had a motorcycle mechanic who loved to walk. Zippy and I would come in for our visits either to repair accidental damage or replace worn out parts. My mechanic had a permanent grimace. Being new, I assumed it was just me he was irritated by. Usually my consultations began with him looking at my bike, gritting his teeth and saying 'That's neglect, that is. Look at the state of that.' It was as though I wasn't standing beside him.

We were on our friendliest terms when speaking of walking. The concrete walls dissolved; we were on some remote hill in the Peaks, or up on Scafell Pike.

In one of these moments he revealed that he had suffered constant pain since injuring his back in an industrial accident when he was in his thirties. Hence his dourness. One day, though, I came into the workshop and immediately recognised that something was wrong. He was smiling and laughing. I thought at first that he was drunk.

'Last night I went to see this man on a farm,' he began. I expected this tale to be about the discovery of a Brough Superior frame in a haystack. 'Some people I knew had recommended him, though they've recommended so many charlatans I don't know why I bothered. But, anyway, I went. He has no qualifications to speak of, but he reckons he just has the touch for manipulating people's spines. So, I let him have a go. And at first, nothing, then he did something with his hands, strong hands,' he held out his own greasy paws, 'and everything changed. The pain was gone. And it's still gone. Cup of tea?' The transformation made me slightly nervous, but I accepted the tea. He restored my bike, giving it a new exhaust and forks, cursing my neglect throughout the process but - I noticed – not as much as usual. That day, a true artist, he restored the bike to an almost new state – only weeks before it was turned into an ashtray by Oxford arsonists.

I've been telling someone else's story, an easier story than the one I should have been telling. After weeks of both carrying excess weight and losing excess weight, I had developed various skeletal clicks and there was compression of my vertebrae. And so, when aware of others walking the Path, I gravitated towards their flaws and had begun to let out a stream of profanities sometimes loudly like one of those people on Oxford Circus. It was nothing personal – if resenting and cursing a stranger for no particular reason *isn't* personal - and I only hoped they were out of earshot. It was important that they understood, as we parted on the Path and our relationship came to a close, *it's not you, it's me.* It was the discomfort and pain talking, that's all.

'Assonant thistle-sifting itinerants,' I cursed as the three approached. Two men and a woman walked their dogs and the narrowness of the way meant conversation was inevitable.

'You're walking the Coast Path ... all the way?' asked the one not holding a dog. He sounded like a 1930s British Pathé news announcer.

'That's the intention, though ...'

'How much does that haversack weigh?' she interjected, the dog tugging against her lead. Was it my expression? It was just like any pack, only more so.

'It's less than it was, though I never risked weighing it. Once you wear it, it doesn't feel so heavy – it's just getting it on that's the trouble. Want to try?'

'I'll take your word for that.' The remaining walker resisted the offer with the same cheerful newsreel elocution.

'But you're doing it for a reason?' The first man again, also smiling. Curiously, people always expected there to be a reason as though it were penance like climbing a waterfall carrying a sack of swords in Paraguay.

I'm doing it for the interesting conversation about luggage mass. But there was no stopping them and they found the reason and were interested and generous. The irrational anger I had felt began to melt. *I'm doing it because I'm an arsehole.*

The three wished me luck and I watched their dogs drag them onwards. Humbled and shamed by these enthusiastic people and their generosity of spirit, I trudged onwards, awakened to my own meanness and pocketed a tenner.

Soon the land smoothed, and near an estuary an older man with a kindly face, his body slightly hunched, told me I was less than fifteen minutes from the Rock ferry.[34] The weight felt less; I was slightly elevated. As the man promised, Padstow was soon in sight, and after a little meandering through dunes, I saw a girl standing waving a flag enthusiastically at the ferry.

With the ferry ticket still in my hand I wandered into Dennis Cove Campsite which overlooked the estuary. A friendly man with the bleached hair of a surfer picked out the driest spot for me as it had begun to rain. There was a bug hotel for bees and other small animals with the sign 'Bug Glamping'. Small tents for bees.

After cleaning I walked to town. Coloured town lights were beautifully reflected in the still harbour. The woman in the post office, though it was officially closed, exchanged my Swiss Francs, making me fifty pounds richer so I went into a restaurant. Inside, I caught up with messages. Kristiina, my Finnish friend who planned to join me in South Devon, asked me about progress. I replied about the generosity of people along the way. 'So, you talk with random people and tell them about the fundraising and then they participate?' I hoped the tone was lost in translation. She might summarise the Samaritan parable: A guy travels the road from Jerusalem to Jericho without checking security conditions, is robbed and beaten but assisted by a rival sect member for personal religious benefit?

'It's one way of looking at it.' They *participate*.

'Oh, okay.' We would soon be talking face-to-face so there would be no confusion of tone.

There was also a message from Canadian Barbara (who gave me a roof in Appledore). The journey sounded *super interesting*. This was the other end of the spectrum. Each day Santa Barbara sent a message asking me to find something described by an A to Z of adjectives. This was the seventh, and something beginning with *g* was *gorgeous*. I sent a photograph of the Bug Glamping hotel. Little things kept my spirits up. She *participated*.

By the time I reached the site, the rain had stopped, and I slept under the stars and a crescent moon.

Crossed paths
Day 17. 26ᵗʰ September

At the entrance to woods two long-bearded men with staffs stopped me to ask directions for the Saints' Way. The two wizards walked off with their sticks. The Saints' Way crosses Cornwall from Padstow to Fowey, so they had just begun.

The town was quiet except for a few early morning walkers, street cleaners and sailors readying their boats. It was the town, according to locals, that Rick Stein bought. Fish and chips at £21.95[35] seemed a bit pricey to me.

The Path passed a memorial to the men of Padstow killed in World War I, and a steel outline of a soldier, facing out to sea. There, I encountered a man and woman. 'Are you walking the whole Coast Path?' she asked. Her partner was silent.

'Yes, I'm trying to get to Treyarnon today.'

'Go down to the beach. The tide is out. You can stick close to the sea. It's more interesting than the track through the fields.'

To most people Doom Bar is simply the name of a beer brewed at Rock on the far side of the estuary. The route down to the beach led to the actual Doom Bar, a sand bank that had shifted over the centuries and had a reputation for wrecking ships. I watched the couple as they carefully helped each other down the steep bank behind me.

As I took photographs they caught me up. 'We're walking up to the lookout.'

'Is it far?'

'We've never had any problems so far. We're not *that* old.' I wasn't sure that's what I had implied.

'I'd be careful on the slipway, it's got a lot of weed on it.' I'd been struggling myself.

'Oh, I think we can manage, I've been doing this for as long as I can remember.' She had quite an edge. I let them move ahead and watched as they took a detour up to a small hut with an antenna. I assumed they knew someone who worked there.

Beyond Stepper point stood an old tower, a daymark for navigation in which I sheltered from the wind. The sky was blue, with clouds like a fine dusting of chalk on a blackboard. As I walked on, rain began and there was little shelter. Despite this, I felt that things were going well. A short run of bad luck had ended.

It was Abba *The Complete Singles* that did it. Having rediscovered my iPod only days earlier, it went wobbly, froze and then, like my e-reader, reset itself to the factory state and offered me Chinese, Czech or Danish. 'That's entertainment,' I said, looking over my shoulder, but of course Zippy wasn't there. There was no fixing this; the volume of information was too large for Mags to email and the challenges of downloading music software onto a library computer were beyond my hacking abilities. I resolved to cope without music, to listen to the sea and birds, and talk to people. In retrospect I wonder, what might I have lost of the journey had I been plugged in?

A world without music requires adaptation. When alone - or when I thought I was alone - I soon began to sing loudly to myself or the animals. My mental register of songs was not exactly a radical mix, but what remained was what I could retrieve from my melodic and lyrical memory. Seven tracks. I had thought that my mind was stuck in their groove merely because I could recall their words and music, yet something did connect these particular earworms to the journey.

In the Harlyn Inn, the bartender asked, 'Are you staying?' as she handed me my drink and wiped the counter.

'No, just passing through. You have rooms?'

'We do have, until the weekend. We get a few walkers through.' She pointed to a poster.

The poster read: 'As You All May Know The Harlyn Inn will Be Closing Its Doors On Monday The 30th Of September. However Before That Happens We Would Love Nothing More Then To Invite You All To Come And Celebrate This Well

Loved Pub And Create Some More Memories With Us Before We Close'. Only Middle English had less restraint in the use of capital letters.

'Closing permanently?'

'There's talk of demolition.'

'I'm sorry.'

'Believe me, so am I.'

I left wishing I could have stayed for the final party. On the beach in front of the Inn an RNLI life guard explained to me his rapid distress scanning technique. Even as he explained it, I noticed his gaze drift across the shoreline and pause on the couple of people he had identified as weaker. He pointed me in the direction of the Path, which was partly hidden and inaccessible at high tide.

Beyond Trevose Head Lighthouse the crashing waves of Constantine Bay contrasted with the stillness of the water to the north. White water crashed on jagged rocks and slid from them as sand through fingers. Yellow RNLI wellies were positioned for a rapid exit on a lookout station welcome mat. Windsurfers, spectacularly airborne and then landing on waves, always appeared to move towards the shore but never reached it. After a time I came to the hostel, which was being sprayed with thick foam from the beach.

Wind blew a pile of leaflets from the front desk as I entered. The woman behind the counter picked them up and put them back where they had been. I was about to point out the futility of this, but she would work it out for herself. For thirty minutes I sat as she attempted to retrieve my record from the system. Eventually the manager arrived, quickly located the record and led me out to the site as the leaflets blew from the counter. I turned to watch her placing them back in a tidy pile.

As protection from the wind I put the tent between shepherd's huts and a large circular tent on a wooden platform, and after cooking I took the food to the bar. One other person sat, reading.

'Are you camping?' I turned to see if the question was directed at me. She had a big smile and sandy-coloured curly hair tied back off her face. I would have guessed mid- to late-twenties.

'Hello. Yes, that's my tent out there, about to take off.'

'Great. Me too. Except not today. Thought I'd try to get a room. I'm still waiting to see if there is one. They seem a little confused.' She nodded to the bar.

'I had the same experience earlier. Are you walking the Coast Path?'

'No. Something else.' She held out her hand. 'Freya.'

'Oscar. Pleased to meet you.'

She was walking the Cornish Celtic Way and my expression must have revealed that I'd never heard of it. It was new, combining the Coast Path with the Cornish Saints' Way and St Michael's Way - a sort of pilgrim's greatest hits. Starting in St Germans near Plymouth the Celtic Way heads west, crosses Cornwall on the Saints' Way, follows the coast roughly and at Hayle crosses the peninsula south to St Michael's Mount. Freya explained that churches provide accommodation along the way. Sometimes, if there was no church, you could substitute a hostel or a bivvy. Denying being a 'proper pilgrim' she was doing it for a friend who had put the guide together.

Over drinks she told me that she had studied life sciences, entomology, and had an interest in bees.

'Is it true what Einstein said, about the bees disappearing and the end of human life?' I asked.

'The end of the world as we know it? That's a myth. Einstein never said that.'

'No?'

'Well, they are a main pollinator and our crops rely on them. It would be bad. I'm not sure it would be the end.'

According to Freya someone called Maeterlinck claimed, in *The Life of the Bee*, that a hundred thousand varieties of plant would disappear and possibly even our civilisation.[36] That was bleak enough.

She smiled a big smile. 'It's not all bleak. Colony collapse disorder only affects honeybees and other bees also pollinate. As do some bats, butterflies, moths and hummingbirds.'

'Great, so it's fine.'

'No, we're pretty much screwing them all too.'

'Oh. I came through Padstow,' I said, changing the subject.

'I did too.'

'At the camp I stayed there was a bug house.'

'Interesting. I saw that too.' She showed me a photograph on her phone of the bug glamping shelter.

'Snap.' My own was almost the same image. 'And I thought I was original.'

'And I was just passing through. By coincidence I took a wrong turn and found it.'

Her favourite insect was the solitary bee. They burrow in the ground and leave eggs and food in each hole. They live solitary lives. It sounded sad to me, but then life in a colony is not a bed of roses.

'Does your pilgrimage take you along the coast tomorrow or inland?'

'The coast for a while and then inland, then the coast again. There is the odd church along the way, which means a detour. We could walk together for a bit, if you like.'

'That would be good. So long as you're not a solitary bee.'

'I can do company too.'

In the hostel, with the atmosphere and the company I felt simultaneously young and very, very old. We said goodnight, I showered and then went to the tent with the clear night and the sea foam sticking to my tent like white blood cells to a foreign body.

Something told me that Freya would be gone by the time I entered the hostel that morning. The weather had been a little troubled when I packed and wiped the foam from the tent; rain hadn't yet started.

It was quiet in the hostel except for a YHA worker getting ready for the breakfast run. I guess it was inevitable that she wouldn't want to be walking with an oldie. There was no hurry if I'd been left behind, so I put down my pack and stared at the darkening clouds through the window.

'How was your sleep?' The voice was behind me. It was Freya.

'Windy.'

'You ready to walk?'

'I am.' I grabbed my gear before she changed her mind.

We started walking in the early morning light, pacing to get ahead of the storm.

She explained how she knew the author of the Cornish Celtic Way, a reverend near Marazion. He planned the route, though it wasn't just for Christians but also those with different or no religion. Perhaps she could smell the unbeliever on me.

The cold rain began and we covered our packs and heads with waterproofs then walked in silence over the soft ground, occasionally complaining to one another about the conditions. I didn't feel like I needed to make conversation; it was enough to have company.

At Porthcothan Freya said we should keep in touch in case our paths crossed so we exchanged numbers and hugged goodbye. She walked up the walled lane towards farmland without looking back. On the cliffs, the Path marker signs had become small upright rectangles of slate. Ever-present fox moth caterpillars prepared for overwintering but in this weather they were curled up for warmth on the Path, beaded with rain.

The rain stopped but the wind remained strong with sudden unpredictable gusts. Twice I was caught unaware and thrown to the ground.

At the National Trust café at Bedruthan Steps where I had stopped for coffee the women I had met near Port Quin stumbled in. They were gasping, windblown and surprised to see me. I made room for them to sit. 'She was just airborne,' one said pointing to the smallest in the group who I had seen filling her bottle. 'We had to grab hold of her to save her being blown away.'

'Yes, I could have used your pack,' she said, laughing but clearly shaken.

'It wouldn't help. I've fallen myself, only harder.'

I said my goodbyes, but looked at them through the window, imagining them as the girls they once might have been. In the gift shop an American woman approached the counter, asking loudly, 'Excuse me, how do you say *harbour* in Cornish?'

The woman behind the counter leaned forward to say 'Well, I don't rightly know, my love. I'm from Yorkshire you see.' The visitor nodded and smiled questioningly.

I heard several Yorkshire accents in just this shop. After the tourists departed I asked to leave my pack and then queried what had brought them there. 'We'd come down on 'olidays, liked it and decided to move down. So much nicer. We never looked back.'

'Yorkshire has its own beauty.'

'You're right there. It does. Just that this has the sea, and the drama. We'll look after your bag if you want to see the beach. It'll be fine there.'

So, I walked down - was partly blown down - the Bedruthan steps to the beach. Where the metal handrail would meet the sea, it was rusted through. I could not have managed the descent with the pack in the wind.

It was a shame that Freya had missed this. The beach was sheltered from the wind and with the tide out I could walk between the stacks to observe them. Each of them was grey-green but jet black at the base to the high tide line, surrounded by miniature moats of greenish saltwater. All were pointed crumpled witches' hats. On closer inspection the black band became a living mass of mussels.

Back at the top the wind was still strong. I retrieved my bag, thanked the Yorkshire contingent and moved on across the cliffs then down onto a beach beside Trenance. At Mawgan Porth a message came through from Freya. 'I went to St Eval.' I imagined her saying this as *evil*. 'There was a church. Weird monoculture, military wasteland for miles – a bit depressing. Just left St Mawgan – had a pasty – heading back for the coast.' St Eval was built around an abandoned RAF base and the community was attempting to shape its own identity in their absence.

Rain hissed across the sea and arrived in a wall of water as the Path approached Newquay, quickly chilling my waterproofs. I considered a series of viewing shelters as refuges, but there was something unsafe about large towns; my residual memory of Newquay at night was of a riot, latent but taking form. Soon I was in town opposite the private island connected by a bridge to the mainland.

'You picked a good day for it!' a voice bellowed from the deluge, the face laughing smugly at me. He was capped and with a dog and standing across the footpath.

'On the contrary, I didn't *pick it*,' I smiled, stepping around him, our faces close. 'I do this *every* day whatever the weather. What's your excuse? You had a choice, and just look at that poor dog. It's freezing.'

'Oh, I, er, well ...' He looked down at himself with an unsure expression as I moved off. It was unnecessary but I couldn't help myself.

Near Towan Head I sheltered in a pub doorway to take Paddy's guidance. There was a place called Pentire Point beyond the town and it looked flat enough to take my tent.

'Are you lost too?' A hooded and heavily laden figure stopped beside the doorway.

It was Freya, looking miserable. 'I'm thinking about Pentire,' I said. 'I don't know why I bother drying my gear if it's only going to get wet again.' I was glad to see her. We could be miserable together.

'Look, there's a church in Crantock, across the river. If you haven't found a place, I'm sure you could stay there.'

The rain stopped beyond Pentire Point but we found the ferry chained off, the café shut. Off season. We stopped a local man and asked the way to the bridge.

'To Crantock? That's tidal. The bridge will be under water now. Sometime around eleven this evening it will be open. It's miles around the estuary though.'

'Thanks.' I looked at Freya. 'A submerged bridge.' The bus was a convoluted route back to Newquay and then another to Crantock so we took a cab to about 100 metres from where we had stood, the other side of a narrow stretch of water. There was a donation which we were to leave in the church hall, so I didn't feel so much an imposter. Another walker, Ollie, arrived from the beach and introduced himself. He had a bright, friendly face with something slightly devilish about it.

After a quick shop supplied by Freya, we cooked something improvised then headed to the pub. Both Ollie and Freya had an ecological spirit. We drank and talked about our two journeys, the state of the planet and horticulture. The two of them were so animated, discussing their outdoor lifestyle, and I was looking in through a misted window. We said goodnight and took our disparate pieces of the consecrated carpeted floor. I found a place near a piano that I hoped might block my snoring.

Over breakfast there was self-conscious polite chat, and it occurred to me that the piano may merely have acted to amplify my purrs. I watched Ollie and Freya with a little sadness as they passed through the lychgate on the Celtic Way, noting that her pack was almost as big as her. Then I took a side exit down towards the beach.

On the sand dunes were patches of luminous magenta. A villager with the same spirit of indignation that leaves post-it notes on taps and thermostats for flatmates, had outlined all the dog shit with red paint like a sanitary Poirot. If you do this in some parts of London it is liable to end badly for you.

After the beautiful sandy beach of Polly Joke (Porth Joke) as it's known locally, the path ascended to the cliffs where an absence of music meant contending with the wind's sound as well as its strength. As though the path was not dangerous enough, a herd of cows crossed my way near the cliff, so I skirted the field, being buffeted from side-to-side by the gale. Out of the corner of my eye a little shape shot along the cliff edge, scattering the herd. When I re-joined the Path the shape was waiting for me; it was a small man, hooded and hunched into the wind.

'You gave them a wide berth,' he yelled.

'I thought it best to avoid them, since they were so close to the cliff,' I explained, squinting as the wind increased in intensity.

'Probably wise,' he shouted. 'Perhaps I should have too. I normally walk with my wife.' I wondered whether this was relevant; was his wife a cow whisperer? 'She's back in Germany so I'm filling in some of the stretches we haven't done.' His accent was English, neutral, not German.

'Roighppupp.' My mouth filled with air, flapping my cheeks.

'Er, yes. Okay, I'd better be off. Bye.' With that he was gone like a little wind-up toy racing across the cliffs.

At the next beach I stood my pack in a prominent position near the dunes and took a dry path down to the waves over the shining wave-wrinkled sand. The split rock of Holywell, Carter's or Gull Rocks, was recognisable from the romantic walks of Ross and Demelza in the most recent BBC *Poldark* television series.

Leaving the beach, I recognised white boards used in filming, across the sand. What were the chances? I was reciting in my head what I would say when I met Aidan Turner. I would make an introduction casual yet profound.

One of the crew told me what they were filming and, alas, it was a Netflix series called *Cursed.* 'It's a re-imagining of the King Arthur legend ... and there are horses,' he said. Curses. There was already too much re-imagining of Arthur on the Path, mostly injection-moulded plastic re-imagining in Tintagel gift shops. So, no *Poldark.* Not so much as Eleanor Tomlinson or Jack Farthing in sight.

The exit from Holywell was via a film studio diversion across a stream, where I again passed the British man from Germany who was watching the sea and the production crew. Perhaps the expatriate didn't yet know it wasn't *Poldark,* and was rehearsing his own opening line to Ross. Not having the heart to disappoint him, I said hello and quickly walked on.

Decaying grey Nissen huts littered the hill above the beach, barracks displaying signs of dereliction. From the top, looking down on the camp behind its high fence, it was hard to believe that it could still be in use. Mould grew inside windows and the metal casement frames were rusted, yet there were prominent army danger signs.

I later read that the whole camp was for sale. It had been abandoned since 2010 when the Afghan conflict was declared 'over' (my Afghan colleagues would be happily surprised to hear that the war was over). If I were to buy the camp, I wouldn't turn it into a holiday village. I'd leave it as a camp so that tourists could experience life as a POW, a sort of Cornish *Fantasy Island.*

Stalag Luft XIII wasn't much worse than some of the commercial holiday camps that could be seen along the coast. Dereliction came naturally here. The salt air, the clawing wind and rain found gaps where none could be seen. Once vacated and without heating, dampness set in and structures softened. The chain-link fences to my right, on the cliff side, were rusted and shredded by wind, falling away from crumbling concrete posts, revealing their red steel skeletons.

As I contemplated this dereliction, a fast-moving silhouette, a small robot, appeared far below me, walking at speed along the cliff edge. There is something unnerving about being followed by someone, ordinarily, but these rapid jerky movements made me want to stand on a chair. I moved quickly around the point.

A concrete seat provided me refuge from the wind and I was crouched behind it having tea when the British German approached. He came to an immediate halt without slowing, like a subject in an old hand-cranked film running at unnatural speed. It occurred to me that I was cowering behind a bench, a fact I attempted to disguise by smiling and looking casual.

'Hello. I'm not hiding, you know,' I shouted into the gale. 'Wind.'

He frowned. 'Hello again. I'm Kent,' Kent shouted above the wind. 'I live in Frankfurt and come back for holidays. We're walking the Coast Path.' I glanced about for anyone small enough that I may have overlooked, looking to explain his *we*. 'Normally I come with my wife but this time I'm walking alone as I have some free time.' This all came out in the first few seconds as though he'd said it many times before. Of course, I had already heard much of this.

There was something a little sad about him. I wondered if Mrs Kent was busy or if she just didn't feel like walking. With this wind, I could appreciate that. Perhaps she just wanted some time alone. I thought about Mags, and probably both of those things were true of her, so perhaps I was just projecting myself.

We exchanged our stories in a volley of shouting. No doubt I left him with the impression that I was a sad person walking alone in this military wasteland without vocation. Something bothered me, and that was the possibility that there was no Mrs Kent. It was something about the way he had brought her into the conversation too early, uninvited like a fond memory, a revenant. As he left, I regretted having avoided conversation. He had grown on me. Clearly conversation didn't come easily to him; he craved it yet was suddenly driven on as though shocked by the fire of discourse he had ignited with his casual words. He was heading to Perranporth, so perhaps we would see each other again.

Kent moved off in his mechanical way, from stationary to ten kilometres per hour without accelerating. I followed a few minutes later though I didn't fear catching him up. Two day-walkers approached with their child as I was tossed about by the wind and had to cling to a barbed-wire fence for balance. 'It's very windy down there,' I warned.

'It's not much better up there, I'm afraid,' she yelled.

He added: 'From a distance you looked like a high-sided lorry'.

It was the rain cover. It was a kite, so I removed it.

Perran Sands was more than four kilometres of white beach, and it made a hard, flat surface. I walked the beach rather than negotiate the wind and the dune conservation area.

The hostel in Perranporth crouched on a cliff edge and had a small seating area on the cliff side overlooking the beach and sea. I stashed my bag in the drying room just as the rainstorm started. By the time I was back in town I realised that my day pack was not only lightweight and collapsible but also highly absorbent. Paddy dripped as I laid him out with my other belongings in the café where I sheltered. Waiting staff offered me numerous non-absorbent serviettes that are unique to low budget cafés. I spent some time looking through charity shops but was self-conscious from my unsociable dripping, and with my bag beneath the front of my hooded raincoat I thought I must appear like a shoplifter. When a woman uncertainly offered to give up her seat for me, I realised instead that all I appeared was pregnant. I responded in the deepest voice I could offer, 'Water retention'.

The seafront offered some solitude until loud music suddenly erupted, and women dressed in red robes and bonnets appeared from the sand in a dour procession. Their faces were ashen, and they wore solemn expressions. They were followed by men in white nightshirts and sackcloth tabards. I looked about, ready to be evicted by a studio hand from this low budget production of Margaret Atwood's *The Handmaid's Tale*.

The procession moved onto walls and benches and then I could see that some of the men wore wooden signs about their necks. 'CORNWALL'S BEACH ECONOMY THREATENED BY EXTREME WEATHER'. Rain ran down their faces and wind whipped their robes. '75% OF ARTIC ICE MELTED SINCE 1990.' 'RISING SEA LEVELS.' Extinction Rebellion. Not a film but a protest, if a theatrical one.

Moving further off for shelter, my pregnant presence beneath an apartment's porch - ignoring the 'Residents only' sign - may have smelled of quiet Stoicism (think *social apathy*). Of course, I was on the moral - if not lateral - side of these ecodoomsters, but they were bound for fossil-fuel-warmed beds. Standing watching these performers in their cold, rain-soaked robes it was difficult to imagine the crisis of global heating, though I knew it was getting hotter. I shivered and walked up the hill.

At the hostel I stood shivering and staring at a dark window of the locked building. It was like looking into a mirror; a drawing of a dead-eyed itinerant stared back at me. The warden's car drew up so I followed her inside.

'You want to camp? There's one pitch out there but you'd need to move the picnic table first. It's heavy. There's a severe weather warning tonight and the wind blows up from that cliff like a hurricane so it's not without risk. There's only that picket fence and then the drop. There are beds, though.' She was really selling it to me.

'What's the price difference?'

'A pound.'

'Which is the more expensive?'

She just smiled and tilted her head. Whether the bed was a bargain or the offer of certain death was overpriced I couldn't be sure, but I imagined the wind and that traveller staring out at me with his pipe and so said 'I'll take a dorm bed, thanks'. Then I tried to dry my gear but lacking heat and imagination I left them on a coat hook to drip.

A group of Belgian men arrived and quickly took control of the kitchen so I hovered uncomfortably in the lounge. Unexpectedly, one of them offered me some of their food. It broke the deadlock. They were on a road trip and had stayed at various hostels along the Cornish coast. 'We are doing the *Poldark* tour' one exclaimed with pride. He pronounced it Pole Dark as though on a pub crawl of exotic dance venues. That Belgians even knew about *Poldark* surprised me. Also, I had assumed it was predominantly of interest to women, so it was refreshing to see men genuinely engaged. Saying that, the series does cover the history of politics, conflict, slavery, mining, workers' rights, justice and scything. Something for everyone, I'd have thought. The one thing lacking in the television series is an honest depiction of Cornish weather, though who really wants to watch what you can see by opening a curtain?

One other man from the north of England was in my dorm, having come down for a rest. I resisted telling him he'd picked a good day for it.

TWO: The End of the Beginning

Forgive us our trespasses
Day 20. 29ᵗʰ September

I arose early to a silent building. The Belgians had somehow evaporated, heading for Heathrow; all their walking clothes and *Poldark* memorabilia had gone. My dorm mate had similarly dematerialised during the night and returned to Birmingham. Not even a staff member remained, the warden residing off-site. It was as though the evening had never been. I felt strangely abandoned, especially having made a special effort to get up early. I showered, packed and opened the door on the unsettled weather. As the Yale latch struck the plate and slipped its tongue in with a swish-click, in a final irrevocable kiss the door shut and I was alone and exposed.

The Path skirted Perranporth Airfield, a former **WWII RAF** aerodrome now in civilian use. Picnic tables, boards missing, lay rotting yet *Perranporth Aerodrome* was displayed on them on pristine shiny yellow plastic ownership signs as though affixed by a lunatic.

Trevellas Coombe was the first example of the famous Cornish chimney, but the weather was too miserable to do it justice. On the far side of the valley two men stood discussing the trail. One leaned on a dirt bike.

'Are you riding up there?' I asked, looking ahead. It was narrow, steep and dangerous.

'We do this regularly, race to the top. We'll have about 20 motorcycles here soon. Don't worry, you have a few moments before they arrive.' It took me *a few moments* just to start moving. It was odd for the Coast Path to be used for motocross, but the iron gate at the foot of the slope bore an image of a motorcycle among its filigree; this was official and historical, not a misuse of the Coast Path. The race from London to Land's End, which started in 1908, was meant to test endurance. As roads improved, the riders began using small off-road sections such as this. I hurried as best I could, pushed on by the sound of engines warming up behind me. Soon I was in the next cove, Trevaunance Cove near St Agnes. Watchkeepers of the National Coastwatch Institution station waved to me as I passed beneath their sheltered box. The famous Wheal Coates' restored engine house and chimney towered above as I made my way to Chapel Porth where I asked the National Trust warden if there was time to make it to Porthtowan by the beach. He checked the tides. 'You'll *just* make it. There are a couple of streams, but you'll find your way across. It's flat as a pancake, so the tide comes in quickly,' he warned. The sun came out and there was little wind so I quickly made up time.

From Porthtowan the ground was level and crossed the edge of fields to Nancekuke Common Airfield. The makers of Nancekuke had the forethought to include a chemical weapons factory, decommissioned since the 1970s. It was an outstation of Porton Down which produced CS gas, or tear gas, used in Northern Ireland. It also produced sarin nerve agent. Like CS, SARIN's name is formed from the surnames of its creators, who worked for the chemical company responsible for Zyklon B. At least one was tried at Nuremberg. And we were producing it.

Said Robert Harris (the novelist) and Jeremy Paxman in their enquiry into chemical weapons development in the UK:

> *For the manufacture of nerve gas, the British chose a remote clifftop on the north Cornish coast, where the RAF already maintained an airbase. Nancekuke appeared an ideal site, high on a clifftop, well away from human habitation and with any accidentally released clouds of gas likely to blow out to sea. Many of the same considerations also made the area a popular holiday area, but inquisitive tourists were kept away from the place by eight-foot-tall fences. The Ministry of Defence later described the plant at Nancekuke as a 'design exercise against the event of the UK requiring a retaliatory capability as a deterrent'.* [Ministry of Defence press release, 29

87

> October 1970] *By 1953, this 'design exercise' was*
> *producing 6 kilograms of GB nerve agent every*
> *hour.*[97] [GB was the NATO designation for Sarin]

Paxman and Harris documented accidents and illness related to the site which were, naturally, played down by the MoD. In a facility which manufactured death not by accident, but by design, incidents are inevitable.

At the end of the Nancekuke base were derelict concrete buildings that would have made good overnight accommodation. They were dry and sheltered, but I had doubts. I would try my chances in the woods near Portreath which would place me further along the Path with fewer opportunities for premature death. In retrospect I should have taken my chances with the nerve agent.

The sun was shining when I left the convenience store in Portreath and bumped into an uncharacteristically-still Kent. He had stopped for a beer in a pub by the water, which he recommended, so his stillness may have been the effects of alcohol. I said I would come back when I had pitched the tent; I could pitch discreetly and then return to town. Having a drink with him on his last night seemed a good thing to do.

A piece of unpopulated flat land in a perfect circle sat adjacent to Illogan Woods, if only I could find a way across the fence. This was my safe alternative to nerve agent, but my plans quickly unravelled.

Climbing to the top of a damp, leaf-carpeted bank and crouching beneath low branches, I sought the easiest section of fence to vault then lifted the pack across. It dropped on the far side of the wire with a thud. The next five minutes were spent snagging my waterproofs repeatedly on the high barbs until I finally cleared the obstacle. The field led to a stile and then another field of cows. They were between me and the flat circle of grass I had seen on the satellite image. It was then that I saw the dead trapped badger. It had been deliberately killed. The rights and wrongs of badger culling aside, what occurred to me was that a farmer who was willing to kill a badger - which is cute and furry -

is hardly going to think twice about putting the wind up me. It wasn't a theory I was willing to test.

The idea of trespassing on what was clearly farmland didn't appeal so I backtracked, moving towards a distant house where I could ask permission. It was then that a thought formed – where there are cows there is a bull, usually in an adjacent field. I was in an adjacent field. There were countless hoofprints around me. In fact, this seemed to be a wide expanse of field with no fences. The bull could be anywhere, and with a section of the Berlin Wall on my back I had little chance of outrunning it. By this time my feet were firmly bogged in the mire. I moved, as best I could, dreamlike through treacle towards the nearest fence separating me from the woods.

Barbs tore at my waterproofs as I straddled the fence on tiptoes, the weight of the pack straining my muscles. A stream had to be crossed and then a composite of crumbling wall and earth which entailed lifting the pack atop and retrieving it from the far side. When I reached the path on the bank above, my legs had the tell-tale signs of strain.

Clouds of midges in Illogan woods were revealed by the sun streaming through trees. At last I came to the farm driveway and there, on the pillar, was a small YHA hostel sign. *No!* At the farmhouse a tree doctor was packing his truck. 'She's away, but I can let you in.'

The sun had set by the time the owner arrived. She could have walked out of an Agatha Christie novel, formal and aristocratic in tweeds. She lived in the large house that I had seen from the field.

'I'm sorry, you can't camp but I can give you a bunk. There's a bull in those fields you see,' she said, pointing to where I had been trapped in the Grimpen Mire, 'and I have no idea where it is. It's the tenant farmer's'. I didn't feel quite so paranoid, only increasingly sore and nauseous from the thought of the bull.

We talked of the old days of hostelling and how things have changed but soon the conversation moved to *Poldark*. The attraction of European tourists to *Poldark* seems to be a recent theme. 'You should see the church at Illogan. There's a *Poldark* story there. Winston Graham lived in Perranporth, where you've just come from. Demelza was based on his own wife. She was born in "Illugan".' I would pay it a visit in the morning.

My legs were cold and ached, but I felt sleepy. Events had overtaken me and in exhaustion I accepted that I wouldn't make it back to share that drink with Kent. I would never meet him again. It was a haunted night in the old house, with dreams of things on the brink of change.

To the lighthouse
Day 21. 30th September

The hostel owner met me outside the mansion. 'I spoke to our resident tree doctor and he tells me there'll be a storm coming in this afternoon, about one o'clock. Best make haste.' I thanked her for letting me stay on the farm without a booking, and then headed to the graveyard in Illogan village.

Inside the cemetery walls a dog-walker asked if she could help. 'I'm just browsing,' I explained. She fixed me with a reproachful look and left, tugging her dog behind. The grave I sought – of the Basset family, Francis Basset being a political character in the novels – was a large elongated urn. It was an impressive urn and Francis Bassett no doubt looked elegant in a red coat, but I couldn't help thinking that he had done little for me but cause delay and ensure I was to be walking in a storm.

Leaving the cemetery it was now clear why the Belgians were in Perranporth. Graham wrote there, but more than just *Poldark*; he contributed plays, thrillers and psychological dramas. Most famous was Marnie,[38] which, like Daphne du Maurier's *The Birds*, was both adapted by Hitchcock and starred Tippi Hedren. The book is bleaker than the film, but then it would be. It's set in England.

On the flat expanse of Caravennel Downs my shin started causing me pain. Like the fear of ghosts, thinking that pretending it was not there would make it go away, I walked on, squinting into the rain.

Carparks were spaced over several kilometres and in each sat drivers, sheltered from the gale behind glass, staring out at the hunched figure trudging, soon limping, by. Something wasn't right. That bull. A needle jab in my left shin came with every step, and it was increasing in intensity in the cold. A dull ache crept across the left of my chest. There was some respite as the Path moved between high hedges but mostly it was exposed. The wind blew uncharacteristically towards the cliff edge as I made my way past Deadman's Cove, towards Hell's Mouth. Heights are not my favourite, but as with all horror you can't help but stare, so I peered over the edge. *Hell's teeth.*

At the foot of the hill, I noticed a building on the far side of the road. It looked like it might have been a café or a toilet block. There was no reason to expect it would be open on this day at the end of the world. In desperation I staggered down to the car park and pushed at the door. It gave! A sliver of light sliced into the gloom.

Inside was modern and stylish; not what I would expect from a café in such a remote location. There was one other table occupied and a friendly Londoner behind the counter offered me a menu.

'You aint so wa'erproof, bruv. Come up when you like. Take yo time.' A succession of windblown and damp people slid in after me. The door closed on the screaming wind, the tail of Hurricane Lorenzo scouring the cliffs of Deadman's Cove behind them.

The thought of leaving was ghastly but my friend David would soon be arriving in St Erth and I was to join him near St Ives. The wind tugged me towards Hell's Mouth as I rejoined the Path, and Godrevy lighthouse gradually came into view, though its island was veiled in mist. It took an age to reach. Rocks on the Point provided me with a seat for tea. Really, I rested because of the pain, which had become intolerable. My hip clicked and a tightness gripped my chest; my body had reached its limit. I stared at the lighthouse which appeared and disappearing in the drifting cloud. I knew this place.

In her novel *To the Lighthouse,* author Virgina Woolf places her fictional lighthouse in Scotland, but she based it on Godrevy

Lighthouse in Cornwall. My copy of the novel was a gift from friends when I left the West Country to work overseas. I read it during the monsoon, rain pounding the palms and shaking the blue wooden scroll blinds on my balcony – weather not unlike this. The book pages curled like petals in the humidity.

Though the novel is a meditation on loss and grief and the changing class structure after the First World War, the parts of *To the Lighthouse* which stayed with me were the descriptions of decay, of the absence of people. These are contained in the second part, 'Time Passes' where she describes a house, now uninhabited, overtaken by vegetation and then:

> ... the roof would have fallen; briars and hemlocks would have blotted out path, steps, and window; would have grown, unequally but lustily over the mound, until some trespasser, losing his way, could have told only by a red-hot poker among the nettles, or a scrap of china in the hemlock, that here once some one had lived; there had been a house.[39]

I read it in Cambodia, where I would spend days wandering places like Kirirom, the abandoned 1960s hill station – its holiday homes with giraffe-paved chimneys and the unnecessarily angled façades of the period slowly being consumed by forest.

This fascination with the reclamation of human endeavour by nature captured me but I didn't understand it. Richard, the Buddhist friend who believed walking was a primeval urge, had a theory. He believed it was caused by the shattering of our illusions. We all hold the belief or hope, however misplaced, that our world is solid and unchanging – that we will be here forever. When we see that the earth, plants, the elements, tear apart the objects of our creation in our absence, that illusion of permanence is disrupted. We stare in fascination at the proof that we are temporary. A red lichen-covered hotel on Mount Bokor in Cambodia. Weed-invaded bumper cars at Pripyat inside the Chernobyl exclusion zone. Time passes.

Woolf, on childhood holidays in St Ives, would have seen this power of nature. But these were her solitary memories, and she offered no welcome to the careless wanderer who might trip upon the remains of former lives. I was just 'some trespasser, losing his way'.

The approach to the beach was flooded and required a detour. Every step felt like a kick in the shin as I limped over the dunes. Walking on sand was excruciating with the injury and the weight of the pack. A kilometre was more like three, battling up and then sliding down each hill of sand, the grass sharp and the rain unforgiving. It was easy to lose yourself in the warren and I was frequently lost.

In this way I moved from Godrevy Towans to Gwithian Towans, Upton Towans and Mexico Towans. A desolate graveyard of mobile homes reached beyond the grassed dunes. It would have been romantic had I not been in it. I limped down to the flat sand and walked to the end of the beach where quicksand warning signs drove me up the dunes past the garden of a lookout. Glass electrical pylon insulators lay on the ground, the discarded tentacles of a Martian fighting machine. The pylons were lifeless, frozen mid stride the way I had come.

In Hayle I entered a convenience store seeking material to stuff my boots. Discreetly placing the pack in the least congested spot I then sought red top sleaze for the task. I opted for an evil little tabloid which prided itself on winning elections for the moderate Conservative and the right-wing Labour. I paid for two identical copies, which caused some confusion, and then struggled to put the papers into my pack at which point the most senior shop assistant said, 'Are you okay?' It wasn't a question out of concern. 'We need space in here for customers.'

'And what am I? I'm just leaving. Thanks,' I added, and walked out. With no hope of a taxi in the mid-afternoon rain I continued to walk beside the main road, playing a limping game of chicken with the traffic to cross to Lelant Saltings where I thought I might catch David's train. The station had a reduced service. The next was Lelant, which I reached only to watch a train fly by. On I moved through suburbia, but on reaching the sea I realised my leg could no longer support me so I retreated to wait for a train. Sodden waterproofs clung to my skin and I shivered.

I had known David for around ten years, in various roles. We had both been in Afghanistan though not at the same time. I had been conspicuous. Sultan, a good friend, had once quickly ushered me along a road, his arm protectively around me. I thanked him for his thoughtfulness as we entered the compound. 'No,' he said, 'you are a big target my friend – but they may miss you and I'm a larger target'. He was joking, or at least I hoped he was. David, though, had the advantage of being able to pass for a local, at least from a distance. As long as he kept his mouth shut, David could pass for an Afghan. Given the insecurity there, it occurred to me that Cornwall was the closest the two of us might come to a short walk in the Hindu Kush.

Eventually a train arrived but heading in the wrong direction. 'Are you heading to St Ives?' the conductor asked as it slowed.

'Hoping to.'

'Look, get on. Better than waiting here. It will be this train you get anyway. There's only one track.'

'Thanks, 'preciate 'at,' I slurred. It wasn't much warmer inside, but at least I was out of the wind. I didn't dare remove any clothes as they trapped some heat and I was too exhausted to find dry ones.

At St Erth, the doors opened and there was David. 'Suppise, Dawid' I said, my jaw quivering.

'Man, are you okay?'

We arrived in St Ives and the conductor advised us on eating options. 'Your best bet is the Wetherspoons.'

I unevenly squelched to the pub's bathroom on my bad and less bad leg, then looked forlornly at my reflection. It seemed that no matter how well my boots were waxed, water found a way in, probably through gaps where the rubber sole met the upper. The easiest thing may have been to buy new boots, but I'd heard so many horror stories about boots not yet broken in (being unable to walk anyway, you might argue I could at least have opted to be dry). So, I hung onto them like Dan to his perished tent and exploded sleeping bag, resolving to patch them up. To take them to the end now seemed somehow important (nostalgia can be needlessly self-destructive).

'Feeling warmer?'

'A little. When I've eaten I'll be fine.' We ordered some sort of Thai vegetable curry with rice and tea. 'Look, you may have noticed my walking ...'

'I was going to ask.'

'I'm not sure I'm going to be able to walk any more. Maybe if we took a day to rest tomorrow and I just hung around town. The other thing is this campsite. It's a bit out of town so we can get a cab.'

'Or we could just get a B&B. If we have to be coming in each day we might as well be here.' So, David found a place near where I stopped walking on the bay. 'All booked. We might be able to get the train back. Have you been to a doctor?'

'It only happened today. I think it may have been the field with the bull.'

'You got chased by a bull?'

'No, not exactly. That is, I knew it was there, in the field, but equally it might not have been. A sort of Schrodinger's bull. The only way of knowing for sure would have been to stay there and egg it on and then I wouldn't be able to confirm it to you. I must have damaged something getting out.'

'To escape from the bull which may not have existed?'

'As it turned out, it did. The hostel owner told me. My own fault really. I was aiming for a nice piece of flat ground. It turned out to be an ancient site, so probably good that I didn't find it.'

After the meal, a conductor ushered us back onto the train and charged us one pound for the journey. 'This must be subsidised. We're the only passengers. It wouldn't pay his salary never mind the fuel.' David was intrigued by such economic dilemmas.

On account of a shortcut, we got to the bed and breakfast slightly more tired than anticipated.

'Hello. Is a double room okay?' she asked as the door opened. We looked at each other.

'I could take the floor - I'm used to it,' I offered.

'Oh, okay?' She said slowly, leaving an audible question mark. 'There *is* a twin room.'

'Thanks, a twin is fine,' David jumped in.

'You can always move the beds together if you want,' she chimed in, then chatted about her business while making tea.

Jay was an interesting woman. She'd been in security and then a carer/foster parent. She clearly cared about people, and over the years she'd helped some of the more troubled. She showed us to our room and let us feel at home.

In our room, we tried not to make eye contact, but the silence was stifling. David remarked, 'Oh, one thing. I forgot to mention she thought we were a couple'.

'That's fine.'

'Do you want to move the beds together?' David asked, smiling.

'Funny. I don't know what you're looking so pleased with yourself about. I don't feel comfortable being cast as the older predator. Do you think we can rig up a washing line in here? I really must get some of this mud out of my stuff.'

I stuffed my boots with the newspaper while David read some of the hideous headlines. He scanned a particularly xenophobic commentary. 'This paper is vile,' he said, scrunching it for me to stuff.

'Yes, vile, but surprisingly absorbent and comparatively the lowest price by volume. And, I almost got thrown out of the shop before I could buy it. They couldn't understand why I would want two copies of the same tabloid.'

'A reasonable question, I'd have thought. One is too much. What are you writing?'

'Just notes. Keeping a record.'

David held me with a look of concern. 'Oscar, before I leave Cornwall ...'

'Yes?'

'... I must ... have ... a Cornish pasty.' I could tell that he meant it. My boots swollen, and socks on the line, he extinguished the light.

David read reviews of the Tate St Ives while I dressed that morning. '"A waste of money." This person doesn't beat about the bush. "This was not our cup of tea. My *husband* described it as like the *Emperors' New Clothes!* Staff frosty. Best bit was the view out to sea." The review is from November 2018. Perhaps it was a bad patch.'

'That was a pretty accurate description. It's a matter of taste.'

'We should go. I really want to see it.' I suspected that he would take an unusually practical approach to artistic criticism. He would be looking for function over form. David may not know much about art, but he could tell you what you could do with it.

After some essential shopping we planned to hit the gallery. I lit candles in the church for Mags' father and my mother, then we visited the Tate St Ives.

We were welcomed in the entrance hall by a palm tree composed of aluminium in chipped white paint with coloured incandescent lightbulbs, most of which did not work. Torquay in winter, I guessed. No, but close. It was Moroccan Yto Varrada's *Palm Sign*, a comment on western tourism, which 'brings a different perspective to ideas of the light and landscape traditionally associated with Cornwall'. The Light traditionally associated with St Ives.

One local painting in particular made an impression on me. *Tol Pedn* is an abstract rendering of a coast watch station and day marks. Artist John Tunnard left London and became a coastguard in West Cornwall during the war. *Tol Pedn,* painted in 1942, was a headland not far from here. He had been captivated by two concrete landmarks. I made a note to look for them.

David and I sat to watch a 1960s black and white film. Wearing large headphones, we appeared in the black screen's reflection like boys on a very dull school trip. The film was about Cornwall.

'So what is the St Ives' Light exactly?' David asked when the film had ended.

'It's what brings the artists here. Can't you see it? Look, out the window.' It was raining and unmoving dark clouds formed a canopy over the jagged grey sea.

'Yes, I see what you mean.'

'If it's raining here, the rest of Cornwall is in complete darkness.'

David frowned. 'Do you think perhaps it's like organic tomatoes tasting better? It increases the property sale price. It does seem to be a very white, middle-class place.'

'Do you have a problem with that?' It hadn't escaped me either how white the whole county was.

'Perhaps it doesn't sit well with my working-class self-image.'

Comedian and social commentator Mark Steel, speaking of the origins of his *Mark Steel's in Town* radio programme explained: 'I was in Penzance in Cornwall to do a comedy show about 10 years ago, and three times during the day I was told, "Don't go to St Ives, Mark. It's posh and full of snobs." So that evening I mentioned this to the audience, and a woman shouted, "It's true, they are posh – they've even got their own dentist."'[40] Clearly this says as much about Penzance as it does about St Ives. In fact, it says very little about St Ives.

'Self-interest in maintaining the idea of The Light doesn't disprove its existence,' I argued.

Sculptor Barbara Hepworth, like many of the women in National Trust shops, came from the West Riding of Yorkshire. She wrote of her new home in 1946: 'The horizontal line of the sea and the quality of light and colour which reminds me of the Mediterranean light and colour, which so excites one's sense of form'.[41] It was almost a complete sentence; a sentence for which the expression *arty farty* had been intended. *All* of the sea, without exception, has shown me a horizontal line. In the same year as Hepworth, 1946, George Orwell wrote 'in art criticism and literary criticism, it is normal to come across long passages which are completely lacking in meaning'.[42] The Light of St Ives owes a lot to the meaningless postulations of artists.

'I can't believe you can't see the quality of The Light,' I said dismissively to David as we left the gallery. 'You haven't been paying attention.'

If there is one artist that I associate with both the South West Coast Path, but also the Tate (Tate Britain), it is Joseph Mallord William Turner. He expressed this country's landscape and atmosphere better than any other artist. There is a reason Turner was the name given to that prize. He was controversial as an artist in his own lifetime, for painting as he saw - not as those who commissioned him expected the finished work to look.

Why Turner's association with the South West Coast Path? Simply because he must have spent more time on the Path than most walkers, in often atrocious weather, given the detail given to his drawings and paintings. Many of these were included as engravings in a book entitled *Picturesque Views on the Southern Coast of England*.[43] Turner reproduced its length, from Minehead and Porlock through to Land's End and on to Poole – thirty-four drawings and twenty-nine separate locations; the main sites along the Path.[44] It is possible to stand at all the places he stood to sketch these views; many of them are unchanged.

'I've got a treat for us tonight. We're going to the pictures.' I dangled this in front of David as we left.

'What's showing?'

'*Downton Abbey*. The film.'

'I've never seen the series. What's it about?'

'It's got everything. Drama, politics, mystery, humour,' I lied. Well, humour certainly; it must be, at its heart, a comedy. 'I just feel this is the place to see it.'

After a hasty meal at a pub we visited the art deco blue and mould Royal Cinema and took our seats. The lights dimmed.

'That wasn't bad,' David said as we left the cinema.

'No, it wasn't.' The plot had included an assassination attempt on the monarch, a raid on a gay club and the oppression of the Irish. Not quite what I had been expecting from a Julian Fellowes costume drama.

Back at Carbis Bay David asked, 'We rise at dawn-ish?'

'Definitely. We're heading to Pendeen which is a full day's walk.'

The End of the World Club
Day 23. 2ᵈ October

A song was stuck in my head, and there it had to remain as David was with me. It made my mental playlist. Track One. Crowded House's *Don't Dream It's Over*.[45] This mourns the lazy human tendency to turn away from the grim reality of half the world and to meaninglessly accumulate *stuff.* The things that really weigh me down are not on my back. We have all the objects we gather over our lifetime: theatre ticket stubs and photographs, the pieces of physical memory with which we will not part - UXEO (unexploded emotional ordnance); furniture to give us comfort; electrical goods and toys to entertain; books and records; carpets and interior decorations; motorised vehicles and bicycles. They are insured against theft, flood and fire. We are willingly imprisoned along with them like prison wardens or the servants of Pharaohs. Our possessions conspire against us. *Are their patterns strange to you?*

The weather was fine as we walked the coastline from St Ives to Pendeen. We passed through the town and gradually moved into a rugged landscape. David raced ahead like a goat, but for me every step was a cutthroat razor in the shin, my hip clicked like a marionette, and a sharp pain crossed the left of my chest. I had to find a doctor.

When I eventually caught up with David we sat on the rocky headland and I removed my boot. The left leg had taken on its shape. 'That doesn't look good,' said a smiling walker heading back towards St Ives. At rest, it felt merely like an itch deep inside the bone. The misshapen leg seemed to belong to another body; my walking days were over.

Chest pain, oedema, a thiamine-low grain-free diet and extreme exercise. Numbness in the feet. Beriberi! None of these thoughts did I share with David. Now, this does seem like hypochondria, but consider Sophia's brother.

Sophia was a friend in Brixham, Devon, who used to make wine from anything vegetable – rhubarb, cucumber, any number of coastal weeds, some possibly toxic - and then she would make me drink them and ask me to offer a verdict. Many were excellent. The experimental variety, we agreed, were awful, having the aroma of turps, but I did tend to get drunk very quickly. Being in my twenties, this was appreciated, and she was great company.

During one such drinking meet, Sophia told me of her adventuring brother Jan (they were of Dutch extraction). A sailor, Jan had deliberately marooned himself on an island in order to beat the record in folklore of Blackbeard and his men. He had a supply of rum but otherwise he survived by fishing. As the Blackbeard story was folklore, he had of course broken the record after ten minutes. Nevertheless, he intrepidly persisted and developed thiamine deficiency. Lower leg oedema is a symptom of beriberi. Rum plus thiaminase-containing fish[46] is not a balanced diet.

I had to find a doctor.

'I'll try to walk with the laces untied. I'm sure that will work. It's probably the pressure from the boot.' I drank rehydration solution and then we walked until the sun dropped. For safety we agreed to move onto the road running parallel to the cliffs.

The lights of the village were visible, but the road meandered and the distance never appeared to lessen. David kindly swapped packs with me, so the pain migrated from my leg to my shoulder which was more tolerable.

Photographs on a wall in Pendeen's North Inn caught my eye and I resolved to show David later. Neither of us felt like alcohol. We ate that mysterious English dish, vegetable curry and rice with tea, before camping in the dark in the least muddy spot. The stars were clear but both of us were exhausted and fell asleep almost immediately.

'Take a look at this,' I called to David in the morning, leading him into the bar to show him the pub wall. 'Hang on. Someone's stolen them. There were dozens of photos here, before.'

'Don't worry, they're safe.' A woman held up a paintbrush. 'Refurbishing. I have to do this wall.'

'Looking for my fan paparazzi pictures from *Poldark*?' An elderly, bearded man popped up from behind the bar. He did look like an ageing pirate.

'Are you famous?' David asked, looking from him to the photographs on the bar. I'm not entirely sure if David knew *Poldark* or if he even owned a television.

'They haven't had me speaking yet. I'm an extra. It's really my beard they want. They won't let me trim it.' He scratched at his neck as though it irritated him.

'Brilliant!' David smiled quizzically, but sincerely. It wasn't Aidan Turner, but it was the next best thing.

The smoking area of the pub was a good tent folding space though everything became slightly ashen. We removed the pack items selected for repatriation to London. They were the solar panel with its one functioning socket (the power pack I could continue to charge by theft of electricity), the empty rum hipflask and cups, the deceased iPod and a few essentials that had become desirables. A bar of antique green Fairy laundry soap (I believed I had the last case in the UK) was now a fragment, the rest having been donated to Jay's B&B.

Pendeen's tiny post office had no packing material so we scrounged a box and tape from a grocery store. The weight saving was around two-and-a-half kilograms, so in total I had sent more than five kilograms back home. Combined with carrying only essential water and food, this would make walking more manageable. Despite the loss, my leg was still in pain so I hoped the terrible weather would take the edge off it.

I limped into the local clinic and asked if I could see a doctor. The receptionist made a wincing expression. 'Our next appointment is November.' A sign on the wall behind her advertised patient choice. 'Your best bet to see a doctor is the Cape Cornwall surgery'.

'We're heading to Cape Cornwall.'

'No, the Cape Cornwall Surgery is in St Just.'

'Of course,' I said. 'Thanks.'

'Embrace the pain,' David said, but he wasn't joking.

We had breakfast in the Geevor Mine café, then headed into the wind and rain. The landscape was monochromatic and apocalyptic. Ruined engine houses, chimneys and wheel towers littered the earth through a grey mist. We kept a steady but slow pace given that we had only to get to Cape Cornwall, the old end of the earth.

'David? What's the name of your end of the world club?'

He was adjusting his poncho in the wind. 'They don't need to know our name, they're not invited.' *They* were anybody not part of this Armageddon survival collective. 'We're calling it the End of the World Club.' The wind moaned ominously as we passed through the ashen wreckage.

'Good choice.' David had the idea that naming the club and even talking about it might make them a target, and here I am writing about it. I asked how it was progressing.

They had a small Whatsapp® group comprised of people with different practical skill sets. No estate agents or beauticians. They assumed that when the end came, technology would be limited so they needed people with practical skills. I suggested that Whatsapp® might cease to function if modern technological society fails.

'You may have a point there, but until then it will work.' I was sure David had thought of this. He wasn't an idiot. Then again, he had stopped walking and was pondering. We began to move on. As survival was one skill, he suggested I could be among their number (all evidence to the contrary). I suggested instead bicycle repair skills.

'That could be useful. Bring your tools.' He said this as though there was a workshop or clubhouse, but I suspected it was all theoretical. A virtual club for a virtual end of the world. The point was, it was going to be a generally apocalyptic scenario. We looked around at the ruins of the Cornish mining communities like a diorama of the end of the world. It really did look bleak, the ash grey detritus where nothing would grow. Half the world's arsenic was produced there at one time. Workers' only protection was clay on their arms and a rag to cover their nose and mouth.

'This is amazing. Arsenic flumes. I love hydraulic structures,' David said as he wandered among the relics of this previous civilisation. It brought out the civil engineer in him. 'Basically, we don't want anybody who doesn't have some useful skill. Unless they can make Nutella® from scratch they're not invited.' This did sound a little like a Douglas Adams planet repopulation scheme and I envisaged disaster resulting from the omission of some seemingly minor domestic assistant or dental hygienist role.

The assumption underpinning this proposed organisation is that, for whatever reason (fuel crisis, conflict over water, nuclear annihilation, disease, Brexit, shortage of confectionary) society as we know it would break down. There is insufficient food in cities for the population, even accounting for farming in Hampstead Heath and chances are the landed gentry of Highgate would purchase a private army and build a wall around the Heath. With its duck ponds and bathing areas as water supplies, they would be able to grow hectares of organic quinoa and avocado in the super-warmed London. Ill-prepared Londoners from the lower reaches would resort to gang warfare as soon as their local supermarket ran out of spaghetti hoops.

Nor should we overestimate survival skills of country folk. To assume that people knew how to farm because they live in a barn conversion is naïve. Large-scale farming is entirely mechanised so things would have to go back to smaller plots with manual labour and the only people who knew about that were ex-presenters of BBC's *Countryfile*. Besides, the voting priorities of country folk suggest we are fighting with the blitz spirit against an enemy in Europe. Organising village hall craft fairs is one thing, surviving after records of our notional digital wealth are erased from history is something else entirely. *Darling, we've just run out of kale.*

Track Two. World Party's *Ship of Fools*[47] was my accompanying mental soundtrack to Armageddon. It had been in the charts when I was still in high school, getting lost on bushwalks. Hearing it in my formative years explained why I was still able to sing it in that howling wind. I would sing it to you now, but the world of lyric copyright law is unforgiving. The song is a warning that the excesses of society will have to be paid for; we are floating blindly towards a place of no redemption. The image is compelling, even more so at the end of the earth where we stood, fearing whatever the future held.

We wandered on through the colossal monochromatic ruins of civilisations past. The day, according to Paddy Dillon, was from Pendeen Watch to Porthcurno, twenty-six kilometres, but we were going only about a third of that given that I was doing an impersonation of Long John Silver and David wasn't used to carrying so much weight. In addition, he was suffering with the wind. Whereas gales had become the norm for me, his attire wasn't entirely suited to the Cornish climate. Like a duellist bringing a knife to a gunfight, David had brought a poncho to a hurricane. It had the advantage of being day-glow orange so there was little risk of losing him in the storm but that was its only virtue.

It only hurt when I walked or laughed. My shin and my chest, respectively, screamed out in agony when I did either. Unfortunately, with David, avoiding walking or laughing was impossible. With a sombrero-like slouch hat strapped to his head, the weightless orange poncho and his South Asian complexion, in the gale he had the appearance of a Mexican being attacked by the Warner Bros' Tasmanian Devil. I would be speaking to him and suddenly his head would disappear. He rotated clockwise then anticlockwise to try to redirect the poncho in the gale. It would simply migrate to cover his head from the other direction so I just talked generally in his direction. I was laughing so much I thought I might faint from the pain. 'I'm really sorry, but I promise this is hurting me more than it's hurting you.'

'I sincerely hope so,' he shouted over the turbulence. 'I can't see a fucking thing. You're going to have to direct me. So, I gave him approximate directions until we could find a ruined engine house behind which we could shelter and tie down his rain gear with guys.

'It's really spectacular here, it's a shame you missed most of it.'

'Why couldn't today have been yesterday?'

'I expected better weather. It's been lovely most of the time,' I lied. There had been the risk, if he'd known how bad it could get, that he wouldn't have come. Like an astronaut marooned on a remote planet, I lured the crew of the rescue ship in to their inevitable fate. It was nice to share some of the bad weather with a friend.

'One thing you missed, David, was a plaque unveiled 20 years ago by Santiago Oñate Labonde,[48] dedicated to the Cornish miners who worked in Mexico. What is it about Mexico and this coast? You know, I heard the town of Real del Monte now has their own version of Cornish pasties. *The man from del Monte says yes.*'

'Look, I don't care what the man from del Monte said. Can't you see I'm in difficulty?' It was as though he was paying homage to the Mexicans. 'This gear was fine on the Camino de Santiago. I may as well be standing under a fucking waterfall.'

At last we were in a valley and then one more hill and we could see the chimney at Cape Cornwall. In the toilet we consulted Paddy, who told us 'refreshments are sometimes available here'. Fat chance. Any purveyors of food and drink were sensibly hibernating, and their potential clients had clearly found a more rational use of their time than walking.

We passed an ancient burial chamber but finding no way in, we sought the hostel, left our packs in one of the campers' toilets then walked to St Just. Two barflies in the pub asked us our destination.

'You should be able to get to Porthcurno easily, I reckon even Mousehole today,' the older man said. He was slightly portly. David raised an eyebrow and gave me a bulging Graves' disease stare.

The man's younger and slimmer companion grimaced. 'I don't think so. I did the walk as part of a Duke of Edinburgh medal and it nearly killed me.'

'Oh, they could do it,' his friend said. The stool creaked under his weight.

'I can barely sit, never mind walk,' I confessed. 'I walked from Lemorna to Porthcurno's Minack Theatre by accident one summer and I remember that being tough.' I didn't mention that I had been carrying very little water but a full bottle of cabernet sauvignon and stem glasses.

I was going to need somewhere to recover and use as a base and the hostel looked fine. As we walked back there David said very slowly, as though his life might depend on it, 'At some point I really must get a Cornish pasty'.

The next day I left David in search of a general practitioner. 'Will you be okay with the stairs?' the locum asked as he watched me cross the floor.

'I may be some time.'

Inside, the doctor looked at my leg. 'Ouch,' he said. 'You're walking the Coast Path, you said?'

'Yes, and I think I've come to the end of the journey.'

'Hmmm. You're doing the *whole* Path?'

'That was the plan, but as you can see ...'

'Yes, it doesn't look good. How much are you carrying? Weight-wise.'

'Well, I'm camping and cooking so a bit, but I have lightweight gear.' He held my leg on a stool. Was the background information simply a distraction while he readied me for the pain – a verbal piece of driftwood between the teeth?

'Aha. Tell me where it hurts. Does this hurt? No. Does this hurt? No. Does this ...'

'Jeeesus!'

'That hurt. Okay, I'm just going to move your ankle.' After some investigation and frowning he said, 'What you have is pitting oedema. You see how when I press here, it stays depressed?' I stayed depressed. 'You might have injured the muscle.' No mention of beriberi. Besides, I'd run out of rum days ago.

'There *was* this field with a bull that I had to exit very quickly while wearing a very heavy pack.'

'That might do it. Pain is an indication of damage – so you have probably damaged the muscle - but occasionally the body overreacts to stress which does more harm than the original damage. Now I'm guessing that if you took anti-inflammatories and rested for a while it would calm down and it will help with any other inflammation you may have. I saw the way you walked up the stairs. Weird.

107

'However, there is a remote chance that it won't correct itself. There is a condition – I'm not saying this is what it is but I should warn you – involving the muscle and the bone which, if it is the case, will continue to worsen and will result in excessive pain. It's an underdiagnosed condition. Compartment syndrome. The compartment being an enclosed bundle of muscles. It can lead to disability and it's very painful.' Pain that is compartmentalised surely has to be a good thing.

'How will I know?'

'Oh, you'll know. The pain you will experience – and again, it's a very unusual condition and I don't want to unduly alarm you, it's very unlikely – but the pain you will experience will be of a scale that ... you will ... know about it. But I don't think it's anything to worry about.' He gave what I assumed he thought to be a reassuring smile.

Beriberi now sounded like a lifestyle choice. That only needed a daily supplement. This involved David amputating my leg with my Swiss army knife while I bit down on seaweed. I left the surgery both relieved and unnerved. Drugs were purchased and consumed, David met me and we took a bus. From Sennen Cove we walked to Land's End just so he could say he'd been there. And to get a Cornish pasty. Sennen Cove had sun and wind – a pleasant fishing village which, uniquely for these parts, still seemed to fish. David carried his pack as this was his final walk.

On reaching Land's End he looked about him in disbelief. 'I was expecting a rocky outcrop and maybe a signpost. Not a shopping mall.' This is everyone's first reaction. 'Let's go to the pub.'

We left the candy floss and plastic toys for Sennen village, slightly inland. The First Inn in England had a smugglers' tunnel where former governor, Anne Treeve, presided over smuggling and wrecking. Wrecking is the pillaging of wrecked ships. In popular culture it includes luring them with lanterns into unsafe waters; the evidence for this is weak and probably never happened.[49] Treeve became informant for the Crown, providing evidence against the smuggling agent. Her punishment was to be staked to the beach and drowned by the incoming tide. This probably happened.

They had no pasties so I was disappointed for David. 'A pasty at Land's End is a bit of a cliché anyway,' I told him. 'Get one in Penzance, it's a real place.'

David was to leave from the Land's End bus stop so we wandered back to wait. 'I've really enjoyed this, in spite of your leg. It's made me want to do this at some point when I have more time. I have to finish the Camino too if you're ever up for that.'

He said he'd try to find a pasty, gave me his lightweight Kermit-green fleece for my endeavour and left me. Feeling a little bereft after David departed, I took my own little bus back to St Just. It passed a small church that used two crossed surf boards for a crucifix.

St Just was closing so I window shopped. Among pith helmets and lamps in the window of an antique shop was a painting of a dodo. Part feather, part flesh, part skeleton, the dodo was framed against a clouded sky. Mauritius, another island where Dutch sailors had become ill from eating toxic fish. It was their habitation that destroyed the bird. The dodo, that oversized parrot, is a reminder of what we are responsible for, how we are making this little rock uninhabitable for all those countless other tenants. Even for the Dutch.

At the hostel there was a message from David. 'I got one! I'll eat it on the train.'

Due to wind, Rebecca cancelled
Day 26. 5th October

In Penzance I found carbon fibre collapsible walking sticks and a loop fleece (which could become a hat or a face mask against the wind). The American shopkeeper said I could take a free winter product, but became angry when I told him *thank you, but no, it's extra weight.* 'But it's free, man. If you don't need it, take it anyway and give it away.'

'Okay,' I said, pulling a scarf from a rack and placing it on the desk, 'I'll take this'. I paid and began to walk off.

'You forgot your scarf,' he shouted.

'I don't need it. It's yours. I'm giving it to you, it's free.' His face looked about to explode, his hands clenched on the countertop, and he made a guttural sound like a slow release of energy.

The Edge of the World Bookshop is a traditional bookshop with an azure panelled frontage. They had at the back a single signed copy of Robert Harris's *The Second Sleep*, of the event I had missed in Appledore. This copy may even have come from the Literary Festival. There is something about a book that has been held in someone's hands and signed, assuming it was not intentional vandalism. The attendant wrapped it for me before I could look inside. Had I just glanced at the endpapers I would have realised that the story and I had common beginnings. There was something within the story that darkly underlined the end of days discussions I'd had with David but I had missed it as I was already in the post office, posting it back home.

That evening at the hostel a couple who had stayed on a farm near Porthcurno remarked that they had narrowly missed a showing of Hitchcock's *Rebecca*[50] at the Minack Theatre on Friday night.

'They show films?'

'Apparently they've started to. It was cancelled due to high winds. The screen would have become a sail.'

'That's a shame. It's a great film and a perfect Cornish setting.'

'Apparently there *is* a film showing on Sunday. Tonight's was also cancelled.'

I would have loved to have seen a film, to lose this feeling of being abandoned. It is always worse for the one who is left behind.

In the morning I walked to Sennen Cove. Mags and I had been here on a rented motorcycle a few years earlier when we rented a cottage in St Buryan. Mags and St Sennen had both been born near Kilrush, West Clare. We were married in St Senan's Church. Sennen is reputed to have come to Cornwall on his way to Brittany or Glastonbury. Mags had seemed to be in a trance that day in the Cove.

110

The walk was beautiful. I carried little and used my new sticks, which soon felt like part of my body. My legs felt like part of someone else's. The ibuprofen seemed to be working, though I wouldn't know for sure until I carried more weight. I took the maximum dose every four hours.

Waves crashed against the shore, illuminated by bright sunlight, filling the air with spray. Two women - Sam and Sarah - photo-bombed my picture and made amends by taking one of me. They spoke of how beautiful the landscape was and I had to agree. There was something in the air; more than just effluent-contaminated saltwater. Perhaps Sennen now meant something to me too.

I arrived in Sennen Cove, thus completing the section of the Path David and I had missed on Friday. There, I telephoned the Minack Theatre to ask if there would be a film showing, and there was. They advised on a taxi service home but said I could get a bus to Porthcurno below the theatre. Miraculously, while I sat watching Sam and Sarah march off into the distance, a late-running bus arrived.

It was a beautiful afternoon. After exploring the tunnels at the Porthcurno Telegraph Museum, I watched the sunset from a cliff and then climbed the steep path to the Minack. 'Hello again. You made it then?' came a voice at the clifftop. It was Sam and Sarah from Sennen Cove, each holding a blanket and waiting for the gate to open. It was good to meet people who have never unlearnt the skill of talking to strangers.

'I hope you're both ready for this high-brow cultural event.'

'It's a classic. I've always thought the lead performance underrated. It was award material,' said Sam.

'Not a little mechanical?' Sarah questioned.

'It was inevitable that they would be typecast,' I suggested.

I could understand why *Rebecca* had been cancelled. It wasn't so much that there was a risk of the screen becoming a sail, it seemed to me that the screen *was* a sail. That, or a tarpaulin used to hold down fish, secured with rope through its eyelets. It reflected in all the wrong ways, showing up every wrinkle. I wasn't complaining though, as it was not every day you had the chance to see a piece of filmic history in an outdoor amphitheatre by the Atlantic.

My seat was a stone throne beside the staircase and had an exceptional view of the theatre, screen and sea. I was seated beside a man whose eating mimicked a wild boar, but I determined not to let him disturb my experience. He loudly and patronisingly explained all things film to his female partner while snorting and spitting food. She was very tolerant. I hoped him rich, with a heart condition and that she was set to inherit.

After a short introduction from theatre staff the lights went down. Lamps of small boats bobbed on the sea below, and the moon rose incrementally higher in the night sky. This is how films should be seen, like *The New Cinema Paradiso*. The audience had its final chatter as the Universal Pictures earth logo rotated and the film began. Everyone was hushed as the title appeared through dark blue water. *Jaws.*[51]

All were drawn into the tension, the playful, competitive banter between the three men on the boat and the references to the violence of this big fish throughout history. It was easy to feel the fear with the boats bobbing on the dark water below us and the perilously steep slope down the cliff towards them.

Contrary to cinema etiquette (which demands that people leave as the titles run, throw their containers on the floor and fight for the exit), there was a sustained round of applause during the end credits. Steven Spielberg, the foley artists, dolly and key grip would have been touched.

A couple staying at a nearby farm shared the taxi with me. Rather, I shared their taxi. 'We're going to need a bigger cab,' he said.

The taxi driver looked around. 'Ah, you saw *Jaws* then. Mind if I drop this man off at St Just first?' The driver was no fool; it was a long diversion and he was based near their site.

'There are too many captains on this island,'[52] he replied, then closed his eyes, exhaling the odour of hops.

'I'll take that as a yes.' He drove into the darkness, turning left not right.

'How is the farm?' I asked.

She paused, considering. 'It's nice. They're very relaxed and seem to be ecologically conscious.'

'I might stay there tomorrow. Do they accept tents?'

'There are none at the moment, but I don't see why they wouldn't.'

'Any idea of the cost?'

Her partner was jogged awake by a bump in the road: 'Ten quid. For that you get the head, the tail ... the whole damned tent'.

THREE: The Beginning of the End

Poacher, pirate, beggar man, thief
Day 28. 7ᵗʰ October

My luggage was tagged and awaited collection by the transfer company in the foyer. I left the hostel, arriving in St Just in time for the first bus to Land's End to continue the journey. Dense fog slept in dips on the country roads forcing the driver to take the journey slowly. We passed the surf church and then arrived at Land's End.

Only my eyes showed in the mirror as I entered the theme park toilet, which was tacky both literally and metaphorically. With sticks and pack I was a Frank Oz creature, four legs, a hump and no mouth. Land's End meant that from here the journey was generally eastward. I no longer had the dilemma of whether to wear my solar panel across my chest in the mornings. With my panel also went any scruples I had about theft of power. To be frank, I never had many of those.

The *Land's End Cat* eyed me suspiciously as I rested beside a farm art shop.

'Goodbye cat.' I hoped it might follow me for a bit, but this was Land's End, and this was where it belonged. At the cliff edge the Enys Dodnan arch and the Armed Knight islet behind it were just visible in the mist. Strange tors were balanced on the cliff, reminiscent of Hound Tor on Dartmoor. One rock had the exact form of a sperm whale.

Beyond Sperm Whale Stone, on a forlorn clifftop above Nanjizal Cove and the Song of the Sea arch, three freshly-placed crimson roses were tied to a lichen-topped barrier, droplets of dew clinging to their petals. No memorial marker accompanied them to explain the subject of their affection, only the barrier to guide walkers away from the crumbling cliffs. I preserved their image as, across the sea, came the deep melancholy chime of a bell.

After some time walking in the mist there was a small coast watch station. Nearby were two strange daymarks positioned on a headland - placed to assist ships to identify the entrance to Porthgwarra. The one closer to the cliff was a crimson cone. Bright green-yellow lichen clung to its paintwork. The one further inland was rocket-shaped and pied. I used this to have lunch though the mist was so thick it had the effect of rain. Through the haze came that mournful, slow peal like the ringing at the beginning of the universe, seconds after midnight.

The sound, like the daymarks, was a warning to ships.[53] A nearby cemetery holds a mass grave to men drowned off these cliffs. Gwennap Head is called *Tol Pedn* in Cornish, the title of the abstract painting in the Tate. In the image were the little daymarks like pawns and the white frame of the coast watch station. John Tunnard had been here in 1942. He died in Penzance the year before I rode the Minehead monorail. If there was a true end of the earth it was here. At one time in history it had been Leven's Land's End, the bleakest and most atmospheric. Tunnard felt it.

The bell rang out again through the unmoving mist. My power pack had only one functioning socket, I realised as I connected my phone. An orange residue lined the other ports just like the solar panel. It was the humidity. If I lost the last socket it was goodbye to my phone and so photographs, GPS, information, outside contact. There was little left to malfunction. I creaked upright, my hip made an audible click, and the bell sent out a deep moan.

Porthgwarra had a tunnel and small caves resembling a skull's eye sockets. The tunnel, hand cut by miners, reached a hidden beach where seaweed had once been collected. The community had made containers with hinged lids – ullies - which the sea covered at high tide, keeping the catch fresh for transportation to Newlyn.

Further on, St Levan's holy well claimed to cure tooth and eye problems, both exceptions to NHS cover. Alas, my teeth and eyes were the only parts without pain. Near the well stood a woman in a pale blue sweater, sandy hair tied back, staring out to sea. She was on a promontory overlooking Porthchapel beach. The sight of her left me in a melancholy mood, and it occurred to me that she might be unhappy. Naturally, I realised I was projecting from my own personal cinema, and the film was *The French Lieutenant's Woman*. More likely, she just wanted to be alone in the landscape, so I walked on towards Minack checking that she was still safely on the bench before being lost to view.

It was only two in the afternoon when I reached the theatre where a sign warned patrons not to attempt the cliff path as it was steep and a road was available. The beach was in use by a few people now that the weather had cleared. Above, on the cliff, three initials and an arrow to the left were etched into a Coast Path marker. It was the farm campsite. The tops of mobile homes came into view and I soon arrived at the reception - closed, as was now the norm - so I waited at a picnic table.

As though from nowhere a man appeared, holding the biggest fish I had seen since last night's film. 'Sea bass! I've just been down to the beach.' The man had the look of Elijah Wood, in glasses and waders. 'I was supposed to be at work but it was such a nice afternoon.'

'It's big.'

'Not *so* big. Within the legal limit but I'd normally throw one this size back. Only, I caught its gills and it would have been cruel to send it back. In any case, there's nobody policing it - insufficient resources. Trawlers digging up the sea floor, people taking a bucketful.'

Under UK law he explained (not English, not British, United Kingdom law) recreational fishers are allowed one bass per day, and it must be 42cm or longer. In February to March and November to December all bass must be released (*the head, the tail, the whole damned fish*[54]).

'What's your technique?' I asked out of curiosity. I had no real intention of queering his pitch, though he was eager to share it. Perhaps he knew I was no fisher, that I would walk on, leaving others like him staring at the sea.

He opened the car boot like a man inspecting the takings after a heist, his face illuminated in the reflecting sun. Inside was an array of fish-shaped lures. 'Any of these will do but this is my lucky charm.' He held up a small fish of some inert metal resembling silver. 'It's a guarantee.'

'That's a small rod.'

'Much fishing culture is ego. Penis substitutes. Sure, you want to get it in the right place across the other side of a river but size isn't everything. Speaking of which, I found my place today, but it was occupied.'

You should aim for the churned water near the rocks, which the seabass prefer, he explained. However, a naked sunbather was lying there. The man had clearly chosen the more distant location out of discretion but it was where the fisher wanted to be. It posed the seemingly impossible problem of how to occupy the same space on an otherwise large and empty beach without appearing lecherous. This he did by keeping his back to the bather and very gradually, over the next half an hour, shuffling sideways across the beach until they were level, giving the impression that he was oblivious to the male member - whereas it was all he could think of. No great discomfort to a Swede or Finn, this is perhaps a very British problem. He then made small casts so as to catch only fish. He wished me well before driving off with his fish in the direction of the village.

There was no sign of my pack through the reception window, so I called the luggage delivery company. 'Just a moment. I'll contact the driver and call you back.' Five minutes later she called, 'Hello, Mr Burton? Yes, he said it was delivered to "a man dressed as a pirate."'

'Dressed as a pirate?'

'Yes, I'm afraid that's the only information we have, but he said the man did work at the farm.' I thanked her and sat down to wait for the pirate, not feeling hopeful. Soon a VW Kombi arrived and a woman with a dog stepped out, but no pirate. Inside, she found my pack. 'Just choose any pitch you like, anywhere you like. No, not there. Or there. No, not there. Or there.'

'Here?'

'No, not there. Try a patch without mud. We're reseeding for winter. No ... no. Yes, that's fine.' I deposited my bag on the site of my choosing.

The little dog followed her back into the van and she drove off, shouting out: 'You can use the kitchen – there's a kettle and microwave. Contact my son if you have any problems'.

After pitching and not wishing to walk further than necessary, I knocked on the reception door in search of food. Standing beside the desk and looking slightly out of place among the propane cannisters, toothpaste and inflatable armbands, stood a pirate. That was the overall impression, although there was no single item which screamed 'I am a pirate' - no sword, parrot or wooden leg. Nor could he be classed as a pirate of the horn of Africa equipped with semi-automatic and a grapnel. There was a mass of dreadlocked hair held with a bandana, long baggy shirt, some sort of rustic outer garment, and possibly eye makeup although this may be recall bias. It was a Cornish pastiche. He had the authenticity of a pirate but with plausible deniability.

'I think I should be thanking you for receiving my pack.' It seemed ridiculous to talk to a seafaring outlaw about luggage transport. I thought I should give it more gravity. 'Not this one,' I pointed at the saggy day pack on my shoulder, 'the large trekking one'.

'Hrgg?' It was a questioning sort of grunt, not requiring the opening of the lips.

'The delivery company said that it was received by a ...,' I had driven myself into a cul-de-sac and so desperately sought an uncomfortable three-point turn, 'by a man who looked like ...' he stared directly at me through outlined and creased lids, '... he ran the place'.

'Uh.' It was a sign of acknowledgment of understanding. I could see this conversation was going to be an effort. It was like he was hung over from aged rum.

'So, thanks.'

'Mmm.' He was busy shuffling papers and looking for something on the desk - perhaps his telescope. At this point it occurred to me that he didn't speak English.

'Could I buy some food?' I said slowly, adding an unnecessary air eating gesture with my hand.

He looked down at his shirt. 'End of season.' It looked more end of century, and not the last, though this at least proved that he spoke English. As I continued staring at his garb he clarified by nodding at the shelves with a raised eyebrow, shelves resembling Eastern Bloc supermarkets in the eighties. 'End of season. Not much call.' They contained the white bread and pasta always found in holiday shops, which I find literally indigestible.

The opposite of spoilt for choice, I browsed uncomfortably. Feeling the intense stare on my neck from the pirate I panicked and grabbed a few things, fumbled for loose change and left him to his treasure hunt. I looked down at my catch. Something proclaiming it was ethically sourced, eggs and a can of rice pudding. Damn.

A breath-taking sunset was followed by a clear evening with clouds of stars and the distant searchlight of Tater Du lighthouse. Never before were so many crane flies found in a single kitchen. In the weak light, eating some was inevitable but it took my mind off the food combination.

The next morning, the Path from Treen was the first test of walking with a full pack. There were occasional twinges of chest pain, and a stabbing in my shin which left me holding my breath and wait for the worst, but it didn't come. The intense pain I had experienced with David seemed to have gone. I planned to take the maximum dose of anti-inflammatories every four hours for the first few days and reduce this gradually.

A white stone pyramid stood on the cliff side of the Path, a memorial to the laying of the submarine telegraph cable connecting France. While taking a photograph I noticed the woman in the pale blue sweater who had been staring out to sea near Porthchapel Beach. She still had that far-away stare, her sand-coloured hair still tied back. She approached, and when at my shoulder said hello, then walked casually down the path to the cliff, alone. Again, I felt sad watching her. Again, I realised how irrational that was. I listened for a splash but it never came.

At Logan Rock a group of older walkers consulted their maps. I moved ahead of them at speed. My leg really was feeling better, and I noticed the difference in the ballast I had jettisoned in Pendeen. Moving fast was important to ensure I made Penzance before nightfall, but I also wanted to stay ahead of the group.

Beyond St Loy a woman and man on the edge of the woods heading to Porthcurno asked my plans, the reason, how much my pack weighed and if I had read that book about the couple walking the Path. The predictability of the questions made me feel a little like a foreign traveller in India. Perhaps it's simply the effect of backpacks; they turn dogs insane, people formulaic. I countered these questions by pointing to the house on the horizon behind them and describing its resident. This, their faces seemed to say, was much more interesting.

Leaving them, I wandered on alone until I was level with the house. 'A desk is a dangerous place from which to watch the world. So, as Smiley proposed, they wandered.'[55] This line had sat on my desk for a decade, urging me to see, not simply to believe what drifted from the field.

The house was *Tregiffian*, the name probably meaning guardian tribe or place.[56] It was John le Carré's house, nothing about it revealing the identity of its occupant other than a sign 'This is not the Coast Path'. His fictional intelligence character George Smiley had been eased out of the service but had remained in London.[57] It was convenient to have him removed. Though le Carré himself had kept one foot in Hampstead, he largely fled to Cornwall once he left the service. This was the house that Alec Leamas bought (the spy who had come in from the cold).

The author David Cornwell, aka John le Carré, had been a long-time advocate for the protection of the coastline and had donated his own stretch of these cliffs to the nation. Five years earlier Mags and I had met a postal delivery driver on the St Buryan side of this stretch of coast. He said that the author probably wouldn't mind us passing through his property, but I didn't feel it was respectful and there was a remote chance he might dislocate my arm, so we walked around. This long detour, longer on account of cattle, meant we were exhausted and thirsty when we reached the Minack Theatre via the Coast Path with our wine. I would have loved to have met him, though not by trespass.

The grassed track descended to the Tater Du lighthouse steps, a suitable place to rest. Tater Du, from torthow du or 'black loaf', perhaps describing the black rock on which it sat. It was the newest in Cornwall and the first purpose-built automated lighthouse in England. It was conceived the year le Carré wrote *The Spy Who Came in From the Cold,*[58] and completed the same year that the improved concrete Berlin Wall was constructed. The lighthouse, though, still stands.

A fern-covered slope was reached by a wooden gate which proclaimed, 'The Derek and Jeannie Tangye Minack Chronicles Nature Reserve – A Place for Solitude'. Recently I had read a book called *The Road to Minack*[59] by Derek Tangye. Mags had picked up the book in a second-hand bookshop after our visit to St Buryan and we liked the idea of the story. Like le Carré, Tangye had worked for an intelligence service, but had been in MI5 during wartime.[60] There appears to be no connection between the two former intelligence workers before the move to Cornwall (though Tangye worked for John Bingham, writer and model for George Smiley), so perhaps it was a coincidence that they were neighbours; that they were all just urban refugees.

Derek Tangye then worked for a newspaper and his wife, Jeannie, worked at the Savoy (she started writing fictionalised accounts of her time there long before Derek began writing[61]). The book describes how they left their hectic life in London to find peace on the cliffs near St Buryan surrounded by animals.[62] When Jeannie died suddenly in 1986, it was their friend and neighbour le Carré who gave the eulogy.[63] Derek died ten years later.[64] Their friendship, according to biographer Adam Sisman, had been 'adversarial', and le Carré also gave the eulogy at Derek's funeral despite Tangye's final words to his friend having been 'bugger off'.[65]

After the Tangye plot, the Path climbed large boulders and the walking poles became essential to move my mass upwards. It was treacherously steep and the ground wet, so I was grateful for the clear weather.

On the edge of Lamorna Cove stood a Celtic cross, its plinth stained with copper from coins left by walkers. It is unlikely that many of those who have left coins were familiar with the story. Wayside crosses are common but often their placement is very specific. This cross with its inscription DWW 1873 was, of course, a memorial. David Watson, aged 23, had been visiting Penzance, and picking ferns when he fell from the spot and drowned.[66] Waves crashed against the rocks below, even on this calm day.

Mags and I had visited the Lamorna Cove Café during our stay in St Buryan (you've seen St Buryan if you've seen the 1971 Sam Peckinpah film *Straw Dogs* about a couple being terrorized on a farm). I had just finished coffee and cake in the café when a couple poked their heads in. 'Are they still open?'

'You're in luck. For fifteen more minutes.'

'A proper walker,' he proclaimed.

'I don't know about proper. Heavily laden certainly.'

'Are you going far?' she asked. 'I'm being nosy,' suddenly apologetic. Her voice was deep, her speech a beautiful received pronunciation.

'That's okay. I'm hoping to get to Penzance. From Mousehole the land is level. Around here it's rugged. I really should get going.'

'Good luck,' she said.

'You too.' I left, though reluctantly, as I could have listened to her for hours.

With dark clouds on the horizon and the beginning of rain I hurried into the shelter of the beautiful woods of Kemyel Crease. A ruined house, overgrown by trees, hid on the edge of the trail, which then opened out to Mousehole and a steep road to the harbour.

Mousehole (pronounced locally *maozel)* is the perfect fairy-tale village, its narrow lanes winding between stone cottages. The harbour wall is split by a narrow passage to let boats enter and leave, and there is even a protected beach within the harbour. Soon Newlyn came into view.

The only thing I knew of Newlyn was that there was a fish riot here in 1896. It's unclear how this attained the title of the 'riot'.

Strictly speaking, it was a demonstration by local fisher-people against the intrusion of East Anglian poachers. While there is a suggestion of violence, questions asked in parliament revealed that, while there were thousands involved, only five civilians and three policemen were injured, one of whom had a cut to the head,[67] resulting from an airborne fish box.[68]

At the approach to the wharf area of Newlyn someone armed with a square brush and a can of beige paint had written: 'EXPENSIVE HOUSES PRICES IN MOUSEHOLE'. The attack of the boring graffitist.

Rain began, and I hurried to the hostel. On the approach, tents were scattered in a copse. They looked to be unofficially pitched. One tent was apart from the rest near a bench. I stopped for tea.

'Do you smoke? Do you have a light?'

He wore a shining white track suit top. 'Sorry, I don't.' Then I realised I had matches and after some searching lit his cigarette. 'You live here?'

'I do now. Tyler.' He held out a hand, ingrained dirt under the nails. Tyler wasn't his real name but it's a good one.

'Oscar,' I responded, taking his hand.

Tyler launched into his story from the middle. 'I had some problems with the mental health services. They said there was nothing wrong with me and that I wasn't eligible for disability allowance. When I explained that I didn't have any problems until they started their investigations, they said I only thought that because I was a paranoid schizophrenic.'

'I can see that must be confusing.'

'I'm a little confused but I'm not a paranoid schizophrenic.'

'Then, good. Do you want some tea?'

'Sure, thanks man.' He went inside his tent where he searched through bags, retrieving a plastic mug. His clothes were surprisingly clean despite an outdoor existence. I poured us tea, apologising for the sugar. 'Thanks. It's hot. That's good.' I casually observed that all the liquid in the tent porch was contained in two litre Strongbow cider bottles.

'It's good to get warm before the sun goes down.' I could already feel a chill in the air.

125

'Under British law it's not legal to receive benefits without a permanent address.' Now, I know this isn't true. A *care-of* address can be used. I mentioned this. 'No, that would be against the law. Scotland is different, since they became independent.'

'But Scotland isn't independent, Tyler.'

'Sure they are. There was a referendum.'

'Yes, and the majority voted *against* independence. Boris is unlikely to allow them a second vote.'

'If they're not independent how do you explain their money? *Bank of Scotland*. He produced a note.'

'They've had their own notes since the late 1600s.'

'No, they're independent.' He eyed me as though I were trying to trick him. He'd seen the evidence. I wondered where his information was from, but then I was unlikely to persuade him. Everything he saw fuelled his world view.

I let it lie. 'What are you going to do?'

'I have a business. I have my equipment in a garage with a woman who was helping me.'

'That does sound like something. You should go with that.'

'I think I will,' he said, for the first time seeming to have a focus on his future.

'Look, Tyler, good luck. I've got to pitch before I lose the light.'

'See you, then. Thanks for the tea.' It would have been good to stay longer but I was growing cold. I'd seen this in people, the creeping paranoia which starts with a trigger event and then is reinforced by a multitude of signs which would have been inconsequential had it not been for that first crisis sending them off kilter. With some luck he would find his balance and some semblance of normality. The trick was retaining the part of the self that his friends would recognise, assuming he still had any. Homelessness is so much deeper than the absence of a building. If threatened with destitution the middle-, articulate- and persuasive-classes have a natural advantage. They're not in the same boat as Tyler; they're not even in the same sea. Tyler asked for nothing besides conversation. Not all who are homeless beg, and not all who beg are homeless.

Comedian Paul Whitehouse, or someone who looked and sounded very much like him, greeted me at the Penzance Hostel. Between several diversions into *Fast Show* sketches he took my details and an order for dinner. 'If you pitch, dinner will be ready when you get back. A good choice. You'll be wearing the tofu curry? Oooh, suits you, sir.' I pitched on the lawn away from the hostel lights, and as the rain came down heavily, jogged inside to eat.

At a nearby table a man was holding a one-sided conversation with a woman. He was a television cliché of a London gangland figure, short but wide, furrowed brow and too much greased black hair intruding low on his forehead for a man his age. An imitation Crombie coat gave him the illusion of stature. She sat submissively while he did all the talking. Occasionally he shouted a question in a lighter tone to the warden behind the counter, but otherwise his monologue was full of bile for his female companion who would occasionally interject cautiously.

'You showed him though, didn't you?'

'Shut ... your ... maaf! I'll fackin' cut you. Fackin' shat aaap,' his whisper screamed, a menacing Bill Sykes with none of his charms.

Once they left the dining room, I discussed the threat with the warden who explained they were staying only one night. It felt better to be far from him in my tent. Far from London's underbelly, I glued my boots.

The road to Manderley
Day 30. 9ᵗʰ October

After breakfast I took some salt to ward off cramp, said goodbye to Mr Whitehouse and headed towards Penzance to pick up the trail. I moved quickly, past the dozing informal tent encampment to the promenade in the direction of Marazion.

127

St Michael's Mount was in shadow against the bright water. It felt liberating after urban Newlyn and Penzance. Kite surfers skimmed across the water, silhouetted against the rising sun. I set up a pace in order to get to the island before the tide came in. It was half past ten when I reached the causeway and I was able to cross, but the tide was beginning to lap the cobbles. The castle grounds were closed for winter, so I peered around the narrow public space. A small stretch of track was visible on the quayside, the start of a little-known underground funicular railway - still used to take goods up to the castle.

Back at the causeway the tide entirely covered the cobblestones, but I had to keep walking. I was able to cross carefully, the water just below the top of my boots. Miraculously, the seal of my newly glued soles had held; I was dry. On leaving the water I met a group of day-trippers in unsuitable shoes stared curiously at the encroaching sea.

'The tide is coming in. You could take your shoes off and wade,' I suggested. 'It's over the top now, and deep.' They looked at their feet then at the water and decided to photograph the Mount from where they stood.

Like Sennen Cove, the west coast of Ireland has a connection with this place and to Brittany. If you take a globe and draw a line from the steep island of Skellig Michael to St Michael's Mount and extend it, it passes through Mont St Michel. Whether this was by accident or design is uncertain; sceptics would call the association wishful coincidence.

The idea of a general line of direction, though, is not so mysterious, it's just common sense. Mediaeval Celts in Ireland, Cornwall and Brittany - indoctrinated into the cult of St Michael and his prophesised role in the End of Times - built fortifications on three islands simply joined by the shortest distances (a straight line).

Some churches take this alignment further and show that an extension of the line takes in Italian and Greek monasteries and finally ends in Megiddo, the place of the final battle of Armageddon. If you trace the line digitally on a globe, though, extending it beyond Mont St Michel, it misses most of Italy - other than the boot tip - clips Libya, bisects Egypt and Eritrea and enters Ethiopia. It goes south.[69] The line goes nowhere near the holy land, as the assumed trajectory is an artefact of the Mercator projection.[70] So, their line didn't go to Armageddon - it's not the end of the world.

Apophenia is the tendency to find connections where none exist; it is the order we take from seemingly random things, to draw straight lines in the meandering landscape, and it is compelling. Our minds naturally seek patterns to make sense of the world.

My own field of professional expertise falls victim to the same compelling search for meaning, the association between any number of social ills and income inequalities being a notable example. Lines fitted by researchers between plots of countries by inequality and homicide or teenage pregnancies are compelling; the more unequal a country, the worse its social outcomes. But these lines are hokum, just very compelling hokum and they've made quite a name for those peddling them.

The simpler explanation is, social problems have social and economic causes: a lack of state investment in health and social care; poverty; guns; gangs; hunger; cultural values; squalor; and, of course, homelessness. And a straight line is just the shortest distance between two points.

The detour from Marazion skirted a quiet and lonely cemetery. At its corner, as I was comfortably squatting, a woman carrying an umbrella and speaking loudly into her phone appeared as though from nowhere. She saw the prone figure before her, stopped and let out a disgusted groan then shielded her view of me with her brolly. I tried to explain but she was too involved in her conversation, and I held only half her attention – the half that was now describing to a friend the sight of a man relieving himself in broad daylight. In truth this was no toilet stop. I was only squatting to let my pack take the brunt of a sudden shower. The impression wasn't helped by my shorts being hidden by the rain jacket. My protestations, though, risked being construed as harassment so I stood and joined the trail back to the coast. I crossed a beach, rounded the shore and didn't slow until the Mount was lost to view.

Above Prussia Cove a derelict low thatched fishing cottage with a rusting winch faced out to sea. The Path, now a roadway, moved into an atrium between two buildings. The circular wall, flanked by two parts of the same house on either side, met a small garden where a woman in black sat at a garden table. Only once I had passed and looked back was the house visible in its entirety. Made of grey stone, built upon a cliff and with a pitched roof, it was an impossible mansion. Its walls facing the sea were flush with the vertical cliff, windows looking directly out onto crashing waves. It was more of Manderley than Daphne du Maurier's own Menabilly. You could be the new bride being received here by the moody and murderous Maxim de Winter: the place could be hired as a wedding venue.

The sun was low in the sky as I passed below the dramatic white art deco building high above Praa Sands and reached the ruined engine house near Rinsey Head where years earlier I had read H.G. Wells' *The War of the Worlds* while the tide came in and drowned my boots. There was cold rain and poor light as I came across a series of chimneys covering the cliffside and held the phone camera up with numb hands. The image before me was an over-optimistic squandering of a classic Cornish landscape - flat and featureless. But then, fortuitously, the storm clouds parted and a shaft of light enveloped one chimney, giving it texture as I pressed the shutter release. As quickly as the light appeared it was gone.

On the approach to Porthleven the dark sky was masked by a darker-still cruciform shape. By the lantern I made out a plaque: 'This cross has been erected in memory of the many mariners drowned on this part of the coast from time immemorial and buried on the cliffs hereabout'. Bodies of unknown sailors would be interred in the cliffs as it was not permitted for them to be buried in consecrated land until the 1808 Grylls Act.

I entered the town in darkness, exhausted and cold. A man leant over the harbour railings beside a Rick Stein restaurant, so I stopped to ask emergency information.

'Excuse me, do you know if there's anywhere to get chips?'

'There's a good place up that hill there.' He pointed across the harbour to a road leading to the left. 'Unfortunately, they closed up at six-thirty.'

'It's just gone that now. Perhaps they're still open.'

'I'm afraid not. I locked up already.'

'It's yours!' He was laughing at me.

'Yes, but at this time of year there's not much call for late eating. Unless you're thinking of this.' He pointed at the blue lights of the Stein restaurant.

'I left my dinner jacket at home.'

'There are still people who want traditional fish and chips. We're open tomorrow.'

'Good to know.' I would be gone by then, though. He showed me the supermarket and a takeaway and then I sought the camp near a rugby field, the grass partly lit by floodlights.

The rain had stopped as I took my takeaway to a harbourside picnic table reserved for a daytime eatery. The Stein restaurant opposite provided illumination, its blue lights reflected in the dark, still water. My shoulders steamed in the icy air. It was peaceful.

At the camp I was ready to hibernate when I heard a West Country voice from the darkness. 'Hello there'. I peered out to see a woman standing rigidly like a servant embarrassed to disturb a guest. 'Hello, I'm down at the carpark in a camper van.' She then began, omitting all punctuation, a story about her and her boyfriend being evicted and living from a van. She had been denied permission to park in the campsite so used the rugby club land. I imagined she was going to ask me for money but then she offered me coffee in the morning. How easily someone can fall out of luck. Then again, maybe they'd never had any to begin with.

131

There should be enough rocks until morning
Day 31. 10ᵗʰ October

With no sign of the particular van (I feared knocking at vans randomly in the early hours), I headed to the harbour. 'You're walking the Coast Path?' a man shouted from a camper van.

'I am. Just under half-way.'

'Would you like coffee?' This was peculiar. Twice in a day. Still, I was conscious that I had arrived in darkness and didn't want to repeat that mistake so I turned the offer down. Later, I wondered if things might have turned out differently had I stayed for just a while to chat.

At the turning from the harbour a plaque on a retaining wall was dedicated to Wing Commander Guy Penrose Gibson. Gibson had led the Dam Buster raids in 1943,[71] but died in action before the end of the war. His mother was from a long family of 'Master Mariners' in Porthleven, and this was his home in England.

Beyond the town was Porthleven Sands and the Loe Bar from which could be seen a cross, mirroring the one on the approach to Porthleven. It marked where 100 of the wrecked HMS Acton's crew were lost. The Loe Bar, a dam holding back the Loe, was notorious for shipwrecks. Loe Pool is a large pool connected to Carminowe Creek. A creek in England is different to the north American one; in this case it is simply a sheltered inlet on a shoreline. Tennyson used this as the setting for the lake into which Arthur's Excalibur was thrown, and where the Lady of the Lake retrieved it.[72]

Beyond Gunwalloe at an outdoor café a young National Trust worker recommended the church to me.

'I can't see a church.'

'Behind those dunes. This is Gunnwalloe Church Cove. It's an odd one.' The church was only visible on skirting the sand dunes. It *was* odd, formed from three parallel pitched roofs. It had a belfry unconnected to the main building, reached by a winding path up a hill.

The sea had encroached from two sides, threatening to leave the little church on its own island. On the approach, through a recessed path among gravestones, a stone figure pointed towards the church porch. Above the door a wooden plaque read rather ominously 'St. Winwaloe the Church of the Storms'. I left my pack on the porch bench and was about to enter when I heard a voice from behind the solid oak door.

'I told you when we were beside that Chinaman,' came a voice from inside.

'What Chinaman?' came a younger voice.

'That creepy statue outside.'

'I think that might be St Winwaloe, Mum. I'm not sure he was Chinese. It says here that he's a phallic saint.'

'What's a phallic saint?'

'He'll get you pregnant.'

'I don't want to get pregnant, not at my age, and certainly not by a saint.' The door opened and a woman supported by a frame looked from me to the pack. 'Oh, hello. Are you walking?'

'Yes, the Coast Path. Towards Poole.'

'I do envy you. You look like you're camping. Are you really camping? That's really something. I would have done that in my day. That looks heavy.' She would have been entertaining company.

'It's not so bad once you get it on.' The pack was still resting in the porch.

'Aren't you worried someone might take it?'

'Anybody who wants to steal it is welcome.'

An elderly man appeared from behind the huge door.

'This young man is walking the coast,' she told him.

'Good for you,' he smiled, then they left.

It seemed a special place so I lit a candle for Mags' father and one for my mother and put some money in the church box. Church of the storms, but not today – the weather had held.

A short walk brought me to Poldhu Cove where a sedan with a noisy exhaust screamed past. When I reached the top of the driveway the car was waiting outside the former Poldhu Hotel (now an elderly care home). It faced me, the engine revving. A voice spoke from the open window as I passed but the message was unclear. I took two steps back, when suddenly the driver sprang out. 'You got a problem, mate? Hang on,' he spoke into the car. 'What the fuck did you say?'

He was agitated. His body made unpredictable jerking movements his eyes stared wildly, a West Country Gollum. I took him in – tattoos on arms and neck, shaved head, not tall but emanating menace. The man took two steps towards me so that his face almost touched my own. It's a move intended to force a retreat, so I stood my ground. This was easy to do, being an elephant to his rat. He was lightning quick, the sort of speed which comes with intermittent explosive disorder or having too many double espressos.

Although his sudden eruption from the car surprised me, I was harbouring hate rather than fear, of this hairless Yosemite Sam. I hated him for his disregard for elderly pedestrians and for the peace of this cove. I hated him for his breath's uninvited proximity to me in his adult tantrum. Mostly, I hated him for speaking with his mouth full of a sandwich he was devouring from one of those non-biodegradable plastic triangular tubs. I offered him my blankest expression and said as a statement of fact, 'You spoke as I walked past'.

'I was on the phone!'

'Were you?' I didn't say more, just waited for the information to register. *Your move.* There was no pain this truculent hoon could cause me that I hadn't already inflicted on myself. The oversized ganglion twitched, rocked from one foot to the other in quick succession. His face indicated the weighing up of whether to add injury to insult. Any resort to violence and I would make good use of my carbide tips on his shins and fall on him with my excess baggage.

During our blank out-staring duel, however, it occurred to me that his upper body was tightly wound cables of muscle and if he chose, he could probably maim me, perhaps permanently. The only witness might be an elderly resident whose testimony would not hold water for reasons of vision or cognition. But my doubts clearly hadn't migrated to my face as he made a huffing noise as though I had wasted enough of his time, and jumped back into his car, presumably either to finish his phone call or continue talking to himself. 'Not worth it,' I heard from the interior.

I slowly turned and walked past the care home, all the time listening for the opening of the car door, then crossed the grass where a wooden hut marked the Marconi wireless field. I stabbed the guiltless earth with the carbide tips and cursed. Past the Marconi transmission station was the monument at which I stared as my head cooled.

My grandmother, whose name was Baird, had traced some of our family tree and claimed that she was related to John Logie Baird, the inventor of the first electro-mechanical television. *Felix the Cat,* the silent film cartoon character, was the first television star (a papier-mâché doll on a phonograph turntable), used in a test transmission from New York to England. So, when I saw the Marconi statue with Felix's head atop, it all made sense to me. Disappointingly, none of the plaques about the transmitter station made mention of Felix, so I compensated by sending a message to all the friends who knew of my interest in the history of photography and of Felix. To find something connecting you to the landscape or to history can make a bad situation better.

It was a little later, but not before I had put word widely about that, on inspecting my photographs while wearing my glasses, I discovered that what I thought was a statue of Felix the Cat was in fact a globe, the ears were transmitting towers and his eye the island of Madagascar. No doubt my family tree was also hokum. I felt my cheeks flush. *O felix culpa.* Nobody must know. People would have to be silenced.

Beyond Polurrian Cove was Carrag Luz or Love Rock, and then the Path led down to fortified Mullion Cove. The Cove was protected by Mullion Island and thick harbour walls. An illustration of the hostility of the sea in this part of Cornwall is that, in the forty-two years of operation there were only three successful active lifeboat launches from the Cove. The conditions were just too rough to put to sea. The south coast was no more pacific than the north. The station closed in 1909 after many years of misplaced optimism. But three launches in forty-two years – seriously?

Mullion and its food were inland from the cove which meant a detour. While asking directions in a bric-a-brac and vinyl record shop I felt a tap on my shoulder.

'Oh hello. You're still walking.' I recognised the beautiful voice.

'You were at the café in Lamorna!' It was the woman whose partner had mistaken me for a proper walker.

'We're staying in Mousehole. It's a good place to see the area. Are you going far today?'

'Beyond the Cove but I'm not sure where I'll drop anchor.'

'Be careful. Are you looking for food?'

'I am.' *Be careful*, not *take care*. I felt I might be missing something.

'Keep going to Mullion. There are some small shops. The only other place seems to be a chocolate factory.'

'Thanks. Check out the vinyl. There's some interesting stuff.' Then I left her and her voice for Mullion.

The convenience store in Mullion displayed a sign that it was permanently closing at the weekend so I bought as much as I could carry believing (correctly, as it happened) I may not see another shop for miles. The county was closing down. The shopkeeper gave me a familiar story of her daughter's overpacking which resulted in her 'wearing the pavement' as soon as she donned her backpack. 'Her boyfriend spent the next two months carrying most of her gear.'

'Is he still available?' I asked.

'Oh, I could check for you but they're not together anymore.' she replied, taking my jest literally.

'No, that'll be fine, but thanks.'

I paid for the goods, wished her luck and, as I was halfway out of the door came her cry, 'Careful how you go'. *Careful how you go*. Once outside, the sun was shining, and I soon forgot about it.

The Potter's Wheel shopkeeper advised me to seek a campsite called Teneriffe Farm. 'Two Fs.'

In retrospect, I could picture the path I should have taken had I not been distracted. As I walked up the hill from the cove, the wind and rain started and soon grew in intensity. The land became marshy and the way was unclear. I passed the last walker as she fought the wind back to Mullion, and then I was alone in an endless expanse of glistening dark green.

As the light begins to die, the itinerant camper's mind becomes a pilot's, scanning the flat ground should the engines fail. You have a mental record of where you have been and a darkening view ahead of where you are bound. You weigh one against the other, though your exhaustion biases you towards the land ahead not behind, which can prove disastrous. The way to the campsite was there, on the edge of my thoughts, and the edge of the Path, and then it was gone.

On Vellan Head the route cut off the point and followed flat land. Paddy Dillon advised: 'The path to follow is the muddy one'. Ahead, in the failing light, were many parallel shining, vertical cuts becoming increasingly bloodied. As the quality of one track worsened I cut another, but it too became clotted and I found I was jumping around like a blunted tone arm stylus. All the paths oozed; it was impossible to see which was true.

There had been no sign of life for miles, except for the occasional boat and a couple of remote farmhouses, their lights warming from orange to white. The promised National Trust Teneriffe campsite was out of view, too far inland or else hidden by trees and I regretted not taking the road.

There approached a hooded figure in the distance along the same boggy lines, moving around the gorse, head lowered. We were now a good distance from Mullion and this person appeared to be carrying very little. Perhaps just a small sack. I didn't fancy their chances, not with this light and the growing wind. It was treacherous. I expected a conversation - for them to ask the advice of a stranger on the conditions ahead or to offer something on my own prospects. Given that there were no other living souls for miles, it was therefore odd when they passed me by, head lowered, not even acknowledging my raised hand. 'One may not greet his fellow at night for fear that he may be a demon.'[73] I watched the silhouette march into the distance behind me like a bad dream.

The widest path wandered left and I let it mislead me even though it was obvious this could not be the way. I was drawn to a ruin on the edge of Kynance Farm, a place sure to be sheltered from the wind coming in from the sea. A sign warned that trespassers would be prosecuted. Worse, there were indications that the route was a cattle thoroughfare. Beyond the ruin were the grey shadows of aircraft and hangars, which in this remote place could only be MoD.

After some backtracking through bog I eventually found my way back to the grooved field and dropped down into a valley, frantically looking for flat and dry ground with some shelter. There were camping places, and ash circled by stones, that others had recently used.

Several high places had flat ground, though some had concrete hazards, remnants of historical soap rock quarrying for porcelain. Too close to the cliff risked shards of rock falling. This place was Soapy Cove, Gew Graze, or *middle hollow* from Cornish mining terminology. Below the ruins was a patch of flat grass on the valley floor sheltered from the sea by a grassed mound. That was it. On one side was a deep roaring ravine with a waterfall emptying into the raging sea. Rocks were everywhere so I used them to hold down the ground sheet and tent in the wind. Only when the tent was all set, camouflaged against the field of dark green, did I place my pack inside as extra ballast. That's when it happened.

Admiring my work amid the roar of the stream and the sea, with a whooshing sound the tent began to flap. Not a gentle flap but a violent shaking that threatened to sweep it up into the air. The wind had changed direction and now used the valley as a funnel directing all its energy at me and my little shelter.

I quickly grabbed rocks and weighted each of the corner pegs and put more inside. In all, ten medium-sized stones at each of the secure points plus my own body and pack, and yet still it lifted. The noise was unbearable, a banshee screaming in the darkness. In my mind a gigantic hooded face howled down through the valley. Then came the rain. I crept out briefly, keeping low, to build a small wall of stone to stop the wind from catching the underside of the fly. I was careful not to look into the darkness up the valley.

One moment the tent was upright, a moment later pressed flat. My lantern bounced, exaggerating the movement so much that it disturbed me. Terrifyingly, the light was also losing its power so I saved the batteries in case I had to find shelter in an emergency. The darkness was pitch, so it was too dangerous to relocate.

Margaret Atwood has a nightmarish short story called *The Tent*.[74] It is pinned between two other stories, *Warlords* and *Time Folds*. *Warlords* says those who have worked for a warlord cannot forget – their occupation's gone, you can't find another or learn something else. The other, *Time Folds*, may be about physics or the effects of time (being given a last kiss and folded up). *The Tent* itself is a meditation on writing. 'You're in a tent. It's vast and cold outside, very vast. It's a howling wilderness. There are rocks in it, and ice and sand, and deep boggy pits you could sink into without a trace. There are ruins as well, many ruins.'[75] Was she there, then, peaking through a pinhole she had made in a pleated ribbon to illustrate time folding? Atwood had written me into the landscape.

As a distraction I read by my e-reader's green light. Having finished a couple of ghost stories, I found the next book that Mags had emailed me. It was by Robert Goddard, a good storyteller, and it would distract me from this place. On the tenth page was the line, referring to the Lizard peninsula near Mullion. I looked forward through the pages and realised the whole book was set between Poldhu, Mullion Cove and the Lizard. It wasn't the sort of surprise I needed. It was highly improbable and I needed the highly likely.

To distract myself from this hurricane and the unsettling coincidence, I forced myself into another place. For the previous five years I had run training courses on surveys and statistics. At the beginning of the course I always posed participants a question to place them in the right frame of mind for what was to come. The question related to stories collected by Wilhelm von Scholz (a favoured writer of the Nazis as it happens) as retold by psychologist Carl Jung in his *Synchronicity* lecture. It involved photographic film used by a mother to take pictures of her child. The exposed film was deposited for processing but forgotten about and it accidentally entered back into circulation. After the war, it was coincidentally bought and double-exposed by the same woman. The image in question had both the woman's children double-exposed on the same frame, four years apart in different towns.[76]

It is a wonderful ghostly story, sending nervous electricity through your skin. My purpose, though, was to demystify it, to give a logical explanation using probability. In essence, I took the magic from it, dulled its power – a statistical exorcism. After some discussion I would reveal various facts about camera ownership, recycling of materials in wartime and recollection in both senses.

The wind by this point was cacophonous and I was sitting in the pool of green light formed by the screen of my e-reader trying to recall the sequence of logic as the tent vibrated. I recalled that some students simply couldn't get past the magical power of attraction of related objects.

What I was really thinking about, with the unsettling howling at my paper-thin door, was not the likelihood of events but the silent hooded figure I had seen on the cliff. The place had somehow entered into my novel. The wind could sweep me into the boiling sea. It might be quick for me, but what a mystery for those worried about where I had gone. There would be no record that I had ever been here; I would simply have vanished.

It was a terrifying night; what little sleep I was to catch would be broken by a sudden burst of turbulence and flapping as a peg broke loose. This had me straining to reach it from inside without risking entering the storm. Exhausted, the next thing I saw was the morning sun.

Mad dogs and Elvish women
Day 32. 11ᵗʰ October

My fear of the night before felt foolish in daylight. I climbed the valley and crossed the top until I found steps down into Kynance Cove.

The ruins in the Cove had been Thomas's Private Hotel in the 1920s. The old sash windows with Georgian bars were broken and those on ground level covered in MDF board. Abandonment, like dead people, was the great selling point of the Coast Path. According to the staff of the National Trust café, the current estate owner had no intention of developing the hotel, something that would attract more crowds into the secluded cove. Over coffee and cake the owner told me about the place and urged me to stop beyond Lizard at Cadgwith.

At the Lizard hostel an officious resident sprang out of a side door as I was disposing of my recycling; he demanded an explanation.

'I've come from another hostel and so I'm just using your recycling. Would you like me to take it back out?' His mouth opened and closed but emitted no sound, then he made a huffing noise and walked back inside. After last night's accommodation I was in no mood to deal with petty officials lecturing me on solid waste management.

The trail passed the squat lighthouse, Housel Bay Hotel, Lizard Marconi signal station, and the Lloyds Signal Station. Beyond Lloyd's white crenellated tower, a large estate warned 'BEWARE ADDERS'. Curiously, the sign was embedded in the perimeter wall and etched into stone. There was nothing temporary about the hazard the reptiles posed walkers.

The Devil's Frying Pan, a crater caused by a collapsed sea cave, marked the beginning of a fairy path winding down to Cadgwith, something from Tolkien. Cadgwith had more than its fair share of thatched cottages. This anomaly is explained by the relative distance of the village from the slate-producing region near Tintagel, yet there was an underlying smugness here - more style than material poverty. I suspect that any attempt to erect my tent would expose a preciousness unrelated to the absence of tiling. It was more middle England than Middle Earth, and though I hadn't met any yet, I was sure that its residents knew it.

But I was prepared to forgive this community pride as there was a public toilet. Sheltering from the light rain I sat in the loo doorway down an alley to glue my boots with the remainder of the tube of rubber adhesive. A man emerged from the street and gave me a disgusted look as he entered the lavatory. Only after he'd left did it occur to me that he may have witnessed a shoeless toilet substance abuser rather than a man frantically intent on sole adhesion. Ten minutes to set is not ideal, but I didn't have the luxury of time if the police had been alerted.

As I left Cadgwith, the final track of Pink Floyd's *Dark Side of the Moon* drifted down from an open window.[77] It lifted me up, though it may just have been solvent inhalation.

After hobbit glen the Path moved through Poltesco, known for quarrying serpentine. Serpentine is an ornate, cheaper substitute for marble, though fragile. Just like marble, only not very good at being just like marble.

The rain was cold and grew in intensity as the Path crossed the cliffs to Beagles Point where a cross commemorated the 1974 deaths of a Sea King helicopter's crew. They had been involved in a night exercise and had crashed into the cliff face. All four of the crew were killed outright. To contemplate the needless loss of life I sat in an old coastguard lookout which sheltered me from both the rain and the large cattle which had the ominous hunched silhouettes of bulls.

The light had all but gone and I shivered as soon as my body was still. Had I been more mentally alert I would have realised that this expanse of darkness was inexorably smothering the land ahead. On my arrival in Porlock Weir, a month ago, I had 13 hours of daylight. Today there were 11 hours and three minutes, a loss of two hours. I covered double the distance with a shorter day.

As the cattle shuffled to a safe distance I made for a gap in the gorse and entered forest with just sufficient light to navigate a stream. Something large and unnatural was silhouetted against the sky in a field. The Guide made no mention of this, so I determined to return in daylight to investigate.

A canvas tent lit by windows was the first sign of the hostel. Alas, I would have to vacate tomorrow as there was a school group. Not even tents would be permitted. The hostel had just enough weather reports with which to stuff my boots.

As I left the drying room in the morning, through a stair window was a flash of something familiar but out of place. On closer inspection I saw that it was, indeed, a Land Rover Defender, orange and with the markings of the G4 Challenge, a global adventure competition which had been cancelled due to the financial crash of 2008. I knew this vehicle. What was it doing here?

The road inland to Little Trevothan Farm was quiet. On arrival, Mark met me at reception and led me to a pitch for the tent. 'You're the only camper,' he said, and I couldn't help feeling a little sad at the thought. Their licence for camping covered only 10 months of the year.

'I'd like to stay a couple of days as I'm going to have some tidal problems.'

'Near Helford Passage. Yes, we've had some walkers who had difficulties timing it. I can drive you if you like.' I wasn't sure if he was just being friendly and I think my face betrayed this. 'Seriously, I've done it for others.'

'That's very kind. I was hoping to go to Helston today for provisions and walk to Helford tomorrow.'

'I could pick you up there, but I would need to know when you expected to arrive and it's quite a journey. It would be easier if I took you there and you walked back and then you could do it in your own time.'

I promised to check the tide times. He gave me his mobile number, I pitched the tent and walked down to the harbour.

The orange Defender was parked outside a bakery so I put my head over the stable door and asked, 'Excuse me, are you the owner of the Defender?'

A man at the counter turned around. 'Erm, no.'

'You're looking for Robin who runs the surf school, love.' The woman behind the counter was stretching around the man's torso. I nodded. 'Take the next left, down the steps to the building on the edge of the harbour.

As I reached the steps there was a white-haired man locking up. 'Excuse me, are you Robin?'

'Yes, how can I help you?'

'Do you own the orange Defender?'

'I most certainly do.' He was fumbling with his keys.

'This is going to sound weird.' And I told him the story. For more than a decade I had visited Mongolia, supporting a programme providing care for older people and those with disabilities in the harshest winter conditions (negative $30\,°C$ was not unusual). Throughout this time we used a bright orange Land Rover Defender with markings identical to this one.

'Really?' Robin now appeared interested. He leaned against the door of Cliff Cottage and crossed his arms.

'It's famous in Mongolia.'

He smiled. 'That model was being sold after the competition and I snapped it up. I haven't seen others. Great vehicle. I use it all the time on the boat ramp. It's the only way to get any traction on the cobbles. The only thing is, unlike the earlier models I haven't found a way for it to leak oil, and the wiper is not operating intermittently. They just don't make them like they used to.'

Dan, the friend with the exploding sleeping bag on that practice run, complained of the same thing. His old Defender was mostly insulating tape and rust. He bought only authentic British parts, guaranteed to fail at night in a storm – usually the wipers. Something always failed so he could delay fixing it. I can only imagine that he enjoyed the suspense.

'You can't be discreet in a day-glow orange four-wheel drive. How did you know it was mine?' he asked.

'I was at the hostel. The cook told me to look for you.'

'That's right. I keep it up there, out of the way. I used to run the place. When I took it over it was running at a loss. By the time I left, it had a good turnover of visitors. I didn't always agree with the way hostels are kept though. You have to keep the uniqueness of the place. These old buildings are special, they all have a character and the place they're in has a character. Its more than having standard menus, posters and toilet paper.'

'I had to vacate today as there was a group school booking. I'm at a farm now.'

'It's difficult for the individual traveller.'

He explained that the halfway point for the Path was Porthallow. He pronounced it *prallow*. There was now a sign there or a sculpture, which was worth a look. Robin was preparing to head off for winter, his other love being photography – wildlife and landscapes.

'It's been good to find you.' And it was. It felt like a connection of sorts. We posed for a photograph in front of the Defender as a souvenir of the chance meeting and I hurried to my bus.

Helston was all out of waterproof flexible adhesive by the time I left.

Back in Coverack I picked up a copy of the tide times then walked to the woods. Two women and a man talked loudly about property prices, a couple of fluffy black dogs running around them, eagerly tugging to go for a walk.

'Can we help you?' She made a whoop sound and laughed.

'No, I'm fine, but thanks.' I smiled and walked by, trying to find the entrance to the woods.

'Are you suuure? We're just going for a walk ourselves.' She displayed signs of alcohol consumption, her speech slurred, her body swaying. I shook my head and walked into what was clearly somebody's garden. Rather than leave, I hovered there to disguise my mistake, pretending to admire the architecture. It was a non-descript bungalow. A woman appeared from behind her curtain and stared at me warily. I smiled my most reassuring smile, she looked shocked and disappeared. Retracing my steps, I walked sheepishly past the three where the drunk woman repeated her offer, laughing. At last I found the lane to the woods and escape.

From the wood I could hear the poodle-like hounds at my heels and the *whoop-whooping* and *hoorays* from the early drinker. She must have had a head start; her companions seemed sober. After crossing the stream a dog shot past, splashing. To the left I found myself in a field confronted by black, white and oxblood red sculptures. Some were steel, some stone. All but a few were animals and had a cubist abstract appearance, though the corners were gently curved.

From the corner of my eye was a flash of black. The dog crossed the field. They were all calling for him now, and I resolved to enjoy the peace of the sculpture garden and put them from my mind.

Terence Coventry had stored the sculptures in these fields in his lifetime and with so many people jumping fences to see them, he opened up the spaces as a garden for the public. He had left London's Royal College of Art when they refused to allow him to change from painting to sculpture, yet John Le Carré had described Coventry as 'a natural born sculptor'.[78] Perhaps it owes to his credentials as a pig farmer, or that he was a sculptor of animals (the visual arts equivalent of genre fiction) that Coventry received none of the recognition of his contemporaries - not even a Wikipedia page.

The silhouetted object I had seen in the previous night's rain was one of the larger pieces, an owl. The owls were hunched, forlorn. One sculpture, a representation of a woman sitting on a bench, connected with the landscape. It told the story of a couple, Reginald and Prudence, who agreed to meet on a bench on the Coast Path. She said she knew the bench. Only, they were thinking of two different benches so they sat together, alone, patiently waiting for the other. Prudence was white. Reginald, in concrete form, sat in another part of the park and could not be seen by Prudence. It had been a Hardyesque mistake.

'Reggieeeeee!' came the distant screech from the Path. A man appeared, out of breath.

'Have you seen a black dog?'

'He went that way.' I pointed back the way I had come.

'Oh dear, he got away from us. It's exhausting.' He wandered off. In the distance could be heard the woman of the pre-prandial drinks, her elongated cry changing pitch several times before reaching her double bar line. Perhaps Reggie had wanted to be alone all along.

My digital map showed a path taking a back route to the campsite, so I walked past Terence Coventry's house and followed lanes to the clearly sign-posted path. Soon the signs petered out and I found myself at a farm lane junction where I took the route most likely to head towards my farm. It was not, however, the way most likely to be a right of way. At the second gate it was necessary to balance on the gate post and swing around to the next field to avoid wading a lake formed by cattle. The water reflected a leaden sky. This was the point where anyone in their right mind would turn back so, having travelled so far, I ploughed on.

Rain fell and one muddy field led to another, the last containing bunkers. On my map it showed as former RAF Treleaver. Perhaps not so former as the lights were on. The sentry boxes closer to me looked like they may harbour bulls, so I moved quietly. The way to the campsite was through the fence to the right. This was topped with barbed wire and behind it was a thicket of trees and brambles. I walked up to the far end but could see no way through. This was embarrassing. I was metres from salvation and yet stuck in a wet field far from roads.

At the end closest to the bunker the vegetation was thinnest. I straddled the wire and, being more agile without my large pack, hopped onto a bush into which I immediately began to sink. The bush could hold my weight only for a moment before it gave, so I hopped quickly from one foot to the other until I made it to a branch which could support me. The sticky vegetation ensnared my waterproofs. Each step I would find my clothing or skin snagged on brambles and soon I would have to call for help. The panic pushed me forward and the thicket eventually gave onto an opening into which I rolled and unwound my brambles. The rectangle of grass was vacant of caravans. This meant that I was able to emerge from the neat dividing hedges into the populated area as though I had just taken a stroll around the camp - had it not been for the blood and pieces of foliage protruding from my rain gear. 'Don't ever take one of his shortcuts.' *Oh, be quiet.*

147

The sky was bright from the waxing moon, if overcast. There was still rain so I cooked in the shelter outside the laundry room while doing my washing. It was a chance to phone Kristiina, my Finnish friend who had promised to meet me in Cornwall (more accurately, she had promised to meet me in Devon). JRR Tolkien had been so excited by Finnish that he had invented an Elvish language based on the pattern of its sounds.

I had hopes for our own unexpected journey. It was important to time our arrivals; my guess was that St Austell would be the place. It was roughly equidistant in time between Coverack and northern Finland.

'I thought you would be in Devonshire by now.' She pronounced the shire like sire. 'How can I plan when it keeps changing?'

'I'm sorry, Kristiina, I had some injuries and they slowed me. Also, it's necessary to take a rest every five or six days.'

'You didn't know you were going to have rest days at the beginning?'

'I wasn't sure. Now I'm sure. I did say it was only an estimate based on walking at the pace of the guidebook.'

'I've looked at the guidebook. Is that guy crazy? The distances. What is he thinking ... isn't it?'

'Don't blame him, it's just a guide. He doesn't know I'm carrying my own shelter.' I was defending Paddy like the neglected child who is entitled to disparage their own parent, but woe betide anybody who does so on their behalf, least of all someone with Elvish blood.

All the right places, not necessarily in the right order
Day 34. 13ᵗʰ October

In reception I casually wove the question of the bunker into a conversation with Mark. He explained that the nuclear bunker was now home to alcohol production, 'they make *artisan vinegar*'. Clearly not a fan of their booze, I thought. I later discovered that they were, in fact, producing, along with beer, artisan malt vinegar and had even won an award for it. It was the only former nuclear bunker-cum-early-warning-station producing artisan malt vinegar. Quite an acerbic working environment, at any time.

Mark dropped me at the Holy Mackerel restaurant in Helford. This was to be a journey in reverse, all the right places, but not necessarily in the right order. A family gathered horse chestnuts in the woods as I left Helford. Fair-haired teenagers, a girl and boy, were exploring a sandy beach. This wasn't real life, it was an Enid Blyton adventure. Sickening.

On the approach to Gillan Harbour an elderly couple stopped to talk. 'Are you going far?'

'Poole.'

'You're going the wrong way.'

'Yes. I have to do this section in reverse because of the tides. To Coverack today, and Falmouth tomorrow.' I got the feeling that there was a bit of something romantic between the two. They described each other as friends. Perhaps I imagined it.

'A good walk, Coverack – in one day? We're just going for a boat ride. At least that's the plan.' He was off to show her his boat and he seemed proud of it.

'He insisted we should take it out. You mentioned the tides.' She seemed to tease him. Perhaps I was right.

'Oh, I assume you need a high tide. I'm heading for the crossing in the harbour and low tide is in about twenty minutes.'

149

Like a scout I consulted my little yellow *Falmouth Tide Times*. 'Yes, this is low tide.'

'Oh, damn. The one time I didn't check the tides and it's low. Isn't that just typical?' He looked deflated.

'Don't worry, dear, we can have a look at it and go to the pub. If there's time we'll take it out later when it will be cooler.' She was very understanding, and it was touching to watch. He struggled with his movement and was out of breath. They were safer on dry land where they could get to know each other without all those knots and swinging booms.

The crossing, according to Paddy, had three options. The first was 'slippery stepping-stones'. The second, a 'tidal ford'. The third was *don't do it*. The difficulty in this stretch if you are travelling the Coast anti-clockwise is that you need low tide for Gillan Harbour and a higher tide for the Helford Passage ferry. The difficulty for me was that I did not have the advantage of having his direction of travel.

The stepping-stones were treacherous, water lapping their worn tops, which were strewn with slimy seaweed. While it was exactly low tide that did not account for a river in flood. The tidal ford it must be. I took off my shoes and realised I had left my water shoes in the tent. No matter, I'd brave the river. It wasn't too deep and I reached the other side without incident.

'Hello there.' It was a walker on the far side. 'How do you cross?' That was when I realised that I was on an island. There was a second channel separating the far side. This was not mentioned in the Guide; perhaps the river had breached the shingle over time.

'The first channel was easy. Can you see a way through there?'

'It looks too deep. I'm going to walk around. Good luck.' And so he disappeared leaving me marooned. *Poop.* I surveyed the area and chose a spot directed towards some steps. The water was much deeper and sharp underfoot so I was happy to reach the far side.

I recall reading a blog that described an exchange between a walker and a Gillan person. Was it possible to cross Gillan Creek?

'Yes, no problem.' And when asked if *they* would do it, 'Oh God no!'

Keeping that exchange in mind, and my recent experience, it was at the next beach that I heard a man in his sixties speaking to two women walking the Path.

'So would you cross it?' One was looking at her map looking contemplatively, like the pathologist from *Lewis*, while the other interrogated the local.

'I do it all the time, yes.' He had the demeanour of the lord of an estate, speaking with confidence and authority.

'Erm, I've just come from there,' I offered.

'Really, how was it?' She turned to me and the man looked agitated at the temporary loss of his audience.

'Well, I walked across without boots as it was much too deep. The riverbed is sharp.'

'You should keep your boots on, man!' He had the indignation of the keeper of all local knowledge, his back straight giving him additional height.

'You *could*, yes, assuming you don't mind walking for the next five hours with wet boots. You two don't look like you're going to the post office,' I said to the walkers. That was for his benefit; he looked as though he was fetching the paper. I looked at their suede low ankle boots.

'I don't think I want that,' said the one with the map.

'It really isn't a problem,' the man insisted, desperate to lead the two.

'There are two ways to cross, but both involve wading,' I explained. 'One, wade the first stretch and then take the stepping-stones which are deadly and you *will* fall in. The river water flows *over* them and through the seaweed on top. Two, wade the first stretch and then the shallower second stretch. But the tide will be coming in soon. At the moment the tide isn't the problem, it's the river in flood.'

'I'm not sure of this,' the first woman looked worried. 'Let's just walk around.'

The man was blustering, clearly disliking an out-of-towner queering his pitch. 'Well it's your choice,' and the tone suggested their life might depend on it. I don't mean to be sexist, but men can be like this, myself included. Perhaps they should have suggested he lead the way.

'It's supposed to be a beautiful walk,' I reassured them, and wished them good luck. We would meet again, though our recognition would be blurred by the fact that I had been walking in the wrong direction.

It was a gentle walk to Nare Point where there was a National Coastwatch Institution station. *Visitors welcome.* So, I went in and was greeted by a Labrador and then a man in semi-military attire, a short beard and glasses. He was probably a little older than me, had a friendly face and said 'Hi, come on in. Are you walking the Path?'

After brief introductions he asked if I'd like coffee. 'I was just making some.' We drank while Dave, as his name tag told me, took sideways glances through the telescope at passing boats. 'How is your eyesight? Can you make that number out?' I was unsure if he was just trying to engage me in the work or whether he genuinely couldn't see it, but I read the number and he confirmed it, neatly recording it in his log.

'I used to be involved in water supply in Swaziland,' he offered.

'Strange. The last programme I worked on was to support the development of a water programme in Swaziland. It became Eswatini when I was working on it.'

'I suppose I'd had enough,' Dave continued. 'So, I started to build a boat. After some months we had finished a Chinese three-masted junk.'

'With red sails?' I asked. I could picture it. There was a travel poster with a red-sailed junk in our living room in London, which I often dreamt of being aboard.

'Exactly. Red sails. Sailing a junk is so much easier. The junk rig gives more drive than these when running downwind.' He pointed to the ones out to sea. 'Bermuda rig sails collapse in light wind, but a junk has fixed battens. Also, it's easier to control solo as you just let out the halyard in strong wind.' He was starting to lose me; I knew as much of sailing as I knew of quantum mechanics. I was still thinking of how those red sails would look in the tropics at sunset.

'So, me and my partner sailed around the world. We harvested rainwater from the deck and had enough canned food so that we didn't need to go into port. Entirely self-sufficient.'

'Like Felicity Kendal and Richard Briers on the high seas.'

'I suppose. Yes, *The Good Life*.'

'What about power?'

'The propeller. There was a motor that we never used, but the propeller could freewheel from the forward movement and this drove a generator. We had electricity for lights and the radio. It was perfect.' He smiled, looked distant, then looked at me and was back in the room. 'Sometimes you just get an impulse to change, to give up whatever it is that you do.' Yes, without a doubt.

'Weren't you afraid? Being on the open sea I mean?'

'We were rarely far out, we'd just follow the coast to the next port.'

'And why Cornwall?'

'We ended up here when I did my back in, so it wasn't easy to work the rig. And now I volunteer. It's not bad, you have great views and meet people. It's not the fast life, but who needs that? What will you do?'

'I haven't decided. I'd like to get out of London. It's a trap.' He just nodded and smiled.

I bought some cola from him, said thanks for the time, and was going to make a donation in the box outside but in my euphoric state sailed right past it. By the time I realised, I was too far up the Path so I resolved to donate at another lookout.

There were more rugged slopes ahead, the trail passing through bracken with views down to the sea. The sky was blue and it was hot. I reached Porthallow, the official halfway point, before three o'clock. The 'Faded Voices' marker, by Tom Leaper and writer Stephen Hall, used words from members of the local community to create a poem to celebrate the Path. It ended 'That's how it was / That's how we're like we are'. I celebrated alone, with tea on a picnic table beside the marker.

Conflicted. That summed up my feelings. I had reached the halfway point so I had to do it all over again. Also, I was alone. There were a few people on the beach who walked past me without acknowledgment and then drove away. Didn't they realise the importance of this point? There was no fanfare. A strange seaweed-covered scarecrow stared out to sea.

If you've ever tried to follow a route guide backwards you will know it's not as easy as it sounds. It's not enough to read the paragraphs in reverse. There are important details hidden within prepositions which must be inverted and turned. Leaving Porthallow I kept to the path closest to the sea, which was a mistake. I eventually found the route but had lost valuable time.

Pipistrelle bats followed me back along the lane. The full moon had risen as I reached the farm. Condensation on my tent glistened in its light. I thought about being over halfway as I made dinner. Last night, possibly while I was on the phone to Kristiina, a person's tent was set alight in Cork, Ireland. The perpetrator, or perhaps someone accompanying them, brutally beat him. He died in hospital from his injuries.[79] It happened in an area of Cork known to be used by rough sleepers. The news quickly forgets; it moves on to politics, celebrity, television licences and singing in the streets. The dead man was Timmy Hourihane, who had once been a chef. A couple of years earlier he had admitted being assaulted three times. '"Wandering around, basically around the whole city, trying to find where can I sleep tonight, is it going to be safe?"'[80] His tent had been pitched off the road on an area of grass. He had owned little more than his life, and in the end not even that.

Tomorrow would be two early bus journeys back to Helford and the ferry crossing then a gentle walk to Falmouth. I slept.

In the light from the shower block I packed quickly. The dark lanes were eerie before dawn; as I passed a farm the twisted face of an old tractor stared from a tunnel of trees. An owl's hoot startled me into the nervous laughter of Sleepy Hollow's Ichabod Crane.

One other dishevelled man waited at the harbour bus stop. Perhaps not as dishevelled as me. He was walking the Path, but in small sections, with a caravan as base. I wondered how he found himself there so early if his base was elsewhere. Perhaps he had walked all night, or else found somewhere to sleep here but my mind was too slow for early morning questions. The bus arrived.

At St Keverne I stayed warm and dry by moving around under the church lychgate. I was pondering whether using the churchyard as a toilet would be inappropriate when what looked like a bread van arrived and the driver jumped out then ran off. Out of curiosity I followed and saw that he disappeared into a small building. A toilet!

I stood at the trough, my kidneys cried out in ecstasy. It took some restraint not to let out a squeal. 'Are you driving the bus?' I squeaked.

'Not at this moment. Leaving for Helford in five minutes.'

Boarding the bus, I leaned my gear against a chair - making a mental note of it all. If you must put something down on public transport, at least ensure it's difficult to leave without it. If you don't, you only have yourself to blame. On the journey the driver asked me about my walking. 'How are you finding the weather?'

'It's been worse. So long as I can keep my gear dry, I'll survive.'

'Are there campsites open?'

'Not so many. Sometimes you camp where you can.'

Two Germans got on at Porthallow and joined in the conversation. So many on our coast; the German coast must be a barren landscape of tank barriers festooned with wartime unexploded ordnance. They had seen no other walkers on their English holiday, which surprised them.

'It's late in the year,' I suggested.

'Late, yes,' he said, 'but not yet winter'. It was true, and I was aware that I had seen fewer people walking. It had been the weekend too and I had only seen the two women near the Gillan crossing. The trail, I realised, had become a lonely one. As we pulled into Helford I stood and did the usual dance to put my pack on. They wished me luck as I stepped down and I shouted goodbye.

Something troubled me as the bus moved into gear and seemed to sob like a child in higher and higher pitch back up the hill. As I watched it slowly disappear around the bend it slowly dawned on me what I had done. My walking sticks were still on board. I dropped my pack and ran after it, shouting, my shin screaming out in pain - but the bus was already out of view. I stood for a moment feeling that the Germans would stop him, but they didn't return. I was pacing now. Walking with the weight of the pack without the poles was foolhardy. Thinking quickly, I fished out my ticket and rang the bus company, explaining the urgency of the situation.

After a few minutes I received a call back. 'Hello, Mr Burton? The driver has already got to the next town and there is no way to turn back.' I glanced up in frustration. A fish-shaped sign above me read *Holy Mackerel*. 'But he said he'd work out a way to get them back to you.' They were words designed to give false assurance and so free up the phone line. She gave me his number and I wrote it down, but without much enthusiasm. I knew I had lost them and I either had to find something else to use or spend a small fortune on carbon fibre sticks. It was such a stupid thing to have done. I had been so careful but then I rarely used public transport.

At least this day's journey was on the flat. I headed for the ferry pier, where I waited alongside a young woman. She was staying in the village and visiting Trebah Gardens, and of course, she was German.

On board the little boat, the pilot explained that the ferry was subsidised. 'One day this week I had no passengers all day, so two is good.' It can't be an easy job to sit all day hopefully watching the shore for customers. The fare was a bargain at £2, when the round trip by land was 36km, but people are addicted to their cars.

We thanked and paid the pilot, then separated at the gardens. A group of international students gathered in the valley by Durgan School House as I passed. At the wooded road where I rested, the students caught up with me, kicking fallen branches and groaning about the walk. Despite the language barrier, 'Moping Adolescent' is universally understood.

I resolved to give the bus driver another fifteen minutes before I called; if he was reluctant to help I would find an alternative crutch, even if it meant kicking one from under someone less able.

A group of men walked just ahead of me. 'I'd be better if I had my other stick,' one of them complained.

'You'll survive.' The leader of the group, as he appeared to be, was a 50-something with a mane of white hair and square jaw, dressed in earth coloured walking gear.

There was something about Silver Mane's posture that suggested army or having sat on the missing walking pole. Not so the rest of his group, who demonstrated less discipline.

'How did you lose your other stick?' I asked of the walker leaning on his pole.

'Snapped.' He shrugged and smiled.

'What he means is, he wedged it between two rocks and then kept walking. Snapped like a wrist.' It was a disturbing, but effective, simile.

'I have a similar problem. I left both of mine on a bus. They're in Helston. I'm hoping to find a way to have them sent on, though I don't hold out much hope.'

'That's rough. How much are you carrying?' Silver Mane was eyeing my luggage in a way suggesting he might suddenly spring into action.

'I'm not sure. Something around 20 kilos. I haven't weighed it.'

'Let me try.' He grabbed it and held it with both hands then let it fall onto one. 'Twenty-five,' he stated as fact, placing it at my feet.

'So much? You think?' Given that I'd already jettisoned more than five kilos, *surely* he'd overestimated.

'Pretty close, not much less. How far are you going?'

'Poole.'

'You started at Minehead? *Not all those who wander are lost.*'

'I was carrying more but ditched some. The sticks help. Helped.' It was nothing more than his guess-the-backpack weight party trick. By the time I knew the truth he'd be gone.

'If you wish to travel far and fast, travel light.' He had an aphorism for every occasion. 'Good luck.' I let them go ahead but I could hear him in the distance for a while as I walked, motivating them with something from Aesop's *Tortoise and the Hare* and then leading them towards a hotel with a restaurant.

In the woods near the church at Mawnan I called the bus driver. 'Hello. You left your sticks. Where are you heading tonight?'

'Falmouth, the hostel. I should be there early. Is there a chance you could put them on a bus to Falmouth and I could coll ...'

'I live in Falmouth. Meet me at Avenue Road, the crossing, at six. I'll be in a car.' I thanked him and rang off. I still wasn't confident, but certainly more hopeful.

It was before four o'clock when I reached Gyllyngvase on the edge of Falmouth, so I waited in the rain until the hostel opened. The manager chatted a bit about the hostel then pointed to a familiar pair of walking sticks. 'Are these yours? A man dropped them off but didn't stay.' I never did get the chance to thank the driver in person.

Coincidences in ruins
Day 36. 15ᵗʰ October

Realising that I'd spent fifteen minutes waiting for the ferry to cross the estuary at the wrong quay, it was important not to appear a dingbat so I pretended to admire the sea view and then casually walked back to the road. Nobody could advise on the correct landing place, so I just checked each pier until I found it. Two other people were waiting when I arrived, out of breath, and within a few minutes the first ferry had docked.

In order to cross the expanse of water known as Carrick Roads,[81] the estuary of the River Fal, and regain the Coast Path, two ferries are needed. The first reaches St Mawes, and the second, Place. There was little time to spare in St Mawes, which was a shame as it had an appealing old seafaring atmosphere. The small boat to Place was waiting for us so we left immediately and soon arrived at a little wood that led to the lawn of an estate.

This must be the Place. Strictly speaking, the village – if it can be called that – was St Anthony in Roseland. At the gate to Place

House I ate muesli from my fluorescent dog bowl while standing beside a private property sign. All potential seating was chained off. While I ate, an elderly woman with an aristocratic air trundled slowly down the Place lawn on a mobility scooter, checked me out without appearing to look directly at me, and then trundled back towards the mansion. She didn't appear to be armed but nevertheless I swiftly moved on.

I passed a half-buried Nissen hut and a mediaeval stone coffin on the path to the church. There followed some traditional beehives, a field of round straw bales, wind-hunched trees, a lighthouse, and a nineteenth-century military battery, according to a sign last occupied in WWII. They were the settings for of an unwritten Arthur Ransome adventure. Growing up here would have meant never having to grow up.

After some time, I looked back to see a couple of women come into view, getting closer by the minute. 'Contemptible flatulent load-shedders,' I muttered. My miserly persona made itself known as I was forced to share the Path. It wasn't hate, just deeply felt resentment.

'We know you!' cried the one with longer hair when they caught up. 'You advised us not to wade Gillan Creek. You're going the wrong way.' And now they were trying to make friends with me.

As I looked at them I recalled the disgruntled man who had urged them to wade a river in flood with the tide coming in, like Moses and the Egyptians. 'Oh, of course. I thought I knew you two. That man didn't appreciate my expert witness.'

'He *was* a bit grouchy. Yours was a very recent expert opinion, which is what counted. The walk around the estuary was lovely. We looked at the water and it didn't look safe so we went with your analysis. Sorry, I'm Annette. This is Jill.' Suddenly they were no longer strangers on my shore, and once again I felt my cheeks burn with shame.

'Oscar,' I held out my hand.

'But you've changed direction. We thought at first it couldn't be you as you were walking clockwise.'

'Time and tide wait for no-one, so I cadged a ride and walked in the wrong direction.'

We talked about the various obstacles we'd faced and how we had overcome them. After a while we walked separately and then talked again at intervals as we came back into sync. I discovered that they were accompanied by another friend, but she was the designated driver who did not much care for walking. Judicious. When we met her, she wasn't at all out of breath.

Once again, I said goodbye to fellow walkers and walked the street alone. The Nare Hotel was under construction meaning I had to take a wide diversion away from the cliffs. The hotel has a promise, which I understand has been honoured, to grant guests a free night if snow ever settled on the ground there. It's a rare thing in this part of the country; given the warmer air brought by the Gulf Stream.

Soon I found myself in a steep valley, at the bottom of which was a path to the left leading to a wood, and to the right the rocky cove. Across a recently constructed oak railed bridge was a ruined cottage with no roof but four preserved walls and flat grassed earth within.

According to the National Trust, the little cottage was built by fisherman Thomas Mallet in the early 1800s. He had married a woman from nearby Veryan, but soon left her to pursue his trade from this cottage. He would leave his boat in the inlet, hauled clear of the waves. Though he returned to Mrs Mallet at weekends with his catch, there could have been little warmth in his relationship for he emigrated to Australia in the 1840s, leaving his wife in Cornwall. The South West Coast Path website mentions a linked occurrence in the 1960s: 'About 120 years later, by an extraordinary coincidence, the National Trust farm tenant for the land picked up two Australian hitch-hikers east of Bristol. One of them was Tina Mallet, the great granddaughter of Fisherman Mallet, returning to Cornwall to visit her roots'.[82] Clearly Mallet had cast his net more widely down under.

Whether or not it was wise to tempt the ghosts of house parties past, it was another immigrant to Australia, now returned, who stayed in the cottage that night. Before making camp I ran to the top of the next hill in the mild drizzle to check there were no better locations. Sheep eyed me suspiciously. One urinated voluminously, as they commonly do when encountering people (I believe this is to avoid fleeing on a full bladder, though I'm no expert on sheep) so I retraced my steps. The wind and rain began as I was putting up the tent, but the shelter provided by the walls of Mallet's cottage allowed me to plant it without losing it to the sea. It was hidden from all angles. I treated the place with respect as it had been someone's home (though at the time not knowing its provenance) and it was comfortable, almost peaceful.

Monuments to deeply unpleasant men
Day 37. 16ᵗʰ October

I had two days to get to St Austell, where my friend Kristiina would be waiting. That meant making haste.

Nare Head has an early warning nuclear bunker from 1962, and another WWII shelter, which was used by British film studios to mount a light display as decoy for nearby Falmouth's rail and docks. The real town, of course, would have been in almost complete blackout. I learned from a sign that the decoy sites were bombed 786 times. Wartime was tough for the arts.

Caerhays Castle Estate, beyond Portholland, was advertising a ten-metre square, earthen-floored lookout as a wedding venue. Perfect for those with loads of cash and few friends. Caerhays Castle itself, in Porthluney Cove, was modelled on a Norman castle. It was closed, naturally, as was the nautically themed café and cocktail bar opposite. Two women were consulting the cocktail menu regardless.

'It's not good to drink in the middle of the day,' I observed as I passed. 'Do they have margaritas?'

'Don't get too excited. It's only a sand mirage. Oh, why can't it be open?' one of them cried. It did feel tragic.

With not a daquiri in sight I felt the need to move on; I was covering one of Paddy's chapters and some more, a ridiculous thirty-five kilometres. After some climbing, near Greeb Point two more women approached and I strayed once more into that embittered area of my mind that ordinarily I reserved for

161

members of the Russian FSB and estate agents. 'Cankerous corpulent pettifoggers!' They were a mother, daughter and granddaughter and they stopped me to ask my plans. Given that my compressed spine was putting me in the foulest of moods I forced my mouth into something I thought must resemble a smile.

'You're camping. Are you eating properly?' The older woman sounded concerned.

'Whenever I can.' There were signs that this might be part of a wider conversation. Resistance was futile so I gently put down the pack, feeling immediate relief.

Her daughter, who I noticed was holding a limp lettuce, joined in. 'You know there are a lot of foods you can eat on the Path. The cabbage we eat can be traced to the sea plants around here.' This I didn't know. She listed a series of plants, pointing at the ground around us and reeling off a Latin litany. It occurred to me that they may have thought me starved whereas I was eating outrageously to no great effect.

'You know a lot about edible plants.'

'I'm a horticulturalist and organic farmer.'

'If only I'd met you earlier.' And when I was more prepared to take notes, I thought.

'You must make sure you eat properly,' her mother said, still looking concerned.

'Yes, I must.' I smiled at the kindness of these two strangers. We were joined by two more, a woman and bearded man. They had walked from Boswinger, a hostel I might ordinarily have stayed at, described as 'a retreat hostel in the traditional style; a tranquil base to discover dramatic clifftops, hidden coves and beautiful gardens'.

'You should check out the little lookout on the point there.' The man pointed towards Dodman Point behind him. 'It's hidden, away from the big cross. It's interesting. Napoleonic era.'

'There are a lot of lookouts,' I replied.

'No, this is different. Trust us.'

'Then I should see it. Have you walked the Path?'

She responded: 'We've done bits, yes. But he's done big journeys in America'.

162

'On a bicycle, not walking. We just had sleeping bags and a light tent - I met some people who wanted to cycle across the States so we travelled on the quiet routes. I was surprised by how well we were received. People were friendly and open. It's much easier there – not as restrictive as here. You could just pitch at the side of the road.'

'It's true, I have to hide and pack the tent in the morning before people start moving about. It's frowned upon.'

'That's it exactly, in England it's as though your movements are being policed. In the States I had great weather and just travelled as far as I liked and then camped.'

It sounded like the Oregon trail, like freedom. Not that I didn't feel free. It was just that you had to be secretive about freedom, as though it was resented, like hitchhiking (the expression 'a free ride' implies 'without having done anything to deserve it'). How much of that is cultural and how much universal I'm unsure.

'Perhaps it's because we live on a small island,' I suggested.

'True, it's a mere 80,000 square miles,' he added. 'We're not a petty people. Check out that lookout.'

The great granite cross on Dodman Point overlooked calm seas and was bordered by fluffy clouds. The cross was a daymark for ships; it was also placed there, though no expected date was given, 'in the firm hope of the Second Coming of our Lord Jesus Christ'.

The lookout was not visible from the point but there was a path between bushes, and there it was. It resembled a small house with a neat lawn and fence, the grass nibbled smooth by wild ponies. Two pines stood at a corner of the lawn, an elderly couple permanently bent by the wind. The lookout had a circular tower rising to just short of the pitched roof. If any smugglers were caught as a result of signals from the watch house, the signallers were entitled to a share of the prize.

And the prize today, a curious shrine beneath a window. It comprised three giant artificial daisies, a miniature Cornish flag, a crucifix with a brass Jesus, two glass ships with an amber-coloured sailor on a wave-painted coaster, and a teddy bear made from artificial Christmas tree material with a bell and ribbon bow tie. I imagined the hideous unreasoning creature who scoured the countryside for trinkets such as these to create their shrine. In my mind, it was something from a Gary Larson cartoon, club in hand and too many fingers. I resolved not to spend the night there. As I left the lookout a shadow passed the window at the front, so I crept out and hid behind the tower. It snorted and was moving towards me. Huge teeth appeared in a hairy face and I let out an involuntary shriek. This sent it off in terror through the ferns. A pony.

Another nine kilometres lay ahead of me before I reached the campsite and it was already mid-afternoon. In Gorran Haven I sought a café but those at the seaside were closed. Down a side street was a grocery store-cum-post office and in the back a crowd stood chatting. 'This seems to be a bit of a social venue,' I commented to the man as I paid.

'It is that. Most people come here. Can I get you anything else? Tea or coffee?'

'You do coffee? Thanks.'

'We can do it anyway you like. A large. Take a seat outside. I'll bring it out to you.' Between buildings was an area with seats and shelter, and a bar. The same man reappeared as bar tender without his apron and gave me my coffee. Shop-cum-post-office (cum-social-club-cum-café-cum-bar). I considered asking for an opium pipe.

A group of people gathered on a nearby table. 'This is the most brilliantly strange shop I've found on the Coast Path,' I said, grinning stupidly.

'It *is* good isn't it?' A man in his thirties with black hair and the look of a 1980s new wave singer turned from his group. 'I've been out of town for months but it's the place to come when you're back. Doesn't take long to meet up with old faces.'

'Enough of the *old faces*,' one woman mumbled, taking a drag on a cigarette. He ignored her.

'East or west? Your direction.'

'That way,' I pointed. 'I saw there a campsite beyond Mevagissey but couldn't get through to them. I'm unsure if they take tents.'

'You mean Pentewan. Yes, they take tents and I'm fairly sure they're open. Just turn up and they should be okay with you camping. If they're closed, camp anyway. There's a lot of beach and you won't get much bother. Don't stop in Mevagissey, they won't warm to you.'

Feeling buoyed up, I walked out of the best local shop in England, past the beach, and around Chapel Point. Daphne du Maurier's *The House on the Strand* (1969) mentions the white houses on the point caught by the western sun.[83] The sun was setting as I passed. One house was on the point and two others were protected by trees closer to the Path. The closer of these two resembled an amalgam of castle and church. Any actual chapel had long since gone but there was reputed to be a hidden private beach on the far reach of the point. It was one of the most beautiful locations I had ever seen, in any country.

Beyond Chapel Point was Mevagissey, a child's imagining of a fishing village but on a larger scale than Mousehole. Three extensive sea defences protected the harbour while three-storey houses with tiled faces looked down on the little boats. Lights blinked on as I walked down the south slope towards the narrow alleys. Though tempted to stop for food the growing darkness worried me, so I looked about the lanes in search of the maze of paths rising to the north.

An audible but invisible gathering of young men in the shadows on the outskirts of Mevagissey forewarned against pitching in the park. I strained to see ahead using the little light reflecting from the sky as the Path descended into a valley and across a wooden bridge. On the next hill the lights of Pentewan Sands came into view, my only guide onwards.

The track was a steep, muddy channel. I could only tell this in the darkness as I was sliding with all my weight, stopped only by gripping at the darkness. It was possible to straddle the channel, standing on dry grass at the edges but this proved more dangerous as an ill-placed step would send me careering forwards. Instead, I took small sliding steps and held onto anything I could feel in the dark whenever my sticks would fail to stop the descent. I was a skier who had mistakenly drifted onto the highest ski jump on the way to the chalet while carrying all his baggage. Had I been able to see anything at all, the experience may have been even more disturbing.

The day had been two-and-a-quarter hours shorter than in September, but I had covered thirty-four kilometres. It was after seven when I stumbled up to the reception office at the campsite, expecting the usual absence of life. To my surprise it was open and would remain so until midnight. Two elderly men stood behind the desk as I strode in on mud platform boots. After agreeing the price I asked them how many years they had run the place.

'Oh, we don't run it. We're just 'curity.' It was sad the way he said it, *just* security, as though they were unimportant. It was self-deprecation typical of people in proper jobs. Imagine a world without them; a world unsafe, cold, bare and dirty.

My head was in the blood-thumping delirium that comes with stopping after energetic activity. There was a Mongolian calendar on their counter and they noticed me dumbly staring. A busload of Mongolian exchange students had come the year before, they explained, and some had kept in touch.

Both men had been invited to visit, but it was beyond their means. The children had, however, shared with them a video from home. The more talkative of the two showed me the video on a tablet computer. It was of the Chinggis Khan monument outside Ulaanbaatar. 'It should be one of the seven wonders of the modern world,' he remarked, gazing in amazement at the images for what was clearly the latest in a number of viewings. I wouldn't speak disparagingly about a national treasure (if Chinggis Khan can be termed a national treasure), but I'd seen this statue from foundations to construction, to eventual appointment as a compulsory fixture on the modest Mongolian tourist trail. It was not the eighth wonder. Throat singing at Khan's 800th birthday was admirable, the maps of his empire were astonishing, the ger shelters of nomadic people were incredible if only that anyone ever survived a winter in them, but this statue was, for me, a reminder of how great empires all eventually end up as kitsch. Reminiscent of the old Anglian Television's knight from the 1970s on its turntable, Chinggis had the sheen of war planes made from unfolded soft drink cans in Viet Nam. Silver and gigantic, he sat atop his horse looking at the desolate landscape while tourists went in and out of his body with their phones on selfie sticks, failing to capture more than a fraction of him. It was hideous.

'Yes,' I replied, 'it's certainly a wonderful thing. Amazing. I haven't seen anything quite like it. Definitely a wonder of the world'. It was a matter of personal taste, like all art. Whatever your opinion, it is something that has to be seen to be believed – and to truly see it you have to be a long way off. They had the video. The view from Cornwall was just fine.

They suggested that I chose somewhere to camp close to the toilet block where the light was good. The air was icy as I pitched, so I showered to warm up and then cooked. Lying in my small square of shelter I considered how we are entranced by the grand monuments of foreign places, yet we miss the beauty and drama of what is right in front of us. Recalling the many hours I sat through Chingghis Khan's 800th birthday party, I considered whether he'd have enjoyed it had he not been dead for over seven centuries. *Probably*, I thought as I drifted off, *he'd have preferred to be conquering worlds.* He was good at that.

Palms were beautifully silhouetted against the rising sun and beach, conjuring the illusion of the Caribbean. After scraping and rinsing my mud-encased boots I held them under the drier long enough to be able to glue parts which had come away. They'd be fine as long as it didn't rain.

A road led out of the Square at Pentewan, then a series of steps up and down and across fields before I reached Hallane Mill, a holiday let with two waterfalls spilling onto the pebble beach. Dense grey clouds cast shadows on a thin sheet of translucent cloud below them, giving the illusion that their shadows were impossibly cast upwards.

On Black Head a stone, like the monolith from *2001: A Space Odyssey*, recorded in a crowded font the life of Al Powsech. The stone proclaimed: 'This wasteland of my contents'. Only on staring did I realised my mistake. It was not for Al Powsech but to Cornish poet and historian A.L. Rowse CH (Alfred Leslie Rowse – Companions of Honour, 1903-97). *This was the land of his content.* Rowse's obituary states that his father was a poor china clay miner and his Oxford education was based on scholarships.[84] He lived in later life in nearby Trenarren House, facing the sea. The whole truth was more dismal.

The real Rowse is revealed in his diaries, published posthumously in 2003. Guardian reviewer Anthony Smith describes Rowse as an egocentric who specifically organised his letters and diaries for publication as a guarantee of his immortality, sexually predatorial and driven by ambition: 'readers of Rowse's many works of history, who delight in his observant antiquarianism and his incisive scholarship (not to mention his gift for evocative autobiography), have had no opportunity until now to realise how deeply unpleasant a man he was'.[85] Rowse himself had something to say about those of slender means: 'I don't want to have my money scalped off me to maintain other people's children. I don't like other people; I particularly don't like their children; I deeply disapprove of their proliferation making the globe uninhabitable. The fucking idiots - I don't want to pay for their fucking'.[86]

David Slattery-Christies' 2017 play *Other People's Fu**ing* was inspired by this embittered quote, and it portrays Rowse spiralling into cynicism following the execution of a friend (von Trott, one of those involved in the failed attempt to assassinate Hitler). The play describes how Rowse had become increasingly resentful about waste, human proliferation and about his own income tax bill.[87]

This all went some way towards explaining the grand stone. The wasteland of his contents. Such a large menhir yet with so little space. Perhaps the mason was having a laugh.

After fields edged by cliffs, the Path descended into woods then onto a road near Rowse's old house. Here the rain began. Hordes of school children were being led on an orienteering day by their teachers. Rowse would have strongly disapproved. The cacophony of their voices faded as I walked across a field and down to Porthpean sailing club. Closed toilets and warnings of rock falls gave the beach a derelict appearance. On the final approach to Charlestown, past the old battery, I had a sudden urge. It is unclear whether this was brought on by knowledge of the village's smuggling heritage, the thought of Rowse, my recent dry period due to imagined beriberi, or trepidation at the approaching meeting. Whatever the cause, I needed rum.

The first thing I saw in Charlestown was the Pier House Pub. However, nearer the harbour was a red and black marquis bearing the fictional soldier's name – *Poldark*. 'Would you like to try some?' A young man was standing behind a display of stone bottles. They were all rum; the company had the sole rights to the use of the *Poldark* name in alcohol. What were the chances? Though I took a tot, I pleaded that weight limits prohibited a purchase of the stone containers (the guilt exemptions of the overladen itinerant).

There was some confusion over which side of the road the bus to St Austell would arrive so I negotiated with a group of pensioners bound in the opposite direction. We agreed that if we were on the wrong side, we would each hold the others' bus for them. At least the rain had stopped.

Yesterday's distance had exhausted me, so I melted into the soft bus seats and stared at the clay industry horizon. Kristiina was visible as we pulled into St Austell train station. Despite being disguised under a yellow beanie hat and dark sunglasses, the smile gave her away. With a grin reaching half the width of her face without showing teeth, Kristiina resembled an acid house smiley. I associated that smile mostly with drinking hot chocolate and marshmallows. It was good to see her.

'Are you hungry, Kristiina?' The transition from electronic communication to speaking was seamless. It was years since we had met face-to-face but that was easy to forget. We'd met in West Africa conducting public health research. Kristiina and I began that journey with a heated argument on a methodological point. It wasn't that we made up and became instant friends. No, the visit was simply a disaster from the start. At least, my part of the visit was. First there were no vehicles then we were unable to purchase fuel due to some bureaucratic system left over from the colonial period. Bedbugs left my face swollen like De Niro in *Raging Bull*, there came industrial action with veiled threats from my surveyors, and finally my room was set on fire due to an overenthusiastic generator and cheap electrical wiring. Perhaps I was just too exhausted to argue further or Kristiina was sympathetic to my state or mildly amused, but somehow the events cemented our friendship.

'I have been in this shop for an hour and I had to eat to stay in the seat so I already ate. Do you think we can sit here?' She looked around as though about to commit some diplomatic offence.

'I'll order, it's okay. I had some rum earlier.' I ordered coffee.

'You drank alcohol in the daytime?' she said when I returned. She had clearly been thinking about this.

'It was free. *Poldark* rum in Charlestown. They were giving it away.'

'Pole dark?'

'The television series. The ex-soldier fighting slavery and political persecution. He opens a mine in Cornwall.'

'The man with long hair and grass cutting sword with no shirt?'

'Yes, that's him. Well remembered.'

'You sent me a picture.'

'It's been some time, Kristiina.' Using a Finnish person's name a lot can make them uncomfortable; I used hers frequently. She admired England, she must know the English ways.

'Since 2017.' Statement of fact. We chatted for a while about the time that had passed before she broke the spell. 'We should go to the bus, isn't it?'

We boarded the bus for the Eden Project. 'Look at that view, Kristiina.' The bus was moving into open countryside with the sea below.

'Please don't talk to me. I'm concentrating, and all.' She looked straight ahead. She had these turns of phrase – *and all, isn't it* - that she had picked up somewhere between *The Catcher in the Rye* and Tottenham high street, but I knew for a fact that she hadn't frequented either.

'Concentrating?'

'Oscaaaar! On not being sick.'

I had forgotten about her motion sickness. At least most of our journey would be on foot. She faced the front of the bus with the expression of a chess master, so I let her be.

St Austell's gigantic slag pyramid of china clay made up the skyline behind the town. 'Don't play on the slag heap,' my father used to warn us. It could flow like liquid, at least the coal version. There was a campaign to have the mountain protected as a heritage site. The Eden Project and many lakes owe themselves to the excavated pits. China clay or kaolinite has many uses including the manufacture of porcelain, skin creams and toothpaste, but the main use is as a gloss coating on paper. Kristiina was not interested in china clay, though, she was focused on not vomiting.

The Eden Project hostel had a pizza restaurant. We ordered and I left Kristiina so I could set up the tent as rain was threatening. Another large tent nearby had been pitched on a considerable incline. I suspected this was its first outing. It was an odd choice for a camping field; did YHA management understand the importance of level ground for those not using Velcro® sleeping bags? A small area of level ground at the bottom of the field offered some promise of sleep so I put the tent there and hurried back as the rain began.

After dinner we found our way to the tent by torchlight. Kristiina quickly spotted the large tent. 'Are those guys crazy? They will be climbing the tent all night. Do you snore?'

'No. Not exactly. I gently purr.'

'Do you "gently purr" loudly?'

'I don't think so.'

'Hmm.'

Leaving Eden
Day 39. 18ᵗʰ October

Kristiina was staring at my neck. 'Were you burned?'

'Is it obvious?'

'Well, yes, I wondered what it was.'

'They're not burns but they're scars.' They did look like burns, I realised. 'Nutritional problems,' I said, and left it at that.

She shrugged to say it wasn't a problem, she had just been curious. I was beyond being self-conscious, they were part of me.

We packed and walked towards the Project. 'Look at the sign, Oscar.' It read *Gateway to Eden*. 'This must be the way.' She wore her wide grin. She had been looking forward to this. So had I.

We found a locker for both of our bags and walked past a sleeping homeless man.[88] He was actually a lifelike statue, placed there by St Petroc's Society (a homelessness charity to which Paul, who I met in Tintagel, had donated seventy sleeping bags). Visitors avoided looking directly at the man out of respect, yet he appeared so close to death, skin hanging from his bones, I just had to stare. Otherwise how would I have known he was not animal but mineral? I photographed him while onlookers tutted at me. *Don't talk to strangers, don't photograph homeless people.* The British might walk past a man being eaten alive by a boogle of weasels, but they would never dare to photograph him. It is a very British discomfort.

The next few hours we spent wandering thermoplastic domes and crossing suspended walkways. I had wanted to come to the Eden Project since I had first seen the 1972 film *Silent Running*.[89] The Project hadn't been conceived then, but when I saw the film sometime in the late seventies, it had such an impact on me that I wanted it to be a real place. The film represented the last bastion of ecological warfare, tropical domed forests floating in space, tended by three little robots and powered entirely by the sun (any good forest is, though they omit to adjust for distance from the sun and the inverse square law). Kristiina had never heard of *Silent Running* and it was too complicated to explain. She raised an eyebrow as if to say *some ancient English language cultural reference.* 'It's like *Wall-E*, Kristiina, only with murder and nuclear explosions.'

The domed forests were incredible, and we were in awe. There were even some small animals. I can honestly say that it was the best £25 I had spent since seeing *Jaws* at the Minack. After lunch we caught a bus back to St Austell and then Charlestown.

'Wow. Old world town.' The harbour had sailing ships and obsolete nautical paraphernalia, though there was a charge to enter. 'We can see it all from here, no need to pay,' Kristiina stated with Finnish frugality.

Icy rain came down heavily as we left Charlestown so we made an impromptu tourist visit to the coast watch station, Kristiina asking unnecessary questions to extend our stay until the rain eased.

The Path moved from the sea and through derelict clay works, overgrown by vegetation. It seemed the end of the world had arrived here too. This was Par.

'We could sleep there.' I pointed beneath a tree at the edge of a park.

'No, Oscar. There are people in the park. They will come and find us.' The campsite no longer took tents so we found a pub to take us. I did not object to the relative luxury.

A pub nearer the beach served food. It was very lively, but we managed to find a table in a corner near the loudspeaker. Once we had ordered, there began a high-pitched squeal of feedback from the public address system.

'Welcome to the raffle for [inaudible screech].'

'What is wrong with her voice?' Kristiina asked.

'I think she may be a little drunk. It is a bit loud,' I agreed.

'And painful pitch. She is breaking my ears. Find somewhere else to sit.' All the seats were taken.

'And number four-hundred and fifty-three, the bottle of spumante, goes to Pam eeeee!' the PA screeched as she let out a squeal. A group opposite, in obvious pain, winced and looked across apologetically. 'Number forty-eight ...' Our food arrived and it seemed that everyone in the pub must have won something. I was beginning to feel left out.

I asked the group, some of whom held their hands over their ears, how long they had been there.

'Since three this afternoon.' He rolled his eyes. 'It shouldn't be much longer,' he assured us.

We had almost finished eating when a table became available in the back room, away from the speaker.

'At last, ear relief,' Kristiina said, smiling. As I sat, there was a popping sound. 'Was that you?' she asked.

'No, it was the amplifier being switched off.'

'It's over?' She sounded disappointed. We stayed for a while and then walked back along the dark streets.

'Kristiina, Kristiina.'

'Stop saying my name!'

'Don't worry, I won't say it three times in a row. Look!' There was a road sign for a village half a mile from the junction.

'Tie-war-dre-ath. So? I'm cold!'

'You *are* a real Finn, *aren't you?* I mean, the stork didn't drift off course? It's almost summer. Tywardreath – and *The House on the Strand*. It must be the translation from Cornish. This was one of Daphne du Maurier's last books. It must have been set near here.' I was staring at the sign in astonishment when I noticed the little figure of Kristiina moving up the street away from me, mechanically like a Victorian wind-up doll. I took a photograph of the sign and jogged painfully to catch up.

Strangely, for a Finn, she *is* very curious about British historical drama and writing, hence her interest in Agatha Christie but also various television programmes, often in spite of a lack of artistic merit. If it was British, in tweeds and had cars with footplates and suicide doors, Kristiina would watch it. I suppose on that night she was too cold, so I resolved to introduce her to du Maurier later.

The book is interesting. For some reason Daphne du Maurier has a reputation for romantic writing yet even *Rebecca* and *My Cousin Rachel* are very dark indeed, and hardly romantic. Menabilly, where she had lived and which influenced much of her most popular work, was restored to the original family, prompting her move to this area. In the new house, *The House on the Strand*,[90] she discovered bottles of chemicals belonging to a previous owner, and she began to devise a story. It involved a protagonist who agreed to be a test subject for a substance developed by his biochemist friend, Magnus. This allowed him to inhabit the world of the fourteenth century, but as a witness only, not to interact. Interacting with flesh would, as Magnus warned, send him crashing back to reality with '"a very unpleasant jerk."'[91]

Well, who hasn't experienced that on occasion? My attempts to interact with flesh usually ended similarly. So begins a period of obsession and addiction – and the book follows similar lines.

Kristiina, though, missed all of this as she was cold. Curiously, after that 1969 novel du Maurier wrote only one other. It was set in the near future after Britain had left the European Economic Community and fell into economic collapse.[92] It wasn't very well received.

'Why are you eating those pills?' Kristiina watched me down a pill with my breakfast. 'You shouldn't take them.'

'Without them I wouldn't be walking.' I left it at that though I did appreciate her concern.

The Path followed a sandy track, then through woods to the little picture-book harbour of Polkerris, where we stopped to explore and drink. Kristiina was entranced by the little port and she roamed around the harbour walls like a curious child. After the harbour we came to open grassland and Gribbin Head, where the sun grew hot. To our left, but out of sight, was Menabilly (the fictional Manderley), home of Daphne du Maurier for many years and the inspiration for *Rebecca* (though in 1938 it was dilapidated and she didn't lease the house for another 5 years).[93] The book of course, opens with 'Last night I dreamt I went to Manderley again'.[94] The first descriptions are in dream, the ruin being reclaimed by nature. The narrator, unusually, is not given a name, but is the woman who marries Maxim de Winter after the death of his wife, Rebecca. The lack of a name says something about how she is seen in the new household. Kristiina raced ahead.

We could see the tower, with its horizontal red-and-white stripes, long before we reached it. A sign explained that it was a shipping daymark. We needed to gather speed, so we made our way down past Polridmouth Cottage, the inspiration for Rebecca's boathouse - though it is simply a cottage with stepping-stones. No boat, no corpse.

There was a sprinkling of rain as we boarded the ferry from Fowey.

I can't even remember the little National Coastwatch Institution station but I know we passed it. I hadn't taken a photo since the Gribbin Head daymark tower. We were determined to reach Polperro while there was still light. Lunch and the ferry crossing had lost us valuable time. The Path meandered across slopes, through rusted ferns and past a little cottage, but it eventually forced us into a miserable pattern of repeated ascents and descents.

'How much farther is it? In kilometres! Give me kilometres!' There was an edge to Kristiina's voice, that Nordic staccato. The Elf was in hiding. Finnish language has a certain bluntness or neutrality to it, and this can sometimes bleed across into their English. Where German, like several other languages, has the delicacy of three genders, male, female and neuter, Finnish has none. It is genderless, making it simultaneously very ancient and very much of the moment. So, of a child in potty training – *it has shat itself.* It. When we talk about someone's baby in English as *it*, to the mother we can come across rude or unfeeling, but to the Finnish we are all equal. You, me, her, them - have all shat itself.

It was at least five kilometres to the campsite but we had food and water so we could stop earlier.

'Five kilometres up and down, up and down? Vittumainen!' Kristiina had introduced me to this word which was a particular type of 'annoying', but which Google chose at the time to translate as 'Fuck Maine.'

Paddy had described this stretch as 'a roller-coaster ride.' That was a bad sign at any time, but especially when the sun was low. We continued to walk but both of us were tiring and dragging our boots.

At the bottom of one of the valleys, near a waterfall, a familiar face looked up at me from the beach path. 'Oscar Barton!'

'Burton!'

'That's what I said, Oscar Burton.'

'And you're Laura.' So, it had finally happened; someone I knew who wasn't aware that I was walking the Coast Path, had met me. And she was crossing the Path in order to get to a car park above. Unlikely, but there it was. How did I know Laura?

There are some events in life that are not so much milestones as daymarks. They are the lighthouses and watchtowers still visible for many kilometres after you pass them. This event marked a change in terrain from gently undulating grassland to a rocky, windswept and barren landscape. The last time I saw Laura that was how things were.

I had been on a field visit and security assessment and a British colleague had subsequently been disappeared. They had called it 'the worst place in the world.' It hadn't been - for me - but it soon became so. Laura was part of the security team communicating with our overseas colleagues. After many months we heard via the media before any formal announcement, that a body had been returned. I avoided the details, not wanting to know. However, I inadvertently glanced at one press report and caught the thoughtless adjective, *mutilated*.

The following year we were occupied with the fallout. Mostly there was a pall over the place. Things weren't ever going to be the same. Like I said, a daymark. There was what came before, and there was what would come after. At some point Laura left and I stayed behind.

Laura had clearly moved on. Today she was with her husband and child, and two friends. We spoke for a few minutes by the sea and then said goodbye, conscious that we were losing the daylight. The first friend I had met by chance on the Path and already we had parted. That remote possibility of meeting someone I knew on the Path had come and gone; it felt like losing Zippy again.

As Kristiina and I crossed the falls, there came a shout. 'Hey, where are you heading?' Laura called out. She had been in a huddle with her friends Daniel and Olivia.

'We're trying to get to Polperro. We might stop before then,' I shouted back.

They were having a discussion. 'Stay with us,' shouted Daniel. Kristiina looked at me and shrugged. *Why not?* So, that's how we found ourselves at the water mill.

On the way up the hill Kristiina (who had taken a slide on the mud and was exhausted) walked behind while I spoke to Daniel. He was a yoga teacher and osteopath, formerly of Venezuela, and Olivia was a British artist. They were an attractive contrast – he Spanish with black beard and hair, and Olivia with wavy fair hair and green eyes. 'You'll come and stay with us – we have a converted barn – and in the morning I'll take you back to where you were. Or stay longer.'

'Thanks, that's very kind.' I explained that I'd worked with Kristiina in West Africa and Laura in *the worst place in the world*, and England. We drove to the mill where Daniel showed us our space. It was a converted barn with mattresses on the floor. Icy from the cool air in the valley floor, but there was a heater.

The mill was in darkness. Olivia and Daniel had recently bought it with the intention of relocating from Wiltshire. Laura and her family had been invited for a few days to see the place. Daniel showed us the original hardwood cogs and shaft of the mill and the mossy wheel outside, visible through a small window.

'Does it work?' Kristiina asked. She touched the ancient machine.

'It would shake the house apart if we connected it. It's too old to support the power it generates, Katrine.' He had already called Kristiina variations on Katherine, which she had accepted, without complaint, as cultural heritage. Besides, she didn't like people using her actual name.

It turned out, over dinner, that we had gate-crashed Daniel's birthday but he seemed glad of the distraction and we were grateful. Daniel discussed the strange politics surrounding Venezuela, the site of population movements and an economic and social catastrophe in South America. It was a distant story; the mill was as much a different continent as a different century.

After dinner we stood and moved to the living room. Kristiina was behind me. 'Why are you walking like that? Walk normally.' It was less suggestion, more command.

'I am *walking* the *way* I am *able* to walk. This is how I walk.'

'It is weird. Try to walk normally.'

'It's not as though I have a choice. I don't think you realise that this is just how I walk now. It's taken me 600 kilometres to master this.'

'Just *try*.'

'It was easier when I was carrying the weight.' So, I walked a few more steps attempting to appear *normal*.

'Noooo, that looks worse!' She suppressed a laugh, covering her mouth.

Olivia sympathetically intervened. 'Don't worry. Maybe Daniel can have a look at you in the morning and give you a little manipulation to make you straight.' I alternately swung my legs into the living room, a marionette controlled by an arseholed puppet master.

Unoccupied for some time, the barn had a dead fly problem. We formed the bodies and the dirt from our boots into a pile before we slept. For a while, lights out, we talked about what Laura and I had worked on in that final year, and how it had all ended. We fell silent and were soon asleep from exhaustion.

In a farewell photograph, beside Laura the yoga teacher, with the morning light behind us we are body twins; I have a woman's waist. A diet of cream teas, chips, ice cream and chocolate made little impact on my weight. This was a life devoid of consequences; the possibility of becoming fat was about as remote as the chance of becoming *hench*.

Daniel drove us to Lansallos where we promised to stay in touch. We thanked him and walked towards the sea down a path by the church.

Although having poor experiences of alternative routes, perhaps because I was tired, I acquiesced to the suggestion of a shortcut. We found ourselves following a track that petered out at a stream and then a cliff. Soon we were climbing fences and entering a steep field of cattle and shit, each cursing the other for their navigation skills.

'Bull or cow?' I said, looking down. As it turned out, horse. Passing through a kissing gate, the wild ponies took a fancy to us, nudging us towards the cliff. This is the reason that people are asked not to feed ponies. We quickly mounted another fence to escape.

'You're lucky with the weather, Kristiina. It hasn't been this nice in weeks.'

'So you keep telling me.'

At midday we reached Polperro and ate in a café across the bridge. It was a welcome rest in a beautiful harbour. The coast east of Polperro has a series of small coves. In 1708 the East India Company ship *Albermarle* was wrecked near the town. It carried a load of indigo, and as it melted, the sea that December was turned a deep shade of blue.[95] What a beautiful thought, seeing Polperro in a naturally enhanced Technicolor.®

At school we were taught that blue dye was something of a rarity before the advent of synthetic colours. So much natural blue, the sky and the sea, yet to be unable to contain it in a bottle. Perhaps if we were still unable to capture blue, we might take more care of this big blue marble.

On the edge of town a panic began. I had used the toilet in Polperro, but Kristiina had not. 'Where is there a toilet?' she said, suddenly a commanding urgency in her voice. We hurried, Kristiina shuffling with her legs close together, towards a single storey pitched roof building in the distance, a shape typical of toilets. On reaching it, it was clearly a storage hut. 'Oscaaar!'

'How was I to know? You'd think there would be one, the town is called *Looe*.'

'Not funny. Ask someone, you're the native.'

'Technically, I'm not. This is Cornwall.' I asked at a nearby café, apologising to the other customers, explaining that my wife was having a baby. As my midwife sister would say, *the head has engaged - prepare for delivery.* Kristiina cast off her backpack and followed their directions, waddling down to the beach. She emerged from the beach loo with a contented smile.

West and East Looe are separated by the East Looe River – that is, before it forks off to the West Looe River. Perhaps it's just called the Looe River in Looe. Or, the River Looe.

Beyond Looe, a shack on Millendreath Beach offered drinks and entertainment. 'Shall we wait for the pub to open? Get cocktails?' I suggested.

'No, we find the campsite.' The bridle path up to Millendreath, through high hedges, was interminable. After some time it looked as though we might have missed a turning. 'This is too far. You said *thirty minutes*, more than thirty minutes ago.' A man descending the hill with his son estimated a further ten minutes, so twenty minutes later we were there.

As soon as the sun disappeared behind West Looe the temperature plummeted, and my hands had difficulty putting the tent up.

'What's that smell?' asked Kristiina inside the tent.

'What smell?' Whatever it was I had developed immunity.

'Mouldy smell.' She bent her elbows, head close to the ground, sniffing in short bursts, her face twisted in repugnance. 'It's this.' She was pointing at my roll mat.

'Ah. It may have got wet. I've since put it in a dry sack. That may have acted simply to contain the moisture.'

She didn't comment, but instead moved her belongings as far away from it as the tent allowed then fixed me with a hard Nordic stare.

'Are those crumbs?' she asked, staring at the space she had just vacated. She jerked her head back to me, her stare becoming more focused. Although she was small and generally harmless, it was a look of such intensity that I put out the lantern.

When I saw the flying thing that morning, Kristiina was far ahead up the track. I mumbled 'Oh my god, look at that,' but she just kept on walking. I didn't want to disturb the creature as it busily collected nectar from deep trumpet-shaped flowers. It seemed to me it was a hummingbird but that couldn't possibly be so. Its wings were invisible, flapping so fast. I had seen hummingbirds in the Caribbean but they didn't exist in Britain. Unless it had escaped from a zoo.

'You won't believe what I just saw. A hummingbird.'

'Oh. How far to this Port Wrinkle?'

'Did you hear that? A hummingbird. They don't exist here.'

'Then maybe it is an immigrant. How far to Port Wrinkle?' Not the response I had expected given her outdoor interests.

Finland has large animals - moose, reindeer, bears. Perhaps these small things aren't impressive to Finns.

We were averaging twenty kilometres each day which was less than I had done solo. Though Kristiina was marching off rapidly in the morning, by the last few kilometres she would tire.

At Portwrinkle, over tea and water, we looked through our meagre rations and decided that we could scrape a meal together from the various condiments. Though we agreed on this, I was secretly fearful of walking without food. The lack of sustenance probably explains what happened. Appropriately, it was in an area on the map marked in red 'DANGER'.

The danger area was a firing range. No warning flags were flying so we crossed. Tarred paths meandered uphill through manicured lawns towards a fort; we were conscious not to take photographs. Beyond Long Sands below us were teams of black clad people in rigid hull inflatable boats with outboard motors. At intervals the people would fall overboard backwards and then another boat would come to rescue them, and this went on.

It was four o'clock.

'How far is it to the fort?' We had found a camp which was also a small fort in Tregonhawke.

'The map shows a couple of kilometres.'

'Noooo. How long, how much time?'

'About half an hour.'

'Why do you use that old map? Why not use Google Maps?'

I opened Google maps and it gave me the same information, 30 minutes. 'In any case we don't know the exact position and it assumes you're walking at average speed, and we are not walking at the average speed.'

'Why do you always use the old ways? Get into the twenty-first century.'

'Why can't you be spontaneous?'

So we walked on and I kept checking the map to give a better estimate in case it was requested. I was tired and she was tired. We were both tired.

'My *god*, this is toooo far Oscaaar. Why are you making these days so long? It's exhausting and you are always using that old book map.'

I could have mentioned that I was making the distances long so she could reach Devon and Agatha Christie country, and that in fact the days were shorter than I usually endured. But, I didn't. Instead, I exploded, electricity passing through my brain and tripping my mouth into automatic. What came was a list of expletives interspersed with 'spoilt child', 'ungrateful,' 'I'm the one carrying all the camping equipment,' 'will you just shuuuut uuuup' and a short educational piece on the global positioning system and Google Maps not being the best for off-road travel as it prioritised roads.

'But we *are* on the road,' her faint voice came to me across the cool, swiftly enlarging expanse between us as I marched up the hill, determined to get to the fort even if it was by myself. That her final cry was logical only made me more determined to make the figurative chasm between us a literal one.

By the time she reached me I had started to pitch the tent inside the fort walls and had already discovered that a wedding was taking place. The bar was closed and there was no food. Kristiina silently helped me to put the tent up. I apologised for my outburst and she explained that she knew she was a 'pain in the ass' but couldn't seem to control it when she was tired and hungry.

We ate what food we had, eked out by sachets of sauces requisitioned from cafés.

'I was going to rent one of the caravans because I didn't think you wanted to be near me,' she said sadly. 'But the reception was closed.'

'I doubt they would have given you one for a single night. You'd have had to stay for a week.' She laughed and slapped her fists against my chest as a chimp might.

'Do you think we should crash the wedding?' she asked, raising an eyebrow. It was exceptionally un-Nordic, but I suspected she was exceptional.

On the rocks
Day 43. 22ⁿᵈ October

The Path from Tregonhawke followed the road before veering south towards Rame Head. 'Look out. Twitchers.' They were on Rame Head harassing a small bird with their lenses, but something bigger had our attention. Rising steeply from a hill at the end of the peninsula were the walls of St Michael's Chapel, dating from the fourteenth century.

'Why be twitching when there is this?' Kristiina asked. The chapel was at the furthest point, a black horse silhouetted beside it in the morning sun. Like other sites dedicated to St Michael it was a fortified chapel with sea and cliffs on three sides with just a narrow saddle connecting it to the mainland. Whatever else the worshippers did, they must have watched the sea as the location guarded the entrance to Plymouth Sound and the River Tamar.

The old county border was marked on a wall in the village of Kingsand. We had reached the limits of Cornwall as the walk moved gently into Mt Edgcumbe Country Park.

I edged through a kissing gate. 'Why do you go through the gate like that?'

'Like what?'

'Turning like that.' There was a distant sound of thunder, but it was in my own head.

I had passed through hundreds of these kissing gates, possibly one for every kilometre. I knew my own dimensions and those of my pack, and the peculiarities of design. I knew how I had to enter and exit these torture devices, always in reverse. Only twice had I been forced to climb the barrier when it had been designed by a numpty.

'I know what I have to do to enter and exit.'

'But you could do it differently.'

'What makes *you* think that you know how my body, pack width, height and depth can pass through this opening better than I can?'

'You're not open to a different point of view.' Few things provoke me more than making the rejection of an idea sound like closed-mindedness. It was as though I hadn't already passed through six hundred kissing gates; that I was a novice.

Seeing my expression she backpedalled, saying, 'I didn't mean that, I was just curious. I just wondered why you moved through like that.'

'Sure.' I walked off through the woods and she trudged behind. The walking calmed me, and I considered the fact that we were arguing about a gate. I took the opportunity to break the atmosphere by asking a walker the distance to the Plymouth ferry.

'Oh, it's not far. Follow the park around, you'll see a green and it's just beyond that.

'Thank you.'

On the way we posed for photographs in a Temple of Venus. The folly had an inscription from Milton's *Paradise Lost*, appropriate since we had walked from Eden. Even in her walking gear Kristiina was more convincing as a Venus. I felt bad now for my anger.

The ferry took us to Plymouth where a blue sign marked 'Admiral's Hard' and showed 352 miles back to Minehead. As we walked onto the main road, a woman's voice came from behind: 'You're walking the Coast Path. With a tent.' It wasn't a question.

'He is, to Poole. For a charity.' Kristiina fished for her to *participate*.

'So you've walked through September and October? I've been here for years and this is the greatest number of severe weather warnings I've seen at one time.'

'Here? Plymouth?' I asked.

'The South West Coast Path Association.'

'You work for the Association?'

'Yes, we're based in Plymouth. You'll see lots of evidence of us here. There are some unusual waymarks. Send me your details and we might be able to run something to promote what you're doing.' She gave me her card. Emily.

The dormitory accommodation was hiding down a side street and looked like it had seen better times. In the time we were there the woman in the reception box rarely moved from her chair though she occasionally rose to peer suspiciously at the occupants of the lounge. Upstairs, Kristiina checked her phone on the top bunk. 'There is a seafood restaurant near here. It looks good. Can we book a taxi to go from the station to Burgh Island?'

I made the booking, the journey involving a convoluted train ride, a station pickup to meet the low tide and an afternoon return from the beach back to Ivybridge station.

Dinner didn't go quite to plan. As they say in Finland, the situation was 'melkoinen soppa', quite a soup, and I didn't even have the soup. By the end of the evening I was standing alone in the freezing cold, outside our dorm building, without my key. I waited to see if Kristiina would let me in.

The issue of the kissing gate had come up again during dinner. Unwisely, I made a comparison between Kristiina's voice, when she was lecturing me, and that of Annie Wilkes in Stephen King's *Misery*. I had confidently assumed she wouldn't understand the obscure reference. My comment must have touched a raw nerve because there were instant tears, she stood and left the restaurant, the cold air blowing across me as the door swung to. Kristiina was no longer my greatest fan. What was worse for my pride was that she had left the money for her half of the meal on the table. The staff had witnessed the whole row, although without the audio, and the two women were now glaring across at me. *That poor woman even paid her own share.* I later discovered that a play of King's *Misery* was showing in two different productions in Kuopio and Tampere throughout September and October, and they had been widely and positively reviewed in the Finnish press.[96][97] What were the chances?

At last the door was opened, Kristiina handed me the key then walked off into the lounge area. Taking this as a signal, I stole off to our room and cancelled the journey to Burgh Island. It was a shame, but that was an end to it.

It was late when Kristiina entered the room. 'I've cancelled the taxi for tomorrow,' I explained.

'Why did you do that?'

'I had to call him before he went to sleep.' Silence. She lay on the top bunk so I couldn't see her expression.

The silence continued, but I could hear her moving, pretending to read. I should have accepted that the four o'clock terrors and arguing were due to tiredness and hunger, and just let them lie. She was one of the very few friends who had made this journey despite the promise of terrible weather, and the distance she had to cover just to begin the walk.

'Look, Kristiina, what do you want to do tomorrow?' A long silence.

'I want to go to Burgh Island.' She pronounced Burgh like *iceberg*.

'Then I'll call the cab driver.'

After the call her head dropped over the edge of the bunk, smiling. 'I'm sorry.'

'I'm sorry too.'

The plan that morning was to take a train to Ivybridge and a taxi would take us to Bigbury-on-Sea in time to cross at low tide to Burgh Island. On the railway platform, Josh Widdicombe and Alex Brooker were entertaining waiting passengers with a game. For Kristiina's benefit I explained that they were comedy television presenters. We boarded the train away from them as they would attract curiosity.

As the train approached Ivybridge I felt a little rising joy; we would finally reach Kristiina's site of pilgrimage without further mishap. I was sorry that we had fought but now it would all be better. The train stopped and I looked down to where the platform wasn't. Perhaps we had stopped at a red signal.

'Let's move forward in case this is a short platform,' I suggested. We passed Brooker and Widdicombe who were in a first-class carriage. They must have got on there by mistake, I thought. At the next carriage we were blocked by a central engine. Moments later the train began to creep forward, and the Ivybridge platform slipped away behind us. My first reaction, naturally, was to get Brooker and Widdicombe to force the train to a stop.

'Oscar? What is happening?'

'Tickets please.' A conductor appeared.

'Seriously? Tickets? Why was there no announcement that this was a short platform?'

'It was on the platform at Plymouth, sir. There's no way through the train anyway due to the engine in the middle, so a train announcement wouldn't have helped.'

'At Plymouth,' Kristiina began, pronouncing Ply like *fly*, and mouth like *mouth*, 'I heard no announcement and saw nothing on the board. If I had, we would have gone to the front of the train. This is very unprofessional.' Sometimes her directness was loveable.

'I'm sorry, the next stop is Totnes. My apologies.'

We passed Brooker and Widdicombe who were showing their tickets to the conductor, so it was clear they were in a different class and we were on our own. 'Don't worry, I've got a plan.'

I made a quick call.

'Kristiina, you will go to the ball.'

'What ball?'

'The island.'

'It is a ball? Really, I think this visit is not meant to be.' Kristiina's head was almost touching the table.

'Since when were you superstitious?'

'There is a point in everyone's life when they face total despair, and this is that point.'

The cab was at Totnes within twenty minutes and we were soon driving back towards Ivybridge. 'Don't talk to me, I'm concentrating,' Kristiina said. She was breathing rhythmic short breaths through her nose, presumably in the oft-misplaced belief that it's not possible to vomit with the mouth closed.

At the beachfront Venus Café in Bigbury I bought food while waiting for the tide. Kristiina's complexion was the shade of mushy peas as she leaned into the sea air, a sunken ship's figurehead.

This was it, the setting of Christie's novels *And then there were None* (the US first edition had the island and hotel on the dust jacket with a skeleton hand[98]) and *Evil Under the Sun*.[99] We took our time walking across the sand spit and exploring the whole island – all except for the art deco hotel which was restricted to guests. In the island pub, the Pilchard Inn, we ordered pizza and sat beneath a green lantern and shark jaws.

'Was that shark from here?'

'Probably, but the sea tractor is high. The water is shallow. It might chew the tyres.'

It was sad to leave the island because I knew it meant that she would be leaving. The taxi took us to Ivybridge and then a train to Plymouth; she slept on both. We made a short trip to collect her things, and I checked into a cheaper dormitory.

The two of us walked slowly to the station and sat in the café until it was time. She pulled hair over her face for a ridiculous photograph, and then walked through the barrier towards the trains. I stayed for a while, hoping that she would come running out, having decided to keep walking with me, but of course I left the station alone.

It had been a good week, despite the need for trans-European conflict resolution. Kristiina's departure, I suspected, spelled the end of the calm weather.

Bad medicine and unicorns
Day 45. 24ᵗʰ October

Shaun, a lonyg-term resident, marked his territory in the dining room. He began to tell me of the many hotels he had worked in around the coast and the varied places in which he had found shelter. They were stories of the military and kitchen sinks, hotels and park benches. His tales were best swallowed with a pinch of sea salt, but I enjoyed listening. The other residents looked comfortable, as though they had been there for some time. What were they waiting for and why were they waiting there?

Another friend, Simone (Sim-moan-aye) was arriving in the afternoon. We'd worked together in public health training and he had been great support to me, with the outward calm of a counsellor or priest. There was time spare to walk the city's coast. The New Palace Theatre, boarded up, looked even less certain of itself in daylight. Buddleia sprouted from a drainpipe and window ledges, and the dark mustard tiles pretended a grandness long gone from pre-Blitz Plymouth. From the ferry terminal the Path led past the wharves and marine barracks. I noticed a man urinating against a storm barrier close to where Darwin's ship, the *Beagle,* had departed for South America in 1831. This voyage planted the seed for *On the Origin Of Species By Means Of Natural Selection*[100] (1859).

On some of the residential streets were plaques in the ground, quotations pressed in brass. They led in two directions to a black door.

It had been a short period in 1882 when a young medical graduate had teamed up with his old classmate from Edinburgh, George Turnavine Budd[101] at this address. After graduating, Budd's 'money had run out, he was dunned by his tradespeople, there were no patients, and what was he to do? ... he assembled them, addressed them in a long and emotional speech, reduced them almost to tears with his picture of the struggles of a deserving young man, and finally got a unanimous vote of confidence from them with full consent that he should pay at his own leisure.'[102] Budd engaged his friend in a medical practice that offered free consultations but medicines at a premium and at an unjustifiable risk.[103] Budd had befriended the young Arthur Conan Doyle.

Budd's inadvertent reading of correspondence from Doyle's mother (disparaging about Budd) put an end to their partnership.[104] He suggested Doyle went into practice himself, offering an allowance of a pound a week covering his accommodation, to be repaid later.[105] Only once Doyle had committed to a year's rent in Portsmouth did Budd write to withdraw the allowance,[106] evidently intending to leave his former friend destitute. Doyle had to find other means of livelihood. These schemings inadvertently prompted the literary career which would create the world's most famous fictional detective, Sherlock Holmes. The quotes of Holmes paved this stretch of the Coast Path to Doyle's former residence.

Plymouth Hoe was watched over by the red and white striped Smeaton's Tower (a relocated lighthouse – and named after its engineer who had perfected underwater hardening cement similar to the stuff used by the Romans in aqueducts). Here was the imagined location spun from Elizabethan publicity, of Francis Drake playing bowls before attacking the Spanish Armada. The ships scattered after Calais and were later blown off course after rounding Scotland, many becoming wrecked. Drake had time enough to finish his game of bowls; the Armada crews would perish over a month later largely from disease, lack of water and bad weather.

On the edge of the Barbican, a wall was littered with plaques. One was dedicated to the ships *Friendship* and *Charlotte,* both of which transported convicts to Australia, to provide slave labour for the new colonies. Another plaque marked the departure of the *Mayflower.* Depending on your perspective, they were reasons for thanksgiving or to hang your head in shame. Looking at a city rebuilt in the 1950s as a vision of the future, it was easy to forget that colonial expansion, the theory of evolution[107] and global exploration began in Plymouth.

At the statue of an imaginary chimeric sea creature I turned inland to meet Simone. Flashing lights and laughter emanated from a temporary fairground as I waited in the park. He was on the far side of a pond dressed entirely in black with a beard and hat. From where I was seated, Simone appeared to walk on the water towards me.

'I've missed you, man,' he said as he stepped off the pond wall, grabbing me around the chest.

'I've missed you too.'

Simone had come from London on a Mega Bus. I introduced him to Shaun who regaled us with stories of commando training and his old haunts through Cornwall and Devon. Simone looked at me, his expressive eyebrows forming a downward-pointing arrow.

Shaun then leaned forward, checked over his shoulder for eavesdroppers and spoke in hushed tones. 'If you're heading to Salcombe there's somewhere you can sleep. I use it all the time.' He described a piece of swampland behind a café, the improbably named *Yawning Lobster*. 'Follow a walkway through the rushes and you come to a bird hide. I carry a screwdriver and screws, and screw the door shut to stop anyone bothering me during the night.' Simone's eyebrows were now so pointed, and his eyes bulging that I had to hold my coffee to my face and pretend to be drinking.

I don't remember everything we spoke about that night over a bottle of wine, but it moved between Orwell's *Homage to Catalonia*, Germaine Greer, Franco, Noam Chomsky, Roy Harper, the state of Europe, and women. He spoke very fondly about some of the people we both knew and loved. Also, we spoke of the dormitory.

'Do Lobsters yawn?' Simone asked casually.

'Only when they're tired.'

'The guy carries a screwdriver and screws, yet he said the benches in the hide can be moved to form a bed. Why not simply put them against the door?'

'Perhaps the door opens outwards?' I suggested, giving Shaun the benefit of the doubt.

'This place is a bit quirky,' he whispered conspiratorially.

'Quirk with a capital Q, and capital Irk. It's a friendly place. I wonder, though, if it's a sort of halfway house.'

'Halfway to where?'

'Halfway *from* where?'

We said no more, but Simone's eyebrows were doing that little dance.

It was still dark when we woke. 'What is the story with the construction?' Simone was whispering so as not to wake our two companions.

'You mean, why do they do it in the middle of the night? Perhaps they are employing vampires. Where did those workers come from?'

We had cereal and coffee with Shaun who wished us well. He might have been up all night. We slipped out quietly, leaving our keys in the box by the door and shortly found our way to the Barbican.

The Path reached the first major site on the route – a rocket-shaped waymark reading, vertically, 'SOUTH WEST COAST PATH'.

'This must be the way,' Simone said, grinning. The same waymark was featured in Paddy's Guide, a shining white and red projectile, a smooth, clean plinth. Our view was of rust and mould-covered concrete. *All go unto one place; all are of the dust, and all turn to dust again.*[108]

'We need to look out for unicorns,' Simone said.

'What was that?'

'Unicorns. We need to look for the unicorns.'

'Yes ... remind me why we need to do that.'

'They will show us the way.'

'The unicorns will show us the way? Have you been eating mushrooms?'

He looked at me as though I were insane. 'It's *in the book.* You know. There's one.' He pointed at a lamppost. At eye level there was a black-on-white symbol.

'An acorn.'

'That's it. Acorns. Not unicorns. We need to look for acorns.'

Beyond a wall covered in poetry, while Simone was on unicorn duty I looked at the Guide. 'It says here we can go up Oreston Road or follow a railway path.' Despite following the signs, we found ourselves lost in suburbia. It was about fifteen minutes before we found our way.

'Unicorn at two o'clock! Look, a castle.' Simone took a photograph. It was a sham castle, a clapped-out lodge separating Cattewater and Hooe Lake. I didn't have the heart to tell him, or perhaps I wanted it to be so. Coming from a village outside Bradford, this probably *was* a castle. My Sancho Panza held his phone out like a crucifix and was snapping pictures of castellated concrete.

The rain was light but persistent as we entered Turnchapel on Boringdon Road, leading to the stuccoed Boringdon Arms. With the pub closed we stopped under the porch of private apartments like Stoics with a bad turnout. 'Shall we have some boring tea?' Simone suggested.

We must have made a sorry sight on our minor trespass. Glistening wet with resigned faces we perched on steps drinking from a folding cup and orange dog bowl – the Boringdon Arms as a backdrop in rain-curtained drabness. 'Look what has become of us,' I said, feeling personally responsible for the weather that had turned out for Simone.

'You might not believe this but I'm having a great time,' he said, and he smiled a genuine smile then slurped tea from his bowl. I was certain he meant it despite carrying my pack for half the journey.

Far beyond the industry of the city we found a plaque to T.E. Lawrence who had been stationed at RAF Mount Batten Point in the flying boat squadron. He had been under the assumed name Shaw on return from India, spurning fame associated with Lawrence of Arabia. It was here, not Wareham, that he served his final years in the military. Wareham was simply where his cottage, Clouds Hill, stood. He had left military service just before he died. Lawrence was fatally injured riding his Brough Superior motorcycle from the post office. Recorded as an accident caused by an obstructed view of dispatch riders at a dip in the road, correspondence immediately before the incident told a different story. The letters were written from RAF Mount Batten, where Simone and I now stood, and they were unambiguous: 'What do I wish? I wish I was dead, I think.'[109] And so he soon was, not deliberately but certainly aided by recklessness. I resolved to pay another visit to Clouds Hill if I ever finished the walk.

Beyond Staddon Point was a blue waymark claiming that there were 283 kilometres to Poole. The Guide provided an erratum for the waymark, that it was actually 368 kilometres. Our calculation was somewhere between the two, simply illustrating the difficulty of knowing true Path distances when there was so much conflicting information.

We were in Wembury ahead of time. A sign announced a seasonal ferry, just not in this particular season. The Wembury pub was also closed for the afternoon, its chef visible through the grimy panes reclined on a bench. We caught the next bus, and I alighted in Pomphlett to be extracted by a taxi to Noss Mayo, directly across the water from Wembury. Simone would carry on to Plymouth and his budget sardine tin on wheels.

It was sad to say goodbye to my friend. He was probably the last I would walk with, depending on another friend's plans. Others had given their apologies as the bad weather became national news. Simone and I hugged and parted on that bus to Plymouth. Before the bus doors closed, he shouted, 'Oscar, you *do* you!'

Now, I had no idea what Sim meant by 'you do you'. To *do* oneself. It was a phrase reminiscent of that now infamous beach with the unfortunate sign 'You can ride your own ass' next to a row of tethered donkeys. I could only conclude that whatever he meant, and I'm sure it wasn't intended as insulting, had been lost in translation either from Yorkshire or Italian Portuguese, or somewhere in between. One thing was certain: it was raining. Even if the sun had shone, it is always worse for the one left behind.

The taxi driver seemed concerned about where I was going so I told him the pub in Noss Mayo. As he drove, he interrogated me about my destination, while I evaded his questions with questions of my own. Only once his cab was out of sight did I approach the pub, in which I had no intention of staying.

'You took your time, sonny. I've been waiting for *tarn* minutes, and I'm wet. It's Baltic.'

The unmistakable Northern Irish brogue belonged to my closest friend, Rodney, who stood beneath the pub awning.

'I wasn't sure you'd make it.'

'You think I'd let you down? Did you not get your messages?'

Rodney was actually from Dublin. This dialogue was an impression of Gerry Adams and something we had used to entertain crowds of amused but baffled Czech men. I moved my mouth to his poorly lip-synced Sinn Fein voice. The reference, lost on our Prague audience, was a 1988-94 UK ban on the broadcast of the voice of anyone connected with eleven organisations based in Northern Ireland. It was a shameful period of censorship initiated by the government, yet comical given the elaborate means by which broadcasters circumvented the rules by using the voices of actors. The choice of our monologue was intended to show the farce of censorship by talking about the weather, a very British convention. It had been raining then, and it was raining now.

Rodney had not only been my oldest friend since I returned to England but he was also my first boss (if you exclude a day temping at Channel 4 mail room checking the names on a paramilitary hit-list). We had worked together in the archives of an international development charity and had soon become friends, having a similar humour and interest in music and culture. As I was also witness to the organisation's culturally offensive historical archive it was also important to keep me close.

Rodney did not wear a duffel coat and moccasins as he stood by the pub but had reasonable wet weather gear and boots. He even had a small pack. Despite his introduction, he didn't appear to be at all wet. I attributed this change to the conditioning I had exposed him to over the years.

We walked to the place where Newton Creek met the river Yealm, through the picturesque village. A sign listed the 'tolls due and payable to Yealm ferry'. These included three pence 'ferriage for every pony or ass'.

'You can ride your own ass,' Rodney muttered. I imagined the small man on an ass, leaning to adjust his stirrup and sending the animal careering off a cliff. As I have said, Rodney was the worst pillion passenger in the world. The road edged alongside a National Trust wood and passed the slip road for the seasonal ferry. Out to sea rose the Great Mew Stone, a rock on the edge of Plymouth Sound. There were a couple of houses and then a track through a wooded area called The Warren. A decent place to camp was immediately on the left, but we needed to cover as much distance between us and the Erme in order to reach it for the early low tide. I asked Rodney to wait at the clearing while I searched for a better location.

The track emerged from woodland onto Gara Point and as I rounded the bend I was struck by a gale. Rain on my face felt like small razors and the wind circled me, phantoms in the fading light. I leant into it to stay upright. In the end I held onto the wire fence for support and at that moment a jogger in shorts came out of the spray. He shouted something.

'Sorry?'

'Are you okay?' he bellowed. I could have asked the same question.

I tried to give the impression I had stopped to admire the view. 'Do you know what that building is, down there?' I pointed at a cube, precarious on the cliff edge below.

'A pill box, derelict.'

'Do you know if it's open?' We were both shouting above the howling wind. It was unnecessary small talk; I had no intention of seeking shelter in the concrete box which was clearly a death trap.

'I don't know. Are you sure you're okay?' As I opened my mouth to respond, my cheeks - inflated by the wind - flapped. I gave the thumbs up, still grasping my sticks. The jogger gave a concerned frown, nodded and turned, racing off in the direction of The Warren.

Out in the raging sea was the Great Mew Stone (another way of saying *Gull Rock*). In 1811, after that approach by engraver William Cooke for the series *Picturesque Views on the Southern Coast of England*,[110] JMW Turner had painted his impression of the Mew Stone. It showed mountainous waves, a dark grey stormy sky and scattering birds. A poem, attributed simply to friend *J.H.* who lived near this wild place, was included beside the engraving and it began:

There, on his grey and wave-worn pyramid
Like spectre Goul in some lone charnel-ground,
His sullen form in misty spray half hid,
Reclines the Spirit of the stormy Sound.

and ended:

The sullen crash, the shriek of wild despair,
One moment swell the gust that whistles by;
The next – no sound of living voice is there,
None, save the waken'd sea-mew's dreary cry. [III]

Picturesque views? What had he been thinking? I could easily have reproduced that image with a camera but, instead, I decided to live.

In the jogger's wake I headed into the woods where all was calm and peace, then retraced my steps to the rare flat ground where Rodney waited. It resembled a former quarry, littered with wet leaves and mud, yet it was luxury after that artist's impression of hell. A large tree gave shelter and a crown in which to place the dry gear.

'I'm afraid there's nothing but a hurricane beyond this wood. We're here for the night.' I was now drenched, and I cursed my stupidity - to be wet *and* stationary. As darkness fell I pitched the tent alone (Rodney claimed never to have pitched one that colour before). My rainproofs hung in the annexes to drip. Rodney sat on a rock and amused me with tales of the Irish records office he'd been working in, and of the last time we were in Devon together. His round lenses had misted over so I couldn't see his eyes.

'You don't suppose this is a turning place for cars?' he said once we were comfortable. I looked at the track and then at Rodney and changed the subject.

'I'll be seeing Tony, you know. He remembers you and your motorcycle skills.'

'I remember. Bearded bloke, salty sea dog with glasses. Big hounds too.'

'That's him.'

Less than a litre of water remained which I boiled. I had been in such a hurry to find a place before dark that I had forgotten about provisions. *Did you not get your messages?* Gathering rainwater in the pot failed, the tent being beneath a tree, so I resolved to look for a stream in the morning. There was a lot of water, just in all the wrong places.

My little book of tide tables showed that the crossing of the Erme would only be possible for about twenty minutes either side of 11am, assuming the river was not in flood. We decided to rest early and wake at 5am. The storm and cold had exhausted me.

A message came from Kenny. 'How is the walk going? Where will you be over the next few weeks?'

'In Devon for a week and half then Dorset.' Kenny had been good to me, not just building me a miniature latrine but sticking around when things were difficult. He was a cultured Scot, frowning on deep-fried Mars Bars which were *for tourists*. Deep-fried pizza, on the other hand. Rodney did not partake of deep-fried foods in Glasgow but he had studied them intently. He was quiet now. It was odd that he lay there with his glasses on yet he appeared to be asleep.

Before I slept, a thought landed like a feather on my brow. It was that all of this - the conditions, the weather and temporary shelter - were distraction and protection from the reality of my life. The reality was, I had no job, my future was uncertain, and perhaps there was no reason to be confident in any talent I thought I might possess. Society might also be on the brink of collapse. It was a fleeting weltschmerz but just enough to disturb my sleep.

FOUR: The End is Nigh

Give up all hope
Day 47. 26th October

A dog's breakfast bowl of muesli mixed with lukewarm tea was followed by packing and putting on my damp clothes, the cold fabric at my neck irritating my scars. Rodney was elsewhere. I balanced my gear in the dry crown of the tree before taking down the tent in the dark, only half awake. He emerged from the darkness to collect his few belongings and we set off.

Sleepwalking in the darkness, we emerged from The Warren woods as the wind hit with its thorny rain. Nothing had changed during the moonless night except that now I could see none of it. Rather than risk my torch to the storm, I allowed my eyes to adjust to what little light there was. Rodney followed close behind; I tried to shield him with my body. We were Scott and Oates tethered to one another. It was to be one of the worst journeys. They say the darkest hour is just before the dawn, but people can be stupid. The darkest hour - at the end of daylight saving - was five past one in the morning.

Ghost-like sheep leapt from the path as this hunched stranger rounded a bend in the dark. Clearly sheep appreciated backpacks no more than dogs. *Please don't let them jump from the cliff.* Most of them gathered near a wall while a few moved onto the field to the right. The walls on Revelstoke Drive were built to prevent horses plunging from cliffs on sharp bends. Giving our ovine friends a wide berth, we stayed on the track, and soon found ourselves in a car park where I consulted Paddy. 'We should have followed the sheep.' The exception that proves the rule.

At that moment the jogger from the night before, in the same day-glow Lycra and shorts, passed. 'Good day for it,' he shouted. He didn't seem to recognise me, probably assuming that the walker from the evening was further along the track or else had drowned. Squinting into the wind I watched him run to the place we should have gone. Sheep scattered as he climbed the stile. We followed, passing beneath a Napoleonic era signal station that ordinarily I would have investigated had there been time. The tidal crossing had to be made at eleven or never.

I used the last of the tea above Little Bloody Cove. Revelstoke, a holiday park, was in a muddy valley edged by trees. Despite the rain I was desperately thirsty and there was nothing between Noss Mayo and the Erme River mouth. Seeing a light on and figures moving inside the Park House, I knocked. A woman, close to my own age, opened the door.

'Sorry, could we trouble you for some water?'

She looked at me a little uncertainly. 'Sure, come in. Do you want a cup of tea?'

'Thanks, that would be lovely.' I removed what was dripping and left it inside the porch. My pack wouldn't fit through the door so I left it.

'I'll wait here,' Rodney said, standing in the porch. 'I'm better insulated than you and I've got plenty to drink.' I nodded.

'Is your park closed for the winter?' I asked as I crossed the threshold.

'Oh, it's not ours. We're just renting the house for the week. There are permanent tenants in the mobile homes, mostly privately owned now. We used to rent one but decided to take the big house.'

'It's a nice house.'

A girl watched television while an older man in the kitchen made tea. He asked 'Walking the Path? How much are you doing?'

'The whole thing.'

'You're heading east?' I nodded. 'So you'll be crossing the Erme. When is low tide?'

'Eleven. Have you done it?' I gulped the hot tea from thirst and my mouth burned.

'I have. The whole path at different times. You have enough time to get to the crossing, though the weather is poor. When you get there, you have to cross from the sand spit. Look for the post on the other side. Aim for the white post. It should be obvious. You can cross further out too, it shouldn't be a problem.'

'Is it deep?'

'It shouldn't be, but with all this rain it's difficult to say. It shouldn't be much higher than your knees. Time it right and you'll be okay.' *Time it wrong and ...*

Thanking them for the tea and water, I made a few silly turns in their small porch with Rodney while trying to put my jacket on and pick up the pack. We peered enviously back at the warm living room with its fireplace and headed out into the cold rain - realising we had wasted precious minutes.

'I've been given advice on the crossing.' The narrow path crossed fields, wind pressing the long grass flat. Paddy had spoken of 'fine coastal scenery'. I opened my right eye to look into the wind and saw only a white haze.

We came to the beach at around ten minutes to eleven and I checked the Guide to see where to cross. It was then that I realised this was not Erme Mouth but Meadowfoot Beach. There was a wooded promontory between us and the crossing, so I stuffed Paddy inside my pack and said 'we'll have to jog'.

'You go ahead, I'll catch you up.'

A boathouse was on Meadowfoot. It had featured in the 2017 film version of du Maurier's *My Cousin Rachel.* Above the beach I crossed a wooded ridge and I didn't stop until I was on the beach at Erme mouth. A dog walker directed me vaguely: 'It's over there, but you can cross closer to the mouth if it looks okay.' Nothing looked okay.

I sent a message on my wet phone to Tony, my old friend from Dartington. Tony now worked in Bantham, across the water from Bigbury, and had offered to help me if I was stuck. 'Tony, this is Oscar. I'm about to wade the river and if successful I should be at Bigbury before dark. Any chance we could meet?' Then I switched off the phone lest it fell into the water.

The sand was soft so I took off my boots, quickly tied them together and hung them about my neck. I considered my water shoes but there wasn't time. This was my first mistake. I looked for the white post but could see nothing. The map was little help; there was nothing to gauge directions at sea level with no compass or sun. The water was high in all directions so I simply walked as far as I could on dry land and aimed for what looked like steps and a Coast Path sign (my second mistake).

Rodney caught up, not - uncharacteristically - short of breath. He removed his shoes then started walking in my wake. The riverbed was smooth at first. In the middle of the river, as I was being whipped by rain and the current threatened to push me over, I suddenly felt sick. It was the sensation of walking on sharp mussel shells with the full weight of the pack pushing me down. Possibly I *was* walking on mussel shells. I also hadn't accounted for the riverbed containing the debris from further upstream bumping into me. Whatever damage I was doing to my feet it was no time to turn back; I was beyond the point of no return. The cold water was deeper than I expected, the pack just above water and my shorts in it. To stay upright I walked with legs apart and swivelled my body; I couldn't risk all my clothes and boots being soaked. Already my body was shaking. Branches and leaves floated by, faster now, hurrying towards the open sea. 'Are you okay or do you want one of my sticks?'

'I'm fine. I've got more mass than you.'

Soon the current lessened, the sand returned and we reached the far side. On the steps I checked for lacerations. There was no blood – my soles were now like leather and most blood had retreated due to the cold. 'Ha! I did it!' I shouted, but there was no-one. Rodney washed in a distant stream like John the Baptist.

There was the squelch of mud inside my boots. I was expecting trench foot. It's important to have something to look forward to.

My phone alerted me to a voicemail. A distorted voice: 'Oscar, whatever you do, *don't* cross the river. You'll drown. It's in flood. *Don't even think about it*'. I called Tony back.

'Hi Tony, it's me.'

'Oscar, don't cross the river! I'll come and get you.' He was frantic.

'It's too late. I already crossed and I'm fine. Cold and wet, but alive.'

'Blimey, how did you ...? I just looked at it and you'd need to swim.'

'I'm at the Erme now and it was only up to my pack.'

'Oh, you're at the Erme! I thought you were crossing the Avon to Bantham. Still, all the rivers are high after this rain. You nearly gave me a heart attack.'

'No, I've got another few hours before I get to Bigbury. You remember Rodney – we came on the bike to Dartington?'

'Sure, of course I remember him. Are you okay, Oscar? You don't sound okay.'

'Yes, I'm well. Where shall we meet?' We agreed to meet at the Venus Café where I had been earlier with Kristiina.

As we left the beach the cold wind exploded as though it had been holding its breath. 'Do you suppose we should try making friends with the wind?' Rodney suggested. Too tired to respond, I stared blankly and walked on.

Paddy wrote of 'a fine view across Erme Mouth.' I squinted into the gale of sea spray and driving rain, digging the poles in as I pushed my weight uphill. There were at least five kilometres of this, up and down. 'Enjoy fine views inland to the high parts of Dartmoor.' Our vista was not unlike the view from the window of a highspeed train. 'The final part of the walk is quite difficult, with several ascents and descents, some of which are very steep.' Of course, I shouldn't have but I blamed the messenger. It never occurred to me to blame the person responsible, myself.

The wire fences whistled and wind grabbed at my pack's rain cover. Twice I was thrown to the ground in sudden gusts. On the second fall I lay there, hoping someone would come for me. Rodney walked ahead and I reluctantly stood and staggered after him.

For a while we were pinned to the fence by the wind. It was like being humiliatingly held down by the school bully; there was nothing to do until he let go of you and you could push yourself off. My skin stung, eyes streamed from the icy spray. 'Enough! Make it stop!' but the howling gale grew so strong it was noise-cancelling. Exhaustion and cold took hold of my decision-making and after another fall I lay in a foxhole, resolving to stay there until the storm passed. Rodney crouched silently against a wall. *This storm is never going to end, it will still be blowing after we leave the European Union.* After I leave. He's still in Ireland.

Track Three. Between shouting at the sky *enough*, I had a mantra in my head. I repeated it over and over as I was assaulted by the storm, a little protective Sanskrit mantra that said that whatever they throw at me I won't be obliterated by it. Of course, it was John Lennon's chorus from *Across the Universe.*[112] The song's opening was famously inspired by a monologue from his first wife,[113] the analogy of torrents into cups. Though Lennon's mantra was becoming less convincing, and though I tell myself I'm not superstitious, I repeated the words as though my life depended on them.

Rodney stood over me, and I saw his stupid moccasins half submerged in a puddle, furry and yellow, but it was just water in my eyes. 'These shortcuts will kill you,' he warned.

'This is not a shortcut.'

'You ought to get moving or you'll die.' He wasn't angry, he just had that slight nagging tone, as he often did when I had invested too much in someone who was going to let me down. It just angered me that he knew before I did.

'You can talk. I'm just resting.'

'Nobody will come by in this weather. It's just us.' He'd developed a much stronger Irish accent than when he was in London.

'Since when were you an expert on walking? *You* came.'

'You didn't give me a choice.' The wind howled and I rolled onto my knees, pushing myself to standing. Nothing had improved. Nothing was ever going to change.

Five kilometres felt like ten as I began counting steps. The sight of distant Burgh Island and the anticipation of the heating in Tony's car kept me going, but I was running on empty, falling down slopes and climbing up hills by focusing on incremental targets a few metres above me. There had been nobody on the Path for hours. Even the birds had found shelter.

I stumbled down the metalled road towards Christie's bar in Challaborough. Losing my speed meant growing colder but I knew I had only a kilometre at most before I was in the car.

'We'll be there around the next bend.' Rodney, though, didn't seem to mind, marching just out of my field of vision.

When last I had been there, Burgh Island had been a luminous white art deco tower on a green field framed by blue and white. Now it was a dark mound, cut off from the mainland by the boiling grey sea, a cacophony of guitars and Indian chanting painted by Lennon and Turner. I shuffled into the car park by the Venus to find it, typical of beach cafés, closed. Tony was nowhere. I looked in the windows of the few parked cars but they were empty. Leaning on the railing overlooking the Island I stared at the sea and thought of nothing, a restless wind inside my mind. Despite my original intentions of having no spiritual insights, I had indeed found myself - in a shivering mess.

'What did you do with your little yellow friend?' Rodney still seemed to be in good spirits, which was irritating.

'Zippy? He blew away.' My speech was slurred.

'The string was old and frayed, you were bound to lose contact. It'll be okay, you know that?'

'No, I should have been more careful.'

Wind and rain slapped at my face and pushed my hood back, but I no longer had the energy to turn myself away. A figure approached, then got into a nearby car and drove off. I began to shake as my temperature dropped. I had to find shelter quickly. There was nowhere.

'I thought that was you. Saw the caf' was shut so I went out to look. I thought I'd missed you.' The weathered face of a sea farer, a straggling grey beard and kind rheumy eyes staring out from a heavy jacket and beanie. A lurcher stood obediently at his side. Tony. I hugged him like he was the last person on earth. It was raining so much he couldn't see that I was crying. 'We better get you inside. We'll go to Sue's gallery, she wants to see you.'

I had rehearsed what I would say when we met, but exhaustion and cold took away any sense of ceremony as I slumped into the car beside Tony. The back seat was filled with dog.

'Were you on the phone, Osc? I thought I heard you talking.'

'Just talking to keep myself awake.' Tony started the car and the two of us drove on through the rain, the windscreen wipers scraping to the sound of the blood pumping in my head.

At the end of visits - in Glasgow, Ireland, Cambodia, wherever - before Rodney left me, we would spend a day bristling. It would sometimes become a heated argument, but I interpreted this as preparation for loss. We would part and I would be left behind, so the fighting was part of the process of separation. Being left behind, everything stays the same whereas the one leaving has new experiences and stimuli. It always feels worse for those left behind. The last time, three years ago, I was on a tube train in London, having just been on the phone to his home. My eyes were tightly closed, my head bowed, when a woman snapped 'Can you please move!' She stood expectantly with a pram, a ridiculous twentieth century hooded thing. I had to open my eyes to know this and so the saltwater dam burst and spilled down my cheeks. The sight of a grown man crying caused her to involuntarily laugh. I stepped aside and she wheeled her perambulator along the platform leaving me standing, ridiculously, in the crowd on the Northern Line.

That was, of course, the day Rodney died. He died in Ireland, the same age and on the same day as the musician Prince, the archivist formerly known as Rodney. A lot of *famous* people died that year, a statistically significant increase I'm told. Like the year we first met, it was a bad year. The last time we met was for a planned walk but it became a painful shuffle around the housing block on the shores of Carlingford Lough. 'You don't battle cancer,' he said angrily, 'it just devours you.' His was a cancer that incrementally ate him up, sapped his energy and made him fart loudly but with great comic emphasis. We took one last trip to a magic road and watched the car roll uphill with the engine off. He wanted to believe.

At the wake I saw his waxy likeness, as I'd seen the embalmed Lenin, Mao and Ho Chi Minh. *All the great communist stiffs*, he used to joke. While Mags held his hand tenderly for a moment, I couldn't bring myself to touch him. Part of me still expected him to open his eyes and shout 'Surpreese!'

I carried Rodney to the church as I'd carried him on the bike, a little unsteadily but no longer complaining about his weight. Our common friends from London carried him out together and celebrated his life. A joint was respectfully puffed. A year later we, his friends and family scattered his ashes and sunflowers into a waterfall. They should have gone into Carlingford Lough and then onwards to the Atlantic, but instead seemed to spend an inordinate time dawdling in pools a few feet from us as we made uncomfortable small talk.

Had he been alive I know he would have joined me here (the worst leg of the journey). On the other hand, he was a humanist and given his intolerance of 'invisible friends', he would have been livid that I had made one of him. But when there are no friends we are forced to make our own.

Tony filled the shivering silence with chatter as we drove to the gallery. The dog sat contentedly on the back seat. 'Come back to ours, we'll get you some food and dry your things out. Then you can spend as long as you like or move on. No pressure.'

In the 1990s I started working in an arts college, Dartington. Tony had been a student of theatre and then became the Welfare and Accommodation Manager. I was in student recruitment. I didn't know much about art, but I knew what I liked.

Tony was 50 then but he looked much younger due to his fitness, tanned appearance, disintegrating Grateful Dead t-shirts and faded jeans.

Tony's partner, Sue, was a counsellor at the college. She was, and is, an artist, who gravitates to representing nature in prints, very beautiful images of wildlife and the West Country landscape.

We had been lucky, having jobs on a mediaeval estate on a bend in the River Dart. It was idyllic. But then something happened. It was not a sudden thing, it was insidious.

I had been saving to go to university to study public health. For several years I lived on fifteen pounds a week after rent. I walked from the village of Harberton across the hills, through Follaton, Cott, Dartington, Shinner's Bridge and up the hill to the Hall and back, thirteen kilometres daily. At last I had enough money so I headed north.

A few months after starting the course in Glasgow I began to feel unusual. One evening, at a dinner party, my legs gave way and I slid slowly down the wall, landing on my behind yet, somehow, did not spill my full glass of red wine over the beige carpet. The carpet belonged to a public health doctor; she had been eyeing me suspiciously all night as a candidate for soiling her décor (though I had consumed no alcohol). She stood over me, observed the red liquid and quickly took possession of my untouched glass, with no attempt to hide her relief. I was carried upstairs to the bathroom where I proceeded to be violently ill over her minimalist 90s ceramic surfaces (though I cleaned up as best I could).

'I wouldn't go in there if I were you,' I advised queuing guests as I departed, and then staggered off to a waiting taxi.

A Department of Public Health Christmas lunch had precipitated this incident. The irony hadn't escape me. The following Monday, everyone who had attended the Christmas jolly was asked by the administrative assistant (armed with a clipboard) as they entered the building, 'Do you have diarrhoea?' Those who weren't in-the-know blushed and hurried to the toilet to check if they'd forgotten to use deodorant. That was fine by her as it was negative publicity she did not have to reveal (she'd booked the rogue caterer herself). Those who responded in the affirmative received the follow-up query, 'Did you have the steamed rice or the potatoes?'

The experience of having diarrhoea and vomiting from *Bacillus cereus* must have pushed me beyond my physical limits. I recall my professor in class at around that time looking at me through thick lenses with pity mixed with a strange curiosity, as though he knew I was at my end but couldn't quite put his finger on which ailment was going to finish me off. He was mentally searching through the textbook of public health, a large volume that he had personally edited. As it turned out, the condition was there under 'P'. He simply said, 'Something's not right,' as my motorcycle mechanic would repeat many years later after sucking in air. *That's neglect, that is.*

My flatmate Rick leaned across after the professor had left and said in mock Sydney *strine*, 'The prof's pointed the bone at you, cobber.' Then, as though to make amends, he added, 'I wouldn't worry. He's still sore about his recent fact-finding trip. Landed in Harare at the weekend and complained about the dodgy airline food. The school secretary answered his call and asked him if he'd taken the potatoes or rice at his own departmental lunch. Her study may go in the Christmas edition of the *British Medical Journal:* Slow-cooked Basmati, a predictor of acute arse piss.'

My speech became slurred, my gait abnormal. The skin on my face scaled and flaked, I suffered intermittent gastrointestinal symptoms and an excruciating headache unrelieved by painkillers. My thoughts were plagued by an uncomprehending fog and my nerves were on a hair trigger. With all senses amplified, the air filled with tinnitus, an uncorrected tape hiss at full volume. Paranoia, fuelled by my oversensitive hearing, had me chasing conspiracies everywhere. My flatmates Rick and John were plotting to have me admitted to hospital (this particular conspiracy was real). While I was probably of more harm to myself than to others, part of me did consider murdering the two of them in their sleep.

Time seemed to speed and slow and I lost awareness of the sequence of events. I felt myself disappearing; my thoughts were no longer my own. The terror that I might die in a strange place had me sleeping with the door open. Rick could, at least, check if I was no longer there. Of course, I had forgotten that he'd moved out, being unable to stand the madness of the flat.

After a theatrical collapse in the street I was isolated in an infectious disease ward, the assumption - on account of the fiasco with the Public Health Christmas meal - being that I simply had an infection. Later, a brain tumour was suspected but then excluded after an expensive scan (the cost borne by the NHS would have paid off my term's student fees). The underlying reasons took years to fully understand but the immediate cause was malnutrition. Malabsorption, walking ludicrous distances and living on a pauper's diet had resulted in neurological symptoms. I had developed *pellagra*, a disease which, though popular in the early 1900s in the southern states of the USA, had fallen out of fashion. In 1990s Glasgow I had taken it out and dusted it off.

My life was going south but my potential demise was averted by taking a vitamin. Well, a lot of vitamins in huge therapeutic doses. I managed to finish my study, not because I felt I had to, but as I had invested so much of myself in it and wanted to see it to the end. A changed person returned to Devon, someone more relaxed, who walked less, and who would learn to ride a motorcycle.

Now twenty years later, as Tony drove me through the back lanes he said, 'I was sure you were going to die out there.'

The house, an old farmhouse inland from Slapton, was shared with their daughter's family. Tony cooked vegetable curry and we talked into the night. 'You've had an unlikely run of weather,' said Sue.

'It's been a bloody awful October. We couldn't think when we've had so many storms.' Tony had the look of a concerned schoolmaster, peering over his glasses.

'Do you ever go back to Dartington?' I asked him.

He shook his head. 'We had it good there - job security, the flat and grounds. We could take the dogs out in the evenings. When the college was at financial risk there was no attempt to save it. They had no intention of keeping the place going. The last time I was there I was in tears. I can't go back.' Dartington. It had been an experiment in *small is beautiful*, and it was over.

Breakfast was with the wider family, Sarah, Angus and their kids who had been kind enough to sponsor me. I had the chance to see their son, Jasper, for the first time since he was a baby. Every time I looked across, he had a different football t-shirt on. It was like being in a student film that had forgotten to hire a continuity person. He seemed eager to please all fans and all teams. I never saw him change, it was just there when I turned, like a superhero change. It was wonderful.

At Bantham beach while Sue and I walked the dog, Tony argued with visitors who refused to pay the entrance fee; his gentlemanly threats had them leaving in what should have been an angry reverse, but because of the narrow drive and other cars it was a slow and painful three-point turn of shame, particularly humiliating.

That evening Sue helped me choose a present for Mags from her art. Some of her animal drawings were moths. She explained that there are hawk moths which have a similar colour appearance to the hummingbird I had seen. We searched and found a photograph of my creature – a *hummingbird hawk moth*, a migrant from southern Europe. It is strange to have lived so long and never to have seen one, and then to glimpse one on a cold morning in Autumn.

This will all end badly, I just know it
Day 49. 28th October

Tony took me back to Bantham in the early hours while the house slept. We hugged and I promised I would be in touch once more before leaving Devon.

At South Milton Sands a beach café was open. Outside were a couple who asked me about my direction. As everyone did, she eventually asked 'Have you read the book?'

'It seems I'm the only one who hasn't. I know a lot of the plot.'

'It's good, but I was expecting a story about the Coast Path,' she said.

'I think the point was, it was about the issues they faced,' her partner explained. 'It was about their situation.'

'Yes, I get that, but it would have been nice to know more about the Path. Have you thought about writing yours up?'

214

'I'm unsure what I'd say.' It wasn't entirely true; I had some ideas. The two gave me some encouraging words which made the walking easier, but they had also planted a seed. If I did write something, it would be about a journey that started with good intentions, but which somehow went wrong. A little like us as an island. Though I wasn't sure how it would end I felt things were improving. They couldn't get worse.

Beyond the beautiful sandy beach was Hope, and this seemed to confirm my feelings. There is an Outer and Inner Hope. From the old Hope Lifeboat Station a steep flight of steps led up and out towards Bolt Tail. There were views back towards Burgh Island, which looked calm and bright once more. The first and final chapters of the island's story were calm, and I could forget the turbulent and torn pages in between.

Just over the brow of a hill I stopped near Cathole Cliff, and before me was a valley with a moderately steep rise at the other side. I was reading the Guide and drinking tea when a man stalked, rather than walked, up behind me. In profile he was the Duke of Edinburgh, with tweeds, a cap and ridiculous socks with red tassels at their elasticated tops ('shooting socks'). And, naturally, a red setter.

'When one stops on the way down,' he stated as though this were the most ridiculous thing in the world, 'one will be *exhausted* on the way up.' He let out a smug laugh as he passed. All of this without once looking at me. You would recognise him as the one who might affect to talk of Abyssinia rather than Ethiopia, and who still discussed the Irish question at his club.

One is hardly going to be tired if one has rested, and even less so if the next stretch is downhill, but he was too fast for me to respond; he was already striding down the hill. Instead of shouting, I demonstrated the fact to him. Packing quickly, I followed the specious squire, matching him step for step despite his lanky stature and my accompanying millstone. On the next hill I was metres from overtaking him with a prepared repartee when he suddenly lurched off inland to chat with a couple of day strollers, leaving me standing at the junction panting, my heart screaming, blood pumping in my ears. I showed *him*.

A woodland walk led down to the first sheltered beach where gift shops and ice cream sellers were still making a decent trade. Another sea tractor took people out into the estuary where they boarded a ferry to Salcombe.

Recalling Shaun's advice in the Plymouth dorm, I checked my phone for the notes I had made. The steep road led to the next beach where the sea fizzed onto the road. In front of me was a café - *The Yawning Lobster.* This lobster was, indeed, yawning. I walked to the back of the public car park and found a boardwalk. It was slippery with growth. Carefully shuffling through the reeds and trees on the slimy timber I made out a small hut, its door minutely ajar.

Opening the hide's viewing slots to let in light I made out three benches at various angles. I moved them together to form a wide platform. 'Simone,' I wrote in a message, 'Shaun was good to his word.' *How had we ever doubted you?*

But for a few dry leaves and a discarded used condom, the hide was clean. I jammed the seats against the door in case someone else was tempted to come in for a nightcap. After dinner the rain grew heavy, thudding onto the roof. I stared at my tent and clothing hanging to dry and contemplated the way ahead; I desperately needed new waterproofs. My dreams were filled with Daleks.

Paddy described a rugged walk ahead with a series of steep ascents and descents down to the southernmost point in Devon.

In Salcombe proper, at a café by a ferry sign, I tripped over a man's morbidly obese dog laying across the doorway. He made no attempt to make it shift.

'Is this the right place for the ferry to East Portlemouth?' I asked as I ordered.

'No, we're a café.' She leaned in conspiratorially. 'I'm kidding. Most of the boats leave from the square in town. It'll be obvious when you get there.'

During breakfast the man with the dog was joined by a woman who spoke so loudly in received pronunciation that all the café's customers - most of whom had also tripped over the lardy dog on entering - were privy to the conversation. Phrases came at me from their side of the room: 'Remoaners trying to undermine the democratic process ... given half a chaaance we'd send the lot of them packing ... hordes of them trying to get into the country.' Looking outside at the rain it was difficult to believe any of this. I thought of Sultan and his family, stuck between Kabul and a safer postcode and I couldn't help thinking that Turkey might be a better prospect than Devon's South Hams.

I tripped over the dog as I left the café, then made my way down to the harbour and the ferry. The man stepping from the boat had a rugged face but friendly eyes. 'Excuse me, are you going to the other side?'

'Leaving in five minutes.'

The boat was small and open but the rain was easing a little. 'If you're aiming for Slapton, there's an easterly coming in. You should be okay on the estuary though.' He gave more meteorological information, but my mind filtered his words, hearing only the possibility of shelter.

'Have you walked the Path?' I asked him.

He steered into the current. 'I used to walk it a lot, but I was into cycling more. I had a motorcycle accident. Landed heavily, broke my leg badly. Complex fracture. At one point they thought I'd lose it.'

'You still walk?'

'It's painful to cover any real distance, or to cycle. I still ride motorcycles though.' He smiled. The one thing he could still do was the thing that had caused the damage, but I could see how it gave him freedom. I missed it.

As I stepped from the boat he took my hand, shook it firmly and wished me luck. It was genuine, though in retrospect I realised also protective. People who work on the water appreciate its power. I watched the little boat move away over to Salcombe.

National Trust volunteers tidied fallen trees in the woods. The volunteers were friendly, but then I wasn't encamped on their land. Near Salcombe Bar was a memorial to those killed when the Salcombe lifeboat capsized in 'atrocious conditions' on 27 October 1916. Last night. The crew had been debating whether to go to Dartmouth or come in, but the decision was made by an enormous wave which pitched the boat stern over bow on the sand bar.[114] Fifteen went out that day, but only two came back, survivors of the worst lifeboat disaster in the West Country.

Rounding the mouth of the estuary the cold rain hit and I struggled against the wind. A thatched lookout belonging to Gara Rock Hotel offered brief shelter but otherwise I kept walking against the easterly wind, my face covered to below my eyes with the windbreak. I took no more photographs for the rest of the day, protecting my phone from the weather. The only respite was a National Coastwatch Institution station. I waved to the watchkeepers as I entered the public building then closed myself in, feeling the wind tug against the door. My gear was saturated, my body chilled, and I just stood dripping until I could bring myself to peel off the outer layers.

'Hello there.' A head peeked around the door. You're walking the Path! Would you like a cup of coffee?' It was a welcome offer. Watchkeepers knew better than to make idle quips about the weather. They have seen it kill. I was very cold, but afraid to put David's fleece on as it was my evening salvation and it would be useless if wet.

When the watchkeeper returned we chatted about the sea life and his work, but he was looking concerned and clearly had something on his mind.

'Look, there is an easterly coming.' *Coming? What was this?* 'It's going to get worse and you're walking straight into it. The track from here is easier up to Start Point, but ...'

'This isn't Start Point?'

'No, this is Prawle Point. It's a fair distance further. Where are you planning to get to?'

'Slapton.' I had made hardly any progress. His face was calm but slightly unbelieving.

'That's quite a way. There are places inland. East Prawle or just beyond Start Point. Consider heading there. It's a long way to Slapton.'

'I will. Thanks for the coffee.'

'That's fine. Think about that detour. Take as long as you like here.'

'Thanks.' I had some tea too, for the extra heat, and ate. Outside sounded like a tornado. Before leaving I wrote a post-it-note to Dave in the earlier coast watch station and put it with ten pounds in the donations box.

As soon as I left the look-out, I regretted it. Though I marched as fast as I could I grew very cold. Walking beneath old coastguard cottages and skirting wet fields, my boots were only slightly less saturated than the rest of me. There was giggling from a group clearly on a circular walk when they saw the masked and hunched man in clinging lime green. Some people say *there is no such thing as bad weather, there is only unsuitable clothing.* Some people are annoying.

At the track to Borough, having lost all inhibitions I urinated at the side of the way as my core temperature dropped. In the wind the wet gear acted like an air-conditioning unit. Near Lannacombe Beach another walker took to the Path but disappeared, and only when I reached The Narrows could I see him on the rocks, recklessly photographing the raging sea beneath a sign that warned, 'Please exercise extreme care when using this section of coast path.'

Nowhere offered any shelter from the incessant wind. The lighthouse should have been visible by now. That's when I looked down onto the beach. Below The Narrows two bodies lay on the sand being pounded by the waves. They were grey and lifeless and my instinct was to get my camera, but the storm would have destroyed it. Instead, I watched, and one of them began to move, then the other. Soon the two seals were rolling around in the surf, playing games with the waves. It was magical, and nobody was there to witness it, just a green scarecrow.

The rocks were slippery leading to Start Point. I was tired but the squall was turning into a storm and if I were to stop, I might not find shelter before nightfall.

The ceiling of cloud was so thick that there was no sign of a sun. As I rounded the Point, lights at a few distant houses blinked on. Perhaps the low light from the storm had triggered the sensors. I slid down the muddied track to reach the relative safety of the deserted tarmacked road. Suddenly, the road plunged into darkness as though by a solar eclipse. My mind frantically sought a reason and then I realised it had been the last Saturday in October; the clocks had changed. I'd had the luxury of the shuttered hide the night before and hadn't noticed the early darkness.

The wind was stronger despite having crossed the spur but now I realised my other mistake; the ferryman had meant I would be protected only within the Salcombe estuary. I was exhausted and cold, my waterproofs no longer deserving of the name. When eventually I reached the buildings, all were private houses - not a pub or shop in sight.

The first wave struck me in the darkness as I crossed the shingle beach. It wasn't the wet that concerned me - I could hardly get wetter - it was being swept out across the black rocks. The houses of Hallsands had been washed into the sea in January 1917 and the village had again lost its pebble beach a century later in January 2016. Waves were suddenly behind and in front of me, their foam luminescent in the dark. Fear gave me energy to scramble forward, my boots digging deep into the loose stones. Frantic, but handicapped by the weight of the pack, I ran sluggishly as one does in dreams from shadows.

A song was in and out of my thoughts, though not one that was easily hummed, nor a lyric which came easily. It was like the name of an old friend which just eluded you, the disturbing recurring dream of a crime committed that you suspect may have actually happened on a drunken impulse. It opens with a gentle guitar riff growing in volume like distant thunder or that buoy with the mournful bell. Track four, *Gimme Shelter,* the Rolling Stones. You don't have to be a clinical psychologist to see why it was often in my head.

Keith Richards wrote the song on a terrible, stormy day in London. He recalled 'I had been sitting by the window of my friend Robert Fraser's apartment on Mount Street in London with an acoustic guitar when suddenly the sky went completely black and an incredible monsoon came down. It was just people running about looking for shelter - that was the germ of the idea.'[115]

The song always sounded to me like the future yet as the opening track of the album *Let it Bleed*[16] it was, in fact, released on the day I was born, fifty years ago. The song's images of conflict and violence captured this place with its relics of warfare, violent weather and absence of shelter.

From the top of the spur a light was visible. It sat at the edge of the blackness where the sea should be. On descent into Beesands the light formed itself into a pub though as I approached it was clear the sea had encroached. Waves dramatically pounded the windows of the Cricket Inn, the road strewn in rocks and weed. I stood, waiting and timing the backwash between crashing waves. I bolted through the retreating water, pulling at the door and squeezing myself and pack between it and the frame.

The wave thudded the windows, a barking dog reaching the limits of its chain. As I slid into the bar I was met by the cold stare of its regulars and the chatter stopped with the wave's impact. Facing my audience I dripped methodically, steaming slightly. The waterproof gloves I had bought, clearly from charlatans, in Plymouth hung ridiculously; sodden flippers on the end of my raincoat which clung to my bony limbs. Balloons of water gathered around the ankles of my waterproof trousers, waiting for an opportune moment to relieve themselves which they now did.

The bar was full and its customers clearly knew one another, a community wary of strangers. With the whole house focused on me I stood framed in the doorway. I had entered a lock-in. A wake. A West Country republican arms deal.

Three people were seated at the bar, two men and a woman who showed signs of having been drinking throughout the storm (it was only six o'clock). The older man - sideburns, slicked back hair and thick eyebrows – rotated his body from the waist towards the crowd, demanding their attention. This was *Key Largo* and he its Edward G Robinson. He spoke loudly with a Devon accent while looking directly at me. 'We've got another one!' The whole bar broke into laughter. I desperately needed to go to the toilet.

'Don't worry, I'll ask Rach if we can get these dry for you,' one of the bar tenders said, walking casually past me.

'Rach?'

'The governor.' She disappeared.

'They'll get you sorted,' said the man with the sideburns.

'If you take your kit off I'll stick it in the drier.' A woman had appeared and was standing beside a table of women in the corner.

'Go on then, we're waiting,' a voice came from the corner. They were quite merry, one in particular. Perhaps they hadn't changed their clocks.

'You'd be disappointed. I'm mostly bones.'

I slipped through to the toilet as a voice escaped the gap in the door: 'There's only one we're interested in.' This was not the welcome I was used to in South Devon. I spent the next ten minutes stripping and wringing my clothes as best I could as men came in to stand at the trough.

'Hi, Rach said I could dry these,' I said, back at the bar. She indicated to one of the waiters who took them from me as though this were an everyday occurrence.

'No worries, love, can I get you a drink?'

I ordered something medium priced and sat at the bar. 'What did the man mean by "we've got another one"?'

'You best ask these two here.'

The merry couple turned to me. 'We had someone a few years back, walking the whole Coast Path, got stuck 'ere in a storm,' he said. 'Oldish fella. Remember, they offered 'im a room. Refused. Said it was against 'is principles. He wants somewhere to stay so we offered the 'ide or the chapel. Where did 'e stay?'

'I think he went to the church,' she answered. 'Or the hide.'

'They offered him a room?'

'Yeah, no charge. 'e just said 'e was doin' it 'is way and didn't want to break the pattern. So goes off to the chapel.' He looked back to his partner.

'Or the hide. Then,' she continued, 'there was a young woman who stumbled in here during another storm. Same advice was given. It's odd how people end up here. Rach is good, she'll sort your clothes out. Then your best bet is the hide.'

'Or the chapel. It's always open. 'e won't mind.' I wasn't sure who *he* was. A priest or someone higher. After a while my clothes were returned and I thanked everyone for their help.

Before I left, Edward G Robinson held me back. 'You stopped somewhere special. Keith Richards played his first public gig in this inn.'

'You saw him?'

'How old do I look? No, my grandfather saw him. You mind yourself.' He nodded and smiled.

The waves crashed across the road as I left the pub. For the next twenty minutes I followed the inebriated directions I had been given, but in the dark and the storm trying to find the hide was futile. I passed a field and along the beach as far as the next settlement, then walked back to the village where all was closing down for the evening. The circuit had been just long enough to ensure I was superficially wet and I could ill afford to get cold. Then, there it was, just as they had described. The door gave. It was unlocked.

When I woke in my golden cocoon the next morning a similarly gilded St Andrew the Apostle looked down on me, I hoped not too begrudgingly. *Forgive us our trespasses.* Inside the chapel it was still dark but light from the street was enough to make out the interior. A bell had been salvaged from the Barrow-in-Furness schooner which was one of five ships wrecked in Start Bay in the great storm of 1891. Near the font was a dedication to seven people who were killed by enemy action in July 1942. Their ages were 54, 49, 23, 13, 4, 2 and 1.

I was grateful for this shelter from the storm, as clearly others had been before me, lost in storms. My waterproofs were chilled as I walked out and witnessed the miracle of an open public toilet beside the chapel.

A council vehicle drove slowly, surveying the damage, the wood and rocks swept in overnight. On the walk to Torcross I saw the pond and hide which had seen no overnight visitors.

The rain was horizontal and I began to chill, my gloves damp sponges on their poles. To generate some heat I marched and soon the Path dipped beneath the embankment of the road, providing some protection from the wind.

A Sherman tank, then, at Slapton Sands, an obelisk, commemorated Operation Tiger and the hundreds of soldiers who died during the exercises. Tiger had been rehearsals for the D-Day landings in Normandy, a period fictionalised in Dartington graduate Mick Jackson's novel *Five Boys*.[117]

Some commentators still report that the deaths were largely due to German torpedoes and a lack of safety equipment.[118] [119] This, perhaps, reflects a desire for a history which is romantically tragic and in which we are blameless. In fact, hundreds of men from the landing craft were mown down by live ammunition in a friendly fire incident (a timing error) and this was kept a secret so as not to affect morale,[120] but not just morale. These failures, on beaches resembling Normandy, both jeopardised the actual invasion and caused embarrassment to senior military planners. "'The orders were, in the hospital, you will not ask these men anything," [91-year-old Paul Gerolstein said]. "You will not ask them anything, you will just take care of them.'"[121]

At Strete Gate, South Hams District Council cautioned 'Please be aware that naturists use the beach to the left of Strete Gate Toilets (when facing the sea)'. A very specific warning or promotion - but the naked truth was, the chances of such an encounter, under these weather conditions, were slim. Above Blackpool Sands an exploded aircraft rocket from Exercise Tiger hung from a Coast Path signpost.

In the Sands gift shop I dropped my bag, telling the attendant, 'If anyone tries to take that, please let them'. In the toilet I peeled off my waterproofs and took them through to the café to drip from the chair. A family stared at me intently as I dripped, and I smiled back like I didn't really mean it, so they busied themselves uncomfortably with their drinks.

In the event, nobody stole my bag. The onward journey was a circuitous route through country roads with no markers for kilometres. Absent signage made for insecurity but eventually a welcome acorn pointed me towards the sea, around Blackstone Point to Dartmouth Castle and St Petroc's Church. From there, tarred roads led to central Dartmouth where I sought an outdoors shop. Now beyond any social graces, I stripped to my shorts, left the wet gear in a pile in the cubicle, asked for the most waterproof trousers and jacket then paid for them. Next, I found a room for the night with a toilet, retrieved the keycode and entered through the cake shop. There was no heater so I hung my gear over doors and hooks, turning the room into a Bedouin, tent and switched on the fan. I left.

In a Thai takeaway the owner looked at me with concern and said, 'You want eat here? I can make table for you. I can make you English tea.' It was as though she knew I was going to seek shelter to eat. I hadn't looked in a mirror for some time.

'That's kind. Thank you.' I ate in the front of the shop on my own little gingham table with a porcelain plate, drinking tea from a cup and saucer. A message from Kenny: 'How's the walk going? Where will you be in the next couple of weeks? Do you realise you chose the Scottish League Cup Final for your fiftieth celebrations? I'll work something out, you eejit.'

As I left, the woman said, 'Enjoy your walk,' which stopped me in my tracks. I hadn't mentioned I was walking, and I had on my best clothes.

Fortified weed
Day 52. 31ˢᵗ October

The first ferry of the day took me to Kingswear. The town's coniferous woods had old-style rubber fire beaters and warning signs. Nobody was expecting anything too serious, not yet.

Beyond the woods a coast watchkeeper, an escapee from Birmingham, pointed me towards Brownstone Battery (1940), which still had rail tracks once used for moving explosives. In the mist I meandered on what I realised were horse tracks until, finally, a stream led me to the true Path where a horse stared with an innocent horse expression. Coleton Fishacre's woods were a beautiful blend of trees in green and brown and I realised autumn had been in hiding in the beautiful but desolate landscape of Cornwall.

Near Scabbacombe Sands a large group of walkers bound in the direction of Kingswear had stopped to rest.

'And where would you be trying to get to?' asked a woman, heedlessly sprawled on the damp grass.

'Berry Head. Is there somewhere with flat ground and shelter?'

An older bespectacled man looked up. 'There's a fort with flat ground. It might give some protection from the wind. You won't be bothered there.'

'You're walking the trail backwards? That's courageous.'

'We started with the principle that you keep the sea on your left but that didn't work, so now we have a book.' He held up a crude manila-coloured samizdat-style binding. 'Reverse-engineered from the real thing. Every instruction, backwards. Every left is right, every up is down.'

'And every hope, despair,' the woman added, taking the copy from him.

'Brilliant! Is that Berry Head?' I pointed at the next headland.

The older man laughed. 'Oh, no. You have that spur, then another, and then Berry Head.' The ghostly outline of Berry Head could just be seen on the horizon. 'It's a roller-coaster,' he chuckled. Had he been reading Paddy Dillon? Roller-coaster, of course, code for *give up all hope*.

'Coast roller,' the woman mumbled, as though in delirium.

'We only have one copy, so we take it in turns getting us lost,' he added. After a short break they stood, bowed in unison like an amateur dramatics group and we moved apart at a sluggish pace.

Man Sands was a beach squeezed between a pond and the sea which, in late afternoon, had become one. I found myself trapped with a dog walker on opposite sides of a tidal inlet joined to the lagoon. Knowing the area, he shouted instructions to me on using rocks as stepping-stones. We moved towards each other but in the end ran out of rocks and just smiled at each other across the expanse, our legs astride, water flowing underneath.

He shrugged, whispered 'Damn, this always happens' and stepped into the water. I followed suit. 'They plan a bridge behind that pool, but I don't see any sign of it happening soon. Good luck. Hope you have somewhere warm after this.' We resignedly splashed past one another.

The next hill was ridiculously steep. By the time I reached a ship's female figurehead eerily leaning seawards, the sky was beginning to darken. It was a tourist park on the edge of Brixham, and small children moved excitedly through the dark in orange-lit costume, led by parents with lanterns. Hallowe'en.

'Do you know where I can find water?' I called to one group.

'Follow us, we're just getting some ourselves.' The family were pale; they had that sallow appearance seen on estates or in 1970s Manchester bands. It was a look from too little sunlight, sick housing and budget nutrition. Still, they were happy and excited by the party spirit in the holiday camp. I stood outside their mobile home while the father filled my flask and Sigg bottle.

'Thanks very much. You're a life saver. Happy Hallowe'en.'

'Happy Hallowe'en,' the father and children said together, smiling shyly. I was grateful as this meant I could go straight to the fort. Children guided me to the Path where a sign advertised 'Luxury lodges for sale.' I looked back at the sad row of portable cabins and then at the photograph of suntans and luxuriance.

As I neared the stile to the country park and the rain began, two small figures dressed in purple approached. 'Are you walking far?' It was now dark; these women were clearly fearless.

'I'm hoping to go all the way. But near here tonight.'

'Great.' Hypnotic eyes stared from beneath the hood. 'You've come from Minehead?'

'It seems a long time ago.'

'A proper walker! It's really inspiring to see someone doing this. We're only doing it in pieces.'

'Keep all the pieces and you may be able to glue them back together. But please don't say it's inspiring. If anyone is inspired to repeat this, then I've committed a travesty.'

They smiled, shrugged and then, 'Well, good luck. Stay dry.' They resembled purple pixies as they waved goodbye in tandem and disappeared into the blackness, one whispering while the other scolded her for talking to the strange man.

The first fort looked most promising as it was far from the visitor centre. After the last dog walker drifted off, I pitched inside a ruined guardhouse and settled down to cook, to read and then to sleep.

The barking dog was the first indication that anything was wrong. It wasn't morning, or at least I was still in darkness. A torch shone directly onto the tent and there were voices.

'Yes, that's what they say.'

'How long?' Both voices were male. I stopped breathing.

'A few days, maybe a week.' If they were talking about me, then they were confused. Perhaps there was someone else taking refuge here and I had been mistaken for them. The torch was still on me. The dog growled.

'If someone's got nowhere to stay ...'

'Look how it's camouflaged. You wouldn't notice it if you weren't looking for it.' Why, then, were they looking for it? This was the first time I'd knowingly been spotted. Were they the authorities? Perhaps a crime had been committed and I was to be the scapegoat, the harmless hobo blamed for a local act of thuggery. Eventually the two left and I waited for the police, National Trust, Natural England or John Craven from *Countryfile* to ask me to leave. I was so stressed, mainly worrying that it might be a camera crew and national shame would follow, that I must have exhausted myself because I don't recall anything after that.

Conscious that there might be curious visitors, or dogs urinating on my ultralight pegs, I delayed breakfast and packed rapidly. To confirm my fears, while I finished striking camp a walker approached and checked on me. It was clear that she was wary but once she knew I was a walker she relaxed. *Just passing through.* Being a squatter now seemed somehow nobler.

Speaking of squatting, waste ground among gorse was a suitable place to do my business, with the islet of Cod Rock silhouetted by the rising sun. There is something life-affirming about going to the toilet with a spectacular view. Are you sitting comfortably? Then you're probably doing it wrong. In a survey of the greatest inventions of all time, the British public voted the flush toilet ninth, above the internal combustion engine and paper (the latter inexplicable as the bidet was not on the list – what did they intend to clean themselves with?). It's an indication of our revulsion of all things poo that we pollute our water in order to hide it.[122]

My life affirmed, I concealed the truth with my trowel then wound my way through the historical ruins and along the edge of Berry Head.

'Excuse me.' A dog walker. He was draped in the same shade of pale as the family at the camp and I noticed that his jacket was thinly quilted and frayed. 'Do the sticks help?'

'I used to think they were for older people, but then it occurred to me that I *was* one. If you're carrying a load or just on steep ground, they take a lot of the pressure from your legs. Try them.'

'I was always worried about tripping over the things but I'm finding walking more difficult each year. Arthritis.' He pointed downwards. The man took the sticks and made a few steps while the small dog ran around him. 'I might get some. Yes, they might help. I'd like to do more. Thanks. Well, good luck.' He gave the impression of having lost something but being unable to recall what it was. It was as though he was startled that his life had run off in an unintended direction while he had been attending to some mundane detail. The sense of this faded and frayed soul was to stay with me for a very long time. Perhaps he was on the brink of a restoration.

A small wooded area led to the outskirts of Brixham and the old stone Berry Head Hotel. Below me a woman walked up to the sign at the sea pool which read 'POOL CLOSED UNTIL MAY. DANGER KEEP OUT.' She irreverently dropped her towel over the sign, climbed into the waves and began doing laps.

Nearer the harbour, graffiti in giant spray-painted stencil font demanded 'LEGALISE FREEDOM'. Someone, but probably not the same magnolia oxymoron, had handwritten by hand faintly below '+ weed' which made so much more sense. As I photographed the wall, a woman walking a dog stopped and looked up. She was smiling, almost laughing. Her dress was sophisticated, with long blonde hair and knee length boots. Nobody that I knew. 'You stayed in the fort then?'

I had been exposed. 'Yes. How ...?'

'You don't know me, do you?'

'Should I?'

'We wore purple last night.'

'That was you? You live here?'

'My mother does. I live near Bristol. This is her dog,' she said, as though being caught in a bar with a man who was just her brother.

'Didn't your mother teach you never to talk to strangers?'

'At one time, but she was worse than me. We might be walking a bit of the path again today. It's put me in the mood.'

'I hope not *inspired.*'

'A little perhaps. Are you doing it for a charity or just for yourself?'

'A "rough sleep walk" for homelessness'.

'Sleepwalk?'

'Rough sleep ... walk.' And I gave my name.

'I'll look you up. Where are you heading today?'

'Food first then Torquay.'

'There's a cheap place on the waterfront.' She pointed across the harbour and started to walk off.

'Thanks. You are ...?'

She turned and walked backwards smiling, 'Rachel,' and then she was gone. My cousin, Rachel. As it happens, I do have a problem with sleepwalking but only when stressed. In the last months of work I destroyed a ceiling lamp believing it a concrete chute intent on burying us alive, as Quixote had cut wine-skins believing them a giant.

Brixham had a working, not a picture postcard, harbour. Two beautifully restored red-sailed trawlers, *Providence* and *Vigilance,* were moored. A controversial ruler, William of Orange watched over the harbour with an inscription 'ENGELANDS VRIJHEID DOOR ORANJE HERSTELD',[123] *England's freedom restored by Orange.* Plus weed. He was Dutch, and this was Brixham. Above me was Dutch Sophia's old flat where I had squandered so many evenings sampling wine made from sea cabbage or other unwanted vegetation which she had endeavoured to turn to alcohol that day. The air was thick with the past and ripe turbot.

I took a picture of William for Glasgow Kenny. If he never turned up it would be some consolation. It was the second orange defender I had met on the journey.

Beyond Brixham the Path crossed Churston Cove's pebble beach and then the shingle ridge of Elberry Cove with its ruined bathhouse. The cove has mention as Elbury Cove in one of Agatha Christie's reputedly cleverest plots, the Poirot mystery *The A.B.C. Murders.*[124] Reputedly because I had never read it. Beyond this, as the rain began, was Broadsands and its long row of beach huts.

'Do you want some coffee?' a voice came from one of the huts. Under a porch were two purple clad figures.

'Hello again. Thanks.' I unfolded my Swedish mug and we stood waiting for the rain to subside.

It turned out they were both teachers from near Bristol and regularly walked together. I tried not to read much into their matching leisure gear.

'I was in education once too, down here. I'm almost back home now.' As the words formed, they rang hollow. Little remained of where I once felt I belonged. The beach, the huts, the amusements. These places were familiar, but they were like pictures someone had shown me as a child. I wanted to believe in them, but they belonged to someone else now.

The rain showed signs of abating, so we couldn't use its excuse any longer.

'Come on Rach, we should be getting on.' They wished me luck and headed off up the cliff. Farewell pixies. It had been a good feeling, to almost walk with someone again. We parted and I let the gap between us widen.

The Path passed beneath the railway (Kingswear to Paignton) and climbed steps to a hillside. On the far side it dropped level with the track where, in Agatha Christie style, an engine came thundering out of the cutting, steam and smoke filling the air and passengers waving at me.

Goodrington Sands looked closed for the winter and I was so close to Paignton that I kept moving. Torbay appeared, stretching to the horizon, long but mercifully flat. Mags had checked into The Imperial Hotel in Torquay, a last-minute decision. She had suggested it as an option and I said I knew it and that it was good. Unbeknown to us, one of le Carré's career *washed-up* characters also booked the hotel in a novel published a fortnight earlier.[125] 'It's fabulous,' came Mags' message. 'There's a sea view.'

'Looking forward to seeing you with antibiotics,' the predictive text chose for me. *Anticipation.* I let her think I was infectious. Probably I was.

'TORQUAY The birthplace of Agatha Christie. English Riviera' a sign proclaimed. It didn't look much like a riviera to me, it looked more like the sea.

The Grand Hotel was a sentinel at the edge of town. My father had briefly been a linen porter at the Grand and once told me of the Agatha Christie Suite which had many rooms and its own foyer. 'If you looked at the dark carpet when the light was right you could make out the stylised shape of a dead body. You had to look closely,' he said, 'and I had difficulty - being colour blind - but once you knew it was there it was quite sinister.'

The room at The Imperial was stunning so I immediately proceeded to introduce it to my tent, sleeping bag and waterproofs. 'Oh, Oscar, what have you done? What's that smell?'

'Nothing. The room probably needs airing.'

She looked unconvinced. 'First thing in the morning they're gone, or you are!' She meant it.

We went to a nearby seafood restaurant and ate and drank until we were thrown out. The meal was Mags' belated birthday; it was great to see her.

Murder by public transport
Day 54. 2ⁿᵈ November

The Imperial was a favourite of Agatha Christie and it appeared as the Majestic Hotel in fictional St Loo (in *Peril at End House*[126]), the Majestic again in equally fictional Danemouth (in *The Body in the Library*[127]), and finally as itself in *Sleeping Murder.*[128] Certainly, it had lost none of its Victorian grandness and there were still numerous upper middle class candidates for slaughter.

Our first stop was Torre Abbey. It had both a poisonous plant garden and an Agatha Christie photographic exhibition, which suggested some degree of premeditation. The exhibition explored her troubled relationships, growing success as a writer and the difficulties that fame brought.

We stood at the Torquay Pavilion beneath a plaque of Agatha Christie. Every site seemed perfumed with the poisons of the writer, details of which I tactfully omitted in updates to Kristiina. One day she would return, if the experience of walking with me had not indelibly marked her.

I had arranged the location not realising that the Pavilion had been permanently closed for the last four years. We waited for Tony and Sue beside its heavily corroded steel girders. When they arrived with their hounds we found a pub that allowed large dogs. Strictly speaking, they didn't actively object to the dogs, perhaps feeling intimidated by Tony. Sue carried a cardboard box the size of a human head.

'This is your belated birthday present from us all,' said Sue as she handed Mags the box. Inside was a lampshade, beautiful gold print on crimson textile. An intricate design of Sue's showed an old stylised fox startled by a flying pheasant under a crescent moon. Somehow it seemed to represent the Coast Path, the landscape and the birds though I had yet to see a fox (a hunt hardly counts, it subtracts). When backlit, the gold of the lampshade mysteriously disappears, the scene becoming a sea of red. Mags loved it.

We drank and talked about our last meeting - when we had taken the round trip by steam train, bus and boat - and what had happened since. Then, as the dogs needed to be walked, we said goodbye for the last time. It was painful and, with everything that has happened, more painful still on reflection.

Forevermore Agatha Christie will be synonymous with train problems. Like the Burgh Island Great Western fiasco, we were destined not to arrive by train. In the morning the station's iron gates were chained and padlocked, the steam engine unattended.

'Oh no, does this mean we can't go to Greenway?' Mags looked so disappointed it broke my heart.

'No, there is always a way.' That said, I predicted that the way would be pricey. Still, we'd saved for a rainy day and it was raining. I made a call, walking out of earshot. Afterwards, I walked back, hanging my shoulders. 'No good, sorry. I guess because it's Sunday.'

'Oh noooo. I was so looking forward to this. I suppose we can finish Torre Abbey or go to the pictures.'

'I suppose so. Still, it would have been good to see her house.'

A man with dark sunglasses and a formal jacket walked up to us and leaned in. 'Mr Burton?'

'Yes?'

'Your taxi.' He pointed to a silver sedan beside the station entrance.

'You found one!' She was smiling and didn't care that I had duped her. My marriage proposal had followed similar rules – *what's the worst thing I could tell you?* If you first hint at a possible infidelity or murder, a wedding sounds a reasonable proposition. You can have that for nothing.

The journey was cheaper than our train tickets would have been, though of course we had no old-world arrival. Some notable items belonging to Christie in the mansion were a Motorola mobile phone (a brick larger than Michael Douglas's in the film *Wall Street)*, a skull biscuit jar and a large wooden lavatory. Christie had insisted on taking the loo with her when she travelled. Was it even plumbed in, or did her business simply flow out into the neighbouring Egyptian marketplace? The ninth technological wonder of the world indeed.

The prize was the collection of fine first editions, first impressions, of all of Christie's novels housed in a glass cabinet. Alas, the cabinet was locked, and the Motorola brick was downstairs. The house itself featured in a number of these novels: *Five Little Pigs*[129], *Dead Man's Folly*[130], and *Ordeal by Innocence*[131] although others were clearly inspired by it.

Greenway's garden reached down to the River Dart and a boathouse/bath house where exotic fruit, with the appearance of rambutans, hung from trees. The weather was warm and sunny, so we strolled along the river until it was time to wait for our taxi.

From Paignton we took the bus to Torquay, ate together for the last evening, and then collected our bags. Our taxi failed to arrive so we hurried to the quay and waited for a bus. As it was Sunday service, Mags missed her train. I didn't mind as it meant we had more time together, using our bodies to keep each other warm on the platform. Mags had been with me at the beginning of my walk and again near its end. Now she was going, and I could already feel the coldness of the small space she was leaving behind. The train drew in and I waved her goodbye.

I made my way to the flat where I was staying that evening and pressed the buzzer. There was no answer so I made a call. 'I'm outside.'

After a while a familiar voice called from twenty metres down the road. 'What are you doing down there, you plonker?' It was Hana, laughing at me. It had been some years since I had visited.

'All these grand Georgian townhouses look the same to me. Hey, I really appreciate this. It was this or the park, and city dwellers aren't appreciative of itinerant campers.'

'It's good to see you, mister.'

'It's good to see you, Hana.'

After dinner, bygone times began to intrude as they often do for old friends who meet after a hiatus. The past is a comforting drug to which all forward-thinking people eventually succumb.

Hana had old world values, though in reality she was a bit of an anarchist when it came to politics and relationships. And driving. She didn't recognise many authorities, though she appreciated kindness. Kindness was perhaps something we hadn't always shown each other, but we were never malicious. When Hana had, for example, locked me in a car boot it was only because I asked her to in order that I might change an infrared film in my camera. That she left me there to chill for some time I attributed to forgetfulness. In reality it may have been something I had said.

Despite the occasional indoor fireworks there was always a special bond between us, and we never lost touch. At least, I never did. I suspected that if I didn't keep turning up like a bad penny, Hana would probably never contact me again. Still, she was always happy to hear from me. At least, that's what she told me when I chose to ask.

Before going to bed Hana helped me weigh myself with and without my pack. I was 10 kilograms lighter than when I had begun. My pack was 25 kilos. The silver mane had been right all along when he had picked up my pack and mentally weighed it outside Falmouth. When I explained this to Hana she said, without thinking, 'Impressive. A true gentleman is someone who knows how to measure the weight of your bag without scales. But doesn't.'

I sat on my folding cot, looking down on Torquay and contemplated the time that had passed and my momentum in kilogram metres per second. My bag and I were 25kg and 63kg respectively, moving at an average of one metre per second. *Torquay in Devon, eight-seven. Two fat ladies, eighty-eight. Bingo!*

'That's just wrong,' I heard Hana saying from the next room, 'Torquay's not in Devon. It's in Torbay'.

FIVE: This Must Surely be the End

Then there were four
Day 56. 4ᵗʰ November

Hana and I said our farewells, hugged and I made my way down to the quay and the Imperial where the Path continued. The town echoed with the faint footsteps of the past, and now so did this hotel without Mags. You should never go back.

In a National Coast Watch Institution station I memorised the different types of boat by their silhouettes, but on leaving I again forgot which was a yawl, and which a ketch. The Sloop was again the pub on the road to Newton Abbot, *The Cutter* just an Echo & the Bunnymen song.

At Meadfoot was a curved white vision of the future as viewed myopically from the sixties. It rose from the broccoli-head trees on Marine Drive, towering above Basil Fawlty's *hoi polloi*. The building's curve ensured that no apartment overlooked another, each alone, a rock, with equitable views. At the foot of the hill a man sat on a bench leaning on his stick. His open expression told me I could sit beside him, which I needed to do.

'I've always wondered what that building was,' I said.

Elderly and slightly hunched, he wore dark sunglasses and for a moment I wondered whether he could see me. 'That's *Kilmorie*, private apartments, gated community. Though, maybe not so communal. It's been there for as long as I remember. You walking?'

'I'm trying. Since early September.'

'I used to walk.' He nodded to himself. 'Now it's only as far as here and then I'm exhausted.' He smiled. 'Used to walk a lot. Just can't manage now. I've got the stick. It helps.'

'This is nice though, right here.' The weather was good, the sky blue.

'True, I can't complain. Can't complain. You're young and fit though, you must be to carry that.'

That made me laugh: *young*. 'It's better not to have to carry it. I need my sticks too.' We sat in silence for a while and then he broke it.

'I wish I were going with you.' It choked me to hear this from a stranger. He wished he was going with me. It was a wonderful and terrible thing. Wonderful, because he felt he would, even without knowing me, a leap of faith. Terrible that he couldn't. We shook hands and he held mine between both of his for a very long time. Even now when I think of him, it stabs in my chest.

At Thatcher's Rock an antique shelter gave me refuge from the rain. Somewhere in my lockup was an infrared photograph of the Rock, dating from the 1990s, the pines luminescent white. It was the same roll of film that led to me being locked in the boot of Hana's car (months apart but on my salary I made a film last).

Above Anstey's Cove I was stopped in the rain. The man told me of a friend in his seventies who had walked the path several times as a whole and knew all the shelters. 'He carries just a sleeping bag. The advantage of local knowledge. One of the shelters is ahead of you. You must check it. Someone is there now but I don't think they're walking.'

As described, under a concrete viewing shelter, on the side by the sea, was a purple square-footprint tent. Some possessions had been laid neatly on the bench beside it, a sign of a sound and ordered mind (or obsessiveness). There was no sign of the owner. It was a beautiful spot, and eminently affordable for someone with no income. It was almost enviable compared to a shop doorway. Not wishing to intrude, I silently wished them luck and moved on.

The Palace Hotel woods hid Redgate beach and bay, inaccessible - ruined by rockfalls and permanently closed. The Path descended into Oddicombe Beach and the Cary Arms. The Cary Arms was not a cry for the US Second Amendment. It was a pub, named after the Cary family of Torre Abbey and Clovelly. The first Lucius Cary, the 2nd Viscount of Falkland, had married the improbably named Lettice Moryson which is, in itself, surely a sign of his working-class credentials in this age of low budget shopping.[132] The marriage had disappointed his father.[133] His father had the last laugh though as, on his death Lucius inherited the title of Viscount and an associated estate which was mortgaged up to the hilt.[134]

The current head of the family was also Lucius Cary. His reputation as a man of the people was tainted somewhat by the Parliamentary 'duck house' expenses scandal of 2009. Politicians of all the major parties and some minor ones had claimed allowances which were either illegal or at least hard to justify, even if they were within the rules for Parliamentary expenses.

'I didn't do it to make £125,000', Cary explained, 'I claimed the expenses in order to be able to meet the expenses of my life.'[135] You could call it a sort of Cary grant. In his defence, he remarked: 'You might say I'm an impoverished peer. My family over many hundreds of years have been noted for their poverty.'[136] Excessive expenses had repeated on the Viscounts generationally in the fashion of Edmund Blackadder.

By Stoketeignhead the sun was too low for me to continue. A distant carpark was visible on the Teignmouth Road, and there were hoof prints nearby. It wasn't good to perch where a farmer and a herd of cattle might trample me in the morning.

At the end of the field closest to the sea was a low wire fence and on the cliff side of the fence was flat ground sheltered by a spreading tree. I wedged the tent between two roots, a sapling and the tree trunk. These would at least stop it from sliding towards the cliff edge. Trees make for a more stable cliff, but should it be the tree's time to fall I would no doubt keep it company.

It had been a good day; only a little rain, and some brief but memorable human contact. Lights of boats anchored in Labrador Bay gently swayed far below my cliff. I had my own small lantern to read by. The sailors would just see an illuminated green bauble beneath a precariously positioned tree. It was a contented and self-contained bauble, proof that you can survive without the multiple lifebuoys we cling to in life. I slept.

Dry gear in the morning was a welcome change. A few overnighters in the car park were visible through the undergrowth as I performed my morning ablutions. In making my hole I was careful not to dig through to the bottom of an overhang. I didn't fancy dying with my trousers down.

Undulating fields overlooking the Teign estuary led to woods and then Shaldon. I had assumed that the Teign Ferry would have ceased operation so was surprised to see a yellow flag and A-board 'Please queue here.' I queued by myself, made a call, and a black and white boat started to move across the gap. From the moment I was aboard, the skipper and pilot, Greg Allen, gave a lightning-fast description of his health and safety responsibilities while carefully steering the ferry to Teignmouth. 'The MCA will probably cripple us.'

'The MCA?' The wind was icy. I pulled my jacket tight.

'Maritime and Coastguard Agency. They're revising regulations on passenger vessels. I'm all for safety and we take it very seriously indeed. We won't go out if it's unsafe. But they're now insisting on vessel survivability. Survivability! You can see this boat. To make this survive a collision we'd be building a completely different boat. All the older boats and ships will breach the new rules. Those working on, or for, the boats will be out of work.'

Prospects sounded grim for all the small ferry operators I had used on my journey – the man with the injury, the small ferries in Helford and Place. We came into shore. 'I hope things work out for you. Good luck.' As an afterthought I asked if there was a good café for breakfast and he recommended a place not far from the landing point.

The café was close to poet John Keats' house. He may not even have resided in that particular house. He had stayed in Devon for only two months while his brother was ill. By letter he wrote to a friend, 'the abominable Devonshire Weather - by the by you may say what you will of Devonshire: the truth is, it is a splashy, rainy, misty, snowy, foggy, haily, floody, muddy, slipshod county.'[137] So much improvement in a mere 200 years.

The café was cosy and had a gorgeous menu with food I could eat. I told the cook that the ferryman had recommended them and then I casually mentioned an error on their menu's ingredients of a famous sausage (I thought it might have been important).

'Are you sure?' she asked.

'One-hundred per cent. I'm funny with ingredients. If there's one thing I do know about her though, she loved to put flour in her sausages - she made a point of it.' The cook looked at me with concern and then ran over to the phone to make a phone call. She gave directions to waiting staff who began to collect the menus from tables.

There followed a conversation with the supplier, and it became more heated as it progressed. I listened to one side of a conversation, the cook calmly navigating a river of disclaimers and carefully placed obfuscation while I ate a delicious breakfast and checked my route. 'So, what you're saying is the stock we hold *does contain it*, or ... *it doesn't?*' After some more clarification there was an exchange of pleasantries and the receiver came down heavily.

When I left the café the staff looked up from the beautiful menus they were systematically defacing with felt tip marker pens. They waved me cheerfully goodbye and I felt a pang of guilt for my careless remark. Some new age customer complaining of IBS may have been less painful.

At Smugglers Lane I looked back on crumbling red cliffs, the concrete breakwater stretching back to Teignmouth. A couple with day packs stood at a bus stop looking at a map and debating directions. They crossed the road and disappeared. When I reached them, they were seated beside a field in Holcombe but were too deep in conversation to chat to me. Some time later I rested on a grassed mound in the sun, and they caught up with me.

'Hello. You must be walking the whole path.' She had blonde hair and her walking partner had a mop of white hair. They were a good-looking couple, and had mastered the rare art of talking to strangers. They clearly weren't from London.

'How did you know?'

'It's all the baggage. Either that or you were a homeless person. I wasn't sure whether to offer you money.' She was clearly the mischievous one.

'I don't look homeless though.'

He chipped in, 'No comment. I'm Andy, this is Kim.'

'Hello Andy and Kim. I'm Oscar.'

'You're going our way. Do you want to walk together?' Kim asked without consulting her partner.

'Yes, if you don't mind me tagging along. At the ferry I'm joining someone who I met walking the Path, back in Tintagel. He was too fast for me.'

Kim and Andy had both recently retired – she from nursing, he from firefighting – and were enjoying walking as an occupation, although not always together. Having a car, both a convenience and burden, made their pattern of walking complex. Often Andy would drop Kim off at one end of a Path section, and he would drive to the other. They would then walk towards one another, meeting in the middle. At the midpoint they would eat together and then continue, walking away from each other in the afternoon. The one arriving at the car would then drive to the beginning of their route and collect the other.

It was a novel method, but it felt a little lonely at times, Kim explained. 'One day the weather was awful. I was walking along those sand dunes at Hayle. Bloody awful wind and rain, and the dunes were exhausting. Eventually I called Andy to pick me up in one of those holiday camps. Mexican Towans I think. Why is it called *Mexico* Towans? I never saw any Mexicans.'

'Nobody knows,' I lied.

'Anyway, Mexico Towans was horrible. I just couldn't go on any longer. Those *dunes*.'

'Yes, I had much the same experience. When eventually I found the flatter beach there were warnings of quicksand.'

We walked on - Dorothy, the Tin Man and the Scarecrow along the yellow brick road to Emerald City, or as it was known locally, Exmouth. We were doing this by instinct; nobody questioned why. 'Sometimes we have to do a thing in order to find out the reason for it. Sometimes our actions are questions, not answers.' So wrote John le Carré in *A Perfect Spy*.[138]

The final scenes of the BBC television series of *A Perfect Spy* (broadcast in 1987) were shot on the promenade of Dawlish, which we were entering. When I had visited my younger sister at her home near the sea wall, the place felt familiar to me though I didn't know why at the time. Le Carré's protagonist Magnus Pym was staying in a B&B on the seafront of a town that the inhabitants had all deserted. Off-season Dawlish made a perfect location. Towards the end of the story, Pym fled here after his father's funeral, to escape not only the authorities but also his past. Compiling his biography, or confession, Pym begins to unwrite himself.

'He returned to his desk and took up his pen. Every line written is a line behind me. You do it once, then die.'[139]

Re-inventing yourself in different settings is a form of deception – but if you are young enough the lie becomes your truth. Pym was a skilled liar and he had chosen Dawlish to disappear, to write out his final confession knowing that his keeper would be his confessor.

The literary world of le Carré is littered with outsiders probably because he felt something of an imposter in his own education and early career. A cod organisational psychologist once suggested to me that a particularly chameleon-like personality type can be explained by repeated disruption in the early years – parents in military or diplomatic service for example (or in and out of prison, as was le Carré's). I wasn't wholly convinced. By age twelve I had attended nine schools, becoming expert at silently mouthing school songs I knew none of the words to. And I'm as honest as the day is long.

'We better get a move on, if we want to get to Exmouth before dark. The days are getting shorter,' said Andy.

Kim, Andy and I walked along roads until we found Dawlish Warren. 'Do we need to stop for a coffee?' Kim asked.

I took this as a signal that *she* wanted to stop for coffee. Andy understood that she wondered if we wanted to stop for coffee.

'I'd like to keep walking. Keep going?' he asked, but it wasn't really a question; he marched on. The road skirted a swampy nature reserve and Kim pointed out a nice pub in vain. We watched the pub recede into the distance as we marched on.

At last we came close to Starcross Ferry, so I sent a message to Paul. He had finished his walk so long ago I couldn't recollect when it had been.

The three of us were approaching the pier when a large figure, dressed identically to me, ran towards us, arms wide like a football coach.

'Paul, am I glad to see you!' He gave me a bear hug.

'You're thinner,' he said, as though he expected this. He was taller than I remembered. I introduced Kim and Andy.

'We're doing the Path too, in random sections,' Kim explained.

'Look,' Paul suggested immediately, 'if you need me to drop you somewhere I can. Or tomorrow after your walk I can drop you back to your car.' That was him, already offering assistance and picking up strays.

'That's good of you,' Andy said. 'We're okay today taking the train but yes, tomorrow that would help.' We exchanged phone numbers and then said goodbye. It had been good walking with others spontaneously. Their train arrived as we got into the car. I had been expecting a Morris Minor or a rusted white van, but Paul drove a BMW Sports Coupé with a dashboard like an airliner.

'How do you feel?'

'The pains migrate. One moment in my hip, the next my shoulder or shin.' He just nodded.

We drove around the estuary and talked about the final days of Paul's walk. By the time he reached the finish line it was dark, but he was met by his partner and friends. It must have been exhilarating. He had raised three times more money than I had. What a great achievement. It occurred to me that my own finish might be a damp squib.

He dropped me at the far side of the estuary on the Exmouth promenade so that I could use the last bit of light to reach our rendezvous in Budleigh Salterton. The rain began five minutes after I had said goodbye to the warm BMW.

Past a rusting metal hull shaped into a shelter, the Path squeezed between a mobile home campsite and a military firing range. Red flags in the sunset served as a warning, should the sound of shooting be insufficient. It was an odd contrast of holiday making and defence. Soldiers were silhouetted against the setting sun while elderly residents chatted on the lawn, unconsciously raising their voices above the sound of gunfire which carried across the water on the cool air.

It was dark as I descended the track towards Budleigh Salterton's promenade, the silhouette of a man moving towards me.

'Sorry mate', said Paul. 'I saw the rain start as I dropped you off. It's a bit further than I remembered.'

We drove to a semi-rural hotel. 'You okay with this? If you're too knackered we can just get food.'

'No, it will be an experience.' So I found myself stripping discreetly in the spa of a hotel and showering until the water ran clear. Then I joined Paul in the steam room.

Two other men sat at the far end. I was ordinarily self-conscious about my body, but as I caught myself in a mirror I was horrified by the signs of infection on my skin and the way my ribs protruded. The Coast Path had eaten most of what muscle I'd owned; a first step in my irresistible descent into decrepitude.

'Oscar, this is Pete. Pete, Oscar.'

'I've heard a lot about you. How are you holding up?' Pete was wiry, muscular. There was something about him, his posture and the way he addressed me, which suggested he might be Army. 'I walked for a bit with Paul, just a day, and I'm not sure I could do it.'

'Oh, I think you could. I can barely walk. I really couldn't do it at Paul's pace. Not in twenty-seven days.'

Pete leaned in. 'So, Oscar, where have you been stopping?'

'Last night was a cliff south of Shaldon. I had to get the cliff side of a fence on account of cows.' I looked to Paul and he nodded.

'Yes, you get what you're given. Then you have to deal with the reality that the ground is uneven. I've spent whole nights climbing to the top of the tent. Shall we take a few laps of the pool?' Pete left first and then we hobbled out. Paul also had a limp and he explained that he had suffered a complex fracture followed by endless surgery. The only time it had not been uncomfortable was when he had been walking. Now that he wasn't, the pain had returned.

We dined, courtesy of Paul's membership, to distant explosions lighting up the sky with rainbow colours. Of course, it was Guy Fawkes' night; I'd almost missed it. It felt like the fireworks were for us, so we drank a toast to our two journeys.

Paul and I drove to a farm on the edge of Ottery St Mary where a mobile unit at the rear had a bare bed and kitchen area. I rolled out my sleeping bag against the chill and boiled water. The toilet block was icy, but at least I no longer needed to have a shower. As is the local tradition on Guy Fawkes Night, people were setting themselves on fire with flaming barrels of tar in the nearby village.

In the morning we drove to Pete's house where he and his partner were waiting with breakfast. Then we drove to the beach, accompanied by Paul's dog Stan.

'We've had some terrible weather. Have you kept dry? Dry sac?' Paul asked.

'Pardon?' The intimacy of the steam room came back to me and I felt my face redden.

'Waterproof bags for your clothes?'

'Yes, well I'm wet but the kit isn't. I changed my waterproofs in Dartmouth as they were just turning to sponges.'

At Budleigh I left my main pack in his boot and we walked together. Stan ran ahead as Paul threw the ball. On the far side of the estuary, sunlight glimmered through stunted trees. A field of kale appeared like gigantic broccoli heads emerging from a ground mist. We looked back towards Budleigh across the water and Paul sighed.

'When I got here I was flying. People were ferrying my pack and I just wanted to cover the distance.' Paul had realised he could finish the walk for his niece's birthday. She had been the reason he had raised the money, the reason he had done the walk. She wouldn't be there for the finish, but it was as much for his brother. It was a generous thing to do.

'I don't think I can go much further; I need to get back to work,' he apologised.

'Thanks for coming with me, Paul. And thanks for last night, for helping me cross and for the spa.'

'Hey, I wish I could do more. You might have a chance to meet your two friends. Give me a bell and tell me where you get to. I'll get your pack to you.'

Far beyond a ruined observation station were three red stacks of Triassic period rock in the sea. I climbed uphill through woods towards two successively higher cliffs. The helicopter could be heard long before it was visible. It hovered below the cliff, metres from the waves. At regular intervals it moved to my eye level then returned to the sea, as though practising a sea rescue. By the time I reached the top there were rescue services in harnesses, and uniformed police. A cross-services simulation. One approached me.

'What's the exercise?' I asked.

'I'm afraid it's not an exercise. Someone drove off there.'

'Off?' He nodded to towards the cliff. Deep tyre tracks stretched from the edge to my feet. The wet earth of a hillock was ploughed by the impact.

The police officer's voice came as a deep rumble but it didn't register.

'Sorry?' I was still looking at the track marks and the crushed bushes at the cliff edge, and I felt faint.

'Are you walking the Coast Path?' he asked.

'Yes.'

'Well, then as you're already here,' he thought aloud while considering what to do with me. 'You should keep going. They're stopping people coming up at the other side, but they'll let you through. Try to stay away from the edge.' I wasn't sure how I would manage to obey that. There was one path, but it wasn't the time to get into a discussion.

'Okay. Sorry.' Gradually the scene made sense, the harnesses and the helicopter, all the different emergency services. My feet were in the trail of evidence. Once I had come down from the cliff I looked at a photograph I had taken of the helicopter and then I saw it – a black mark at the foot of the cliff, a smudged life. It was an easy mistake to make, to confuse this with a harmless practice run. *Post hoc ergo copter prop.*

In town the road was blocked by emergency services and the helicopter had landed on a grassed area. A uniformed group were laughing – gallows humour. Messages from Kim told me that they were in the Fort Café on the promenade and that I should join them.

'They let you through then? Andy's just ordered breakfast.'

'You know what this Path is?'

'No, what?'

'Death. If it's not shipwrecks, it's drownings, people or whole villages washed away by the sea, planes and helicopters crashing in poor visibility, lifeboat rescue disasters and cars driving from cliffs.'

'I suppose there is a lot of it. Three days ago a couple on the Path ahead were walking on the beach and they were washed into the sea by a freak wave. She made it back, he didn't.'

It is difficult to imagine how in reasonably calm conditions this could happen. Someone you know is there one moment and gone the next.

None of us were carrying much that day but we left town feeling a weight. We traversed the cliffs towards Weston Mouth, thin cloud with few breaks meaning we were not at risk of overheating. As Kim was speeding ahead, I was able to spend more time speaking to Andy about fire and some of the recent disasters the country had seen.

'What people don't realise is that everything is flammable. Even concrete burns - at the right temperature.'

'But some things are better fuel than others?'

'Yes, that's true. It's just that people want simple explanations and they want to lay the blame at a single cause. Usually there are many problems which contribute to these disasters.' I could see that.

As we rounded a bend we noticed Kim's head protruding over a hillock. She stood and slid herself back into her trousers.

'Were you taking a wee?' I asked.

'I'm afraid so. I expected you two to take longer to catch up. Desperate,' she stated without shame.

Soon we strayed onto the subject of Brexit, and there was a palpable tension. We were on opposite camps, I knew that, but in reality the whole country was and, regardless of who was pulling the strings, it was foolhardy to make enemies of half the country. Not unless we all wanted to go up in flames.

'How do you deal with cows?' Kim asked. 'Sometimes they can be quite aggressive.' Was she deliberately changing the subject?

'I sing. I sing *Misty*,' I said. My version of Garner and Burke's *Misty* was reserved for the bulls, cows and sheep. 'I love Johnny Mathis's voice. My version makes his version sound so much better. Usually the cows just stare at me, insensible.' Of course, my intention was that they weren't surprised by my approach as they would hear me coming; I was made larger with my voice (and backpack) and the sound was at least gentle, if not beautiful. The song is unquestionably a tearjerker, if occasionally for the wrong reasons.

'Any reason that song in particular?' She looked concerned.

'It was one of my mother's favourites, so I remember the words, it was played so often,' I explained.

'Oh,' and Kim fell silent, walking on. It was odd behaviour, but I put it down to being preoccupied.

At Branscombe Mouth, Kim and I were talking and distracted when Andy went on ahead. At a gate the sign clearly pointed through some mobile homes rather than up to the cliffs, so we walked between the homes until reaching a wooded way. At a sign marked *Path to Beer*, Kim asked: 'Do you think Andy went over the top?'

'I don't hold any grudges about Brexit, both sides were a disaster.'

'No, I mean do you think he went over the top of this cliff?'

'Oh. It does seem strange that we haven't reached him. Would he normally wait?'

'Sometimes he would, though we often walk separately. I suppose we'll meet again.' There was no phone reception as we moved on through the undercliffs. The trees were very tall with hanging moss and liana-like parasites.

We asked a large and jovial group walking towards Branscombe Mouth, 'have you seen a man walking along here alone?'

A white-haired man declared 'We haven't passed anyone. Where would he be heading?'

'Towards Beer. I've lost my husband.'

'It happens to us all dear,' a woman giggled. 'If we see him, we'll let him know where you are.'

As we moved off Kim said, 'I don't know what she meant by that. She's been watching too many films, silly twit.'

It was after the forest, at Beer Head, that Andy appeared behind us out of breath.

'I realised you weren't following so I doubled back and saw the sign through the woods. So strictly speaking I've walked this section twice.'

'Well done,' we both congratulated him.

In Beer we stopped to decide on the destination. 'It's getting dark, so stop here or go on to Seaton?' Andy asked.

'I'm happy. Don't want it to end,' said Kim smiling. I felt the same; I was enjoying their company.

A local offered instructions on walking the coastal route to Seaton. 'Go down to the sea down those steps.' He pointed towards an area in darkness. 'At the bottom, stand on the manhole cover and look across towards Seaton. If you can see the shingle continuously you should be okay.'

The light was gone when we descended the steps. 'Do you see a manhole?' Andy shuffled in the dark.

'You mean the sewer access cover?' I asked.

'I haven't seen a sewer access cover or a manhole. Oh dear, I wonder if we should go back.' It was too dark to see Kim's expression, though I imagined she was smiling. We bumped into one another standing on what was left of the steps.

'In any case it's too dark to see the shingle but the reflection on the water looks a long way off. Let's chance it,' Andy said as he marched ahead, covering considerable ground. Kim and I struggled on the shingle, heading always towards the lights of Seaton.

After some time a figure on the beach came into view and it wasn't Andy. 'Do you think they're walking towards us?' Kim asked in the dark.

'Could be. They're very big.'

Andy had stopped in front of the figure who now seemed massive in silhouette.

'Perhaps we should hold back in case whoever it is tries to kill Andy,' I suggested.

We caught up, our feet digging into the pebbles. 'I've brought your pack, Oscar,' Paul shouted. 'I've found somewhere for you to kip.' On the promenade we made our way past beach huts. 'Look, some of them don't have locks.' He opened one up and shone the light from his phone inside. It was clean.

'You think it will be safe?' Kim was peering in.

'I can lock it.'

'But the lock is on the outside.'

'I have a plan.'

The Vault Bar on the corner looked lively so we went inside. Paul engaged a few customers and staff in the story of our various journeys. It felt like an ending. Being on a high, I pushed the thought of tomorrow, being alone again, from my mind.

'That's weird,' I said, looking at an alert on my phone.

'What's weird?' Andy leaned across to see my screen.

'The team at the café in Teignmouth donated to the walk. They left a smiley face, yet they didn't even know who I was.'

'We might be able to explain. Yesterday, after we left you, we went there for food on your recommendation. It was good. They remembered the issue with the menus. I guess Kim sold you to them.' Andy smiled. A nice gesture.

'You'll be crossing Golden Cap soon. We did that recently. It's a really nice bit.' Kim looked excited for me.

'We probably need to be getting back, so you'll be on you own to the end,' warned Andy. We lapsed into silence and finished our drinks.

Paul broke the tension. 'Let's find you some grub. You've got a long night ahead in a cold shed.'

We drove slowly, Andy leaning out the window as though seeking illicit substances. He shouted to a man drinking in the street, asking if there was a chip shop nearby.

'Aye, there's one down there,' he pointed, 'but it's a bit minteh.'

'Thanks.' He wound the window up. 'A bit minty? What do you think he meant? Minty chips?'

Kim: 'He sounded northern.'

'Pricey? A mint,' I offered.

'That makes sense,' agreed Andy.

The menu was relatively exotic – swordfish, blue grenadier, that sort of fare. I waited in the shop for fifteen minutes while their engine idled outside. 'Sorry,' I said as the car door opened. 'Haute cuisine takes time.'

Andy, Paul, Kim and I embraced on the promenade and they readied to depart. 'Enjoy your minty chips' Paul shouted as they drove off waving.

I scurried along the promenade through the rain to the beach hut. The small padlock that I had dropped in the post office in Lynton had finally proved essential. There were two things I had carried to no purpose until now: that yellow padlock and a shoestring.

A couple of things played on my mind that night. One was being locked in. The other was being set on fire while locked in. Perhaps also being forklifted onto a flatbed truck bound for Scarborough. But it was simple for someone with a bicycle lock or padlock to trap an occupant inside what was essentially a garden shed. There was sufficient hatred of those without fixed abode for the risk to be real.

Checking first that I was not observed, I slid my pack into the hut then locked the door open with the padlock. Someone approached, walking their dog, so I stood at the railings watching the half-moon descend through clouds. It was now raining heavily. The stranger said *hello*, walked by and moved up the ramp towards town. The coast clear, I stepped inside, slipped the shoelace through the loop of the padlock and brought the loose ends inside the beach hut. These I tied to my walking sticks, pressing them across the doorway so that, with everything taut, the door held shut but was easily opened in an emergency. The shoelace, if cut by an intruder, would send the sticks clattering to the floor and wake me.

Homelessness, I reflected as I crawled into my bag, generates a range of human emotion in the same person. Pity, of course. A desire to protect and assist, certainly. Cries of injustice and social inequity, likely. That the government has failed in its domestic economic policies, undoubtedly. Insecurity at having a stranger in your stairwell or doorway, inevitably. And *it's been six weeks, can I please have my couch back!*

I ate my bourgeois fish and chips and thought of the days that had passed, of Paul ferrying me around the Exe, meeting Pete in the spa and walking with Paul, Kim and Andy, just not all at the same time.

My sleeping bag lay diagonally to avoid two determined drips from the roof. It would be fine as long as I didn't move during the night. Did any midnight lovers, I wondered, notice a gently purring beach hut as they strolled the promenade?

Lost weekend
Day 59. 7ᵗʰ November

The hut was left as I had found it. Railings cast long bars on the promenade as the sun rose above distant clouds under a pale blue sky. Though the air was cold I knew this was going to be a beautiful day. The day was to be a journey with no deviation, the Path trapped by cliffs on either side.

I talked to strangers, said good morning to a gaping fish-bush sculpture and moved lightly along the seafront. My present life skimmed the edges of respectable society, never quite in, never quite out.

Across the little harbour spanned Axmouth Old Bridge, built in 1877. It is the oldest standing entirely concrete bridge in England,[140] possibly the world. Though, of course the Romans cleverly built the dome of the Pantheon in 125 CE and that still stands. Bastards.

Beyond a golf course the Path reached fields, where I found a sign: 'Please note that it takes approximately 3½ - 4 hours to walk to Lyme Regis. The terrain can be difficult and walking arduous.

There is no permitted access to the sea or inland along this stretch of the path.' *Are you in or out?*

A sudden transition from field to forest track signalled the Undercliff. This was the site of many landslips, which became grassland and then, over time, woodland. The landslip of 1839 was dramatic, rapid, and the resulting terrain quickly became a tourist attraction. It had been used for crops and grazing sheep but with continued disuse various species of plant grew. The land constantly shifts. Most recently, Christmas to New Year 2013 saw a large collapse which effectively closed the Undercliff and diverted the Coast Path inland for two years.

There were few places on the Path with forest, and this was the most spectacular. If you were not told that it was Dorset you could imagine being in the sub-tropics. It is the place where Jeremy Irons and Meryl Streep met secretly in Harold Pinter's film version of John Fowles' *The French Lieutenant's Woman* (1981).[141] The film was famously passed over by the American Academy as punishment for humiliating the celebrity presenters, who mispronounced its title five times during one awards evening.

This forest with its humid microclimate is probably the closest Britain comes to rainforest. The quiet of the still air amplified my tinnitus and, with the rushing of blood in my ears, it pulsed like the synchronous hissing of cicadas among the trees. That's when I knew what this reminded me of; it reminded me of where I had grown up.

As teenagers in Australia, me and my group of friends would occasionally gather during long weekends and take a train to the Blue Mountains on a 'red rattler', the noisy red train rolling stock. There was no particular reason for it. Why does anyone choose to go walking? We wanted to be with nature, to escape suburbia and to bond in that particularly awkward male way (to bond while not acknowledging it).

We had decided to avoid our usual destination, Red Hands Cave.[142] It wasn't that we didn't like it; it was an amazing place, an

ancient place with meaning. It was a cave with hand outlines left
by indigenous Australians. Darug Aboriginal groups know it as a
place to initiate young warriors. According to their stories, the
cave is the dwelling place of the ghosts of children and many of
the hands were from children. It was really a misnomer; most of
the hands were not red, the outlines were red, as an ochre paint
was sprayed or blown over the hands. There *are* some red hands
though. It was an eerie and moving place, but on this occasion we
just wanted something different so we didn't go there. Fossil, with
his medicine chest, chose the course.

Laden with our hastily selected 'essential items' we began our
walk; the valleys looked much the same - a lot like the Dorset
valley I was walking through now. I remember that the boulders
grew larger, until we were scaling rocks the size of small houses.
Then we were cut to pieces by scrub. The heat was amplified by
the steam train rhythm of the cicadas' synchronised chirps. This,
and the weight we carried, made us unkind to each other. The
map was useless; we were lost.

In the waning light we eventually hit a fire trail. One-by-one
the group emerged from the trees, cut and exhausted. We sat and
talked. No matter where we found ourselves on our forest walks,
a story would always surface about a tragedy, a hanging or murder,
or some forest-dwelling character who appeared simply to
terrorize city dwellers camping on his territory. This gruesome
tale would then stay with us for the whole trip, playing tricks with
our minds as we sat around the campfire in the evening.

The fire trail came out at the place we had tried to avoid - Red
Hands Cave and its ghosts of children. We had come full circle in
our desperate attempt to go somewhere different. Our tales of
murder and mayhem were creepy enough without this sacred site
drawing us in. Nobody mentioned the map or the original plan
again.

And while I was writing this section of my story, I noticed that
signed copy of Robert Harris's *The Second Sleep* that I had
posted back to myself from the Edge of the World Bookshop in
Penzance. It was still lying in its box. I happened to glance upon
the endpapers, the first free page and pastedown against the
cover. In my copy the endpapers were printed with a photograph

of a cave wall covered in many hands dusted over with ochre paint. For some indecipherable reason the publisher included, in a book about Exmoor, a picture of a cave painted in red hands.[143]

Harris's story itself was not, as I'd thought, a mediaeval detective story, but set in the future (not a spoiler, it's early in the novel), and its apocalypse – while not explained entirely – was associated with the fragility of modern city living. An End of the World Club, if such a thing existed, would be wise to include this on their reading list. Immediately after noticing this I switched on the television to be confronted with Pinter's film version of *The French Lieutenant's Woman*. Not just any scene, but Meryl Streep and Jeremy Irons walking through the Undercliff of Lyme Bay. Somewhere, an infinite number of monkeys typed away at an infinite number of typewriters.

One thing I recall about that teenage journey, is that my backpack had been killing me on the return walk from Red Hands Cave. The others told me I should stop whingeing. Only when I unpacked did I discover, wrapped inside the tent and pressing against my spine had been that bloody folding latrine shovel. It was to be the last time we all camped together. Never since do I recall feeling the sense of belonging that I had back then with those friends.

Now, as I walked through the Undercliff forest there was only me, the gang scattered. We all met up briefly in the last decade, irrevocably changed - only a faded image of what we had been. The Undercliff flooded with memories but, with not another soul for miles, they settled in me like a dead weight.

My backpack still killed me as I climbed over and under a couple of large trees felled by storms. I rested at Sheepwash, the pack looking harmless while at rest. The sheep wash dated from 1800 and was incongruous in a forest with no sheep and no grass to graze.

At a peninsula with a rare view of the sea, voices carried. Something about the sound unnerved me; I imagined sinister forest dwellers, stone-throwing ghouls, rednecks stringing up hikers to a tree. I had been alone with my thoughts for too long. As I rounded the bend two men blocked my path, one carrying a chainsaw. Their conversation ceased as soon as I came into view and they stood, staring.

'Are you, er, with the National Trust?' I asked, hopefully.

'No, we're not.' The older of the two replied flatly. My forehead prickled. 'You walking?' There was no other way and I was in no state to run the way I had come.

The younger's introduction was incongruous given that he carried the chainsaw. 'We're *Natural England*.' The whole of it? He did most of the talking while the other eyed me suspiciously. 'Just monitoring access after the storm. Have you seen any fallen trees today?' It sounded as though he had made it up on the spot. Nerves made me speak quickly.

'A couple, after Goat Island. Before Sheepwash I think. One is large – I had to take my pack off – and the other you can climb over. It's a big job, probably bigger than a chainsaw. Maybe.'

'Are you walking far?'

'To Poole.'

'From Somerset?' I nodded 'The whole thing? So you've seen most of it by now. Do you mind me asking what your favourite part was?' Perhaps they weren't burying anyone; perhaps they were just tree poachers.

'It's funny, everyone asks that, and to be frank I haven't been able to say until now. Years ago, I did most of Dorset up to Lyme, in reverse, and that was beautiful, so now I've covered it all. I know there are dramatic cliffs and beaches, but I'd say *this* is my favourite bit.'

'Really? Most people say they hate the Undercliff. The trees block the views.' Perhaps he was right; what was I saying? They had a chainsaw. This was Stockholm syndrome.

'Well, you still have cliffs, to the left, and you can hear the sea most of the time. The forest is almost subtropical, and the sea is still there, just not the shore. There's very little forest on the Path; I've never seen forest like this in England. It's more like where I grew up in Australia.' The weather had been beautiful too, but I suspect even rain would not have spoiled it with so much natural shelter.

'I like it too, thanks.' I had passed the test and they stood aside. The older of the two smiled, no longer looking as though he might assist in the removal of human limbs. Still, I listened for the sound of the motor revving as I hurried through the forest.

A ruined pumphouse stood near the unmarked four-wheel drive belonging to the foresters. Once clear of the forest I came to a second building, half hidden in the undergrowth. This had once belonged to John Fowles.

The author's first novel *The Collector*, published in 1963, is a disturbing tale. Lonely London clerk and butterfly collector Frederick Clegg becomes obsessed with an unobtainable young female art student, Miranda. It's no coincidence Fowles made him a butterfly collector; the ancient Greeks saw the butterfly as the physical manifestation of the human soul. When Clegg wins the Football Pools, he buys an isolated country house, abducts Miranda and imprisons her in the basement.[144] Fowles received the highest advance ever paid at the time for a first novel, and then sold the film rights. Like le Carré he left his Hampstead home and moved to this isolated farmhouse. The buildings were silent as I passed; they slumped, overgrown with ivy.

Open grassland descended to Lyme Regis and the Cobb sea defences made famous by *The French Lieutenant's Woman*. Lyme's seafront had changed since I was last here, the wooden groynes now replaced by stone. The Path crossed fields to woodland from which the whole town could be seen. At my ankles three disfigured heads witnessed as I passed into the impenetrably dark passage, Hallowe'en pumpkins placed there to scare walkers. *Toil and trouble,* perhaps, but I wasn't bothered by a ripe gourd. Steps had collapsed and there were detours within detours every few metres. The coast beyond Lyme was a series of ugly blackened scars where green hills had been, and the original Path had crashed into the sea. Against plan, I had the sea to my left. The circuitous diversion traversed a golf course where I immediately became lost. I waved my sticks in the air to distant golfers but they walked further away, deliberately ignoring me. This was irritating; they were too fast for me to catch up. I found myself on the fairway under a lowering sky with the Chubb safe strapped to my shoulders.

In my mind golfers were rich men in groups, focused on their game at the expense of all else – namely their patients, women in childbirth and mill workers. They talked in an indecipherable language of backspin, birdies and bogeys, and wore stomach-churning pastels and silly hats.

When, eventually, I gained the attention of a man near a green, he said 'Oh, I thought you were a golfer.'

I was out of breath. 'Sorry, I'm looking for ... the ... Coast Path.' I was still very angry.

'Ah, it's not that obvious.' He then did something I hadn't expected. He stopped playing, but away his putter, and walked with me back to where I had lost my way. It was a good distance and he chatted with me about the Path and how strange a diversion it was - through a golf course – as though the inconvenience was mine rather than his (which, let's face it, it wasn't). That is, he was being kind and more than reasonable.

'From a distance,' he explained, 'your walking poles looked like clubs and your backpack a golf bag. When you waved the poles I thought you were playing through.' That's why the other golfers had walked quickly away - they thought I'd brain them. I felt ashamed for my golfing prejudices. A lack of weaponry had been the only thing that prevented me from gunning them all down and burying them in bunkers staked with tees.

'You see that gap in the trees near the hotel sign? Follow this path around the pool and you'll emerge from the woods at the hotel. You'll be on the road towards the sea.' Before I left, I asked him why he was golfing alone. 'Oh, I prefer it. I go at my own pace and I don't have to talk to other golfers.'

Charmouth was closing down for the evening; the last of the beach visitors headed home. I followed signs to a farm holiday park, which appeared deserted. The light was fading, the air already icy on my face, when a bespectacled man arrived in a little farm utility buggy and began answering his own questions.

'You need to camp? Are you walking? You are. Are there many of you? Just one.'

The entertainment and restaurant block slumbered in melancholic hibernation. I pitched as quickly as I could with frozen hands. I held the key for the disabled toilet, but managed to break the hand drier. With the air freezing around me, I got into my bag.

In the protection of my golden chrysalis my phone screen lit up with a message - from old school friend, Fossil! He was fighting fires just eleven kilometres from Red Hands Cave that night. Improbable. Much later, finding himself trapped, he would wrap himself in a tarpaulin and hide from the cold wind in a crevice. At dawn a rescue helicopter dropped him and his team onto a disused golf course where he was helped by another lone man.

We had both been in the landscape of our childhood for a day. True, we had played with fire back then, but the world of our childhood was a much cooler place.

In the morning it was impossible to dry the tent with the sun so low and the camp in shadow. The picnic tables had a layer of ash and everything had condensation of its own. I shook the tent and rolled it up. In retrospect, not my best decision.

Leaving Axmouth meant crossing County Bridge which read: 'Dorset. Any person wilfully injuring any part of this County Bridge will be guilty of felony and upon conviction liable to be transported for life by the court. T Fooks.' This seemed a little excessive, but then I didn't live there. On Stonebarrow Lane a concrete yurt marked the approach to the old Coast Path where the coastal route back to Lyme Regis could be seen, collapsed into the sea. It was the worst erosion on the Path and certainly the ugliest.

Cows looked on warily as I sang my way up the relentless incline. I was relieved when I came to the top of Golden Cap and began the descent. At the Seatown shop, after several unsuccessful and uncomfortable attempts at small talk with the girl behind the counter, I ordered coffee and browsed the newspapers. They were all depressingly about Brexit and the trade agreement but thankfully all looked too heavy to purchase. For a moment I was in the real world, but it was too unbearable so I walked out into sunshine.

A couple resting on the hill up to an Armada beacon greeted me with a raised hand and a wheeze. Over undulating grassland, past the beacon and a circular trough, was Eype Mouth where a sign proclaimed 'café now open'. It felt like lunchtime so I followed the sign's direction. After half a kilometre of trudging inland my energy waned and I walked back to the Path.

In despair I asked a local if she knew where the café was. 'Oh no, that's *long* closed for winter,' she said with a little chuckle.

'Do you *know* the owners?'

'Oh yes, I know them. It's a small place.'

'Then would you do me a favour?'

'If I can.' She offered me a pursed-lipped smile.

'Please ask them to take down their *now open* sign on the Coast Path.'

'Oh?' She stared at me, moved her head back as though detecting a rotten smell, and her smile quivered as though this was the most unreasonable thing to ask.

'They're not *open*,' I reasoned. 'It's only fair, don't you think? I've just walked a kilometre hunting for the thing carrying *these* sash window counterweights,' I pointed a thumb behind me. The woman peered nervously at my pack, her brow furrowed.

'I'll tell them,' she said, the muscles in her cheeks quivering, now less sure of herself. She tugged on her dog's tether and backed away.

'Thank you. The South West Coast Path Association appreciates your contribution,' I smiled back.

West Bay offered provisions. The beach was made famous in 1975 when a man abandoned a stolen jelly-shaped company lorry then walked into the sea. In one version, to his boss he wrote, 'you will have heard about my speech ... I was drunk ... I am not optimistic but then only fools judge things by results'.[145] In another he wrote, 'Possessions bring misery. Absolute possessions bring absolute misery'.[146] There are also two versions of the death – one in which he left his clothes in a pile and swam into the sea. In another he tested the water, found it too cold, and walked off. In both, his suicides were fake (he merely killed off his old self, buried his life's mistakes and moved on). This was, of course, the fictional Reginald Iolanthe Perrin (RIP),[147] aged 46, preparing to adopt a new persona. Staring at the sea I realised this happens to us all in the end; we fake our own deaths, if metaphorically, and force ourselves into different jelly moulds. They sometimes make us look ridiculous.

I followed the Path to Burton Bradstock. Beyond River Bride. Cows ran towards the corner of a field as I approached, perhaps mistaking me for a farmer with treats so I threw an imaginary ball. It failed to send them in pursuit and instead made their interest in me more intense, establishing the superior intellect of cows over dogs. Intellect *and* violence. Cows kill more than dogs and probably sharks, but we tend to spend less time in shark-infested waters than fields. I squeezed through the herd, hoping that they did not breathe in before I was free.

Burton Hive beach buzzed with tourists visiting the café and catching the late afternoon sun. There was no evidence of the tragedy that had unfolded five days previously, as described to me by Andy and Kim, a mother and son dragged out to sea. Holiday-makers now laughed and played as though nothing had happened.

The landscape changed from sandy earth into low-lying marsh. As I left the mobile homes behind, the smooth surface of a pool reflected the purple sky, the sun dipping beneath the horizon. In this saturated land I felt, rather than looked, for a place to camp. There seemed to be no land that would hold a tent. Finally, at the end of Burton Mere was an area of reeds that had been recently cut; now low, dry grass covered the ground. 'Here.' I spoke aloud to no-one.

A voice replied indistinctly and I held still. It must have carried on the cold air, probably fishers on the shingle beach, blocked from view by the reeds.

My breath formed into small clouds though I wasn't conscious of quite how much the temperature had dropped until I unpacked the wet tent and laid out the ground sheet. When I bent to pick it up, it moved as a stiff, solid sheet, like a slice of frozen bread. Even wearing gloves, my hands could barely function to put the tent together.

Ordinarily I wouldn't risk lighting the stove inside the tent, but I was numb. Once I was cocooned, it provided a little heat. Finding myself desperate for a pee, I tugged at the tent's zip. Nothing. Taking the zip and flap in two hands, I pulled and tugged but it would not budge. In the lantern's light I made out fine lines like fungal tendrils on rotting wood: ice. I was frozen in. A bladder primed to expect immediately relief is an impatient child. There was no option but to do my business in the tent. Ironically, though having little else in my world, I did have a pot to piss in. A window from which to empty it, I did not have.

Anyone who has done the act in a confined space will appreciate my predicament. It had all to fit into the single cooking pot. Horrible really, but not as disgusting as the alternative. I could wash up in Weymouth. For over a minute of controlled spurts I possessed the stamina of that pissing manneken in Brussels: Jean-Claude Van Damme. I finished just short of the rim.

With my hands warmed slightly from holding the pot, I pressed them against the tent zip and kept them there until all feeling had left. There were a few millimetres of movement as some of the ice thawed. I re-warmed my hands on my pot and repeated this until the zip moved half a centimetre. This gave room for movement and, as I pulled, it gradually shredded ice until the zipper ran the full length.

The cooking pot was still warm to the touch as I swung it in an arc away from my former prison. 'Gardyloo!'

The morning walk was over bog and grass, but moved onto the shingle beach as the rain began. Cogden Beach was an arrow-straight embankment of stones, a natural extension of the arc of Chesil Beach ahead. The ridge only became Chesil Beach proper once separated from the mainland by the saline Fleet lagoon. From May to August you should not walk on Chesil Beach as it's a haven for rare animal and plant species, and plovers nest on the ground, their eggs camouflaged among the pale stones.

Cogden Beach had to be crossed, though it was easiest to move on the adjoining wet marsh where the ground was firm. A shingle bank can be romantic to view in moonlight But to be *On*

Chesil Beach, to borrow from Ian McEwan, is annoying. Walking the full length of a shingle bank in cold wind and rain while carrying a backpack is pants.

In Abbotsbury there was a refreshment café near the beach but they advised me to visit their branch in the Sub-Tropical Gardens for food. I walked the road to the garden and approached the counter. 'This is your food menu?' I asked, pointing to the board.

'Yes,' she replied. I stood for a while looking at the list of food. She uttered no further comment. It's important that this is understood. I then found a table to begin undressing. First, I removed my gloves, which stuck to my hands and inverted. I inflated them with air to right them. My jacket did the same trick as I pulled off each sleeve. I hung these on a nearby hat stand. After some time I walked across and placed my order.

The attendant, who had been standing watching me undress, said: 'Oh, we're not serving food, no. Not until midday.' It was not yet eleven.

'You didn't think to tell me this when I came in?'

She stared vacantly. I do occasionally despair of the human race. Not wishing to make a show of the same strip routine in reverse, I collected my sodden gear and walked into the gardens to dress. Though I had no ticket for the garden, it would have been a foolhardy manager who challenged me when surrounded by so many sharp plants.

Leaving the village (I'd found a more welcoming teashop), I was conscious of the eerie chapel dedicated to the martyr St Catherine – looking down on me from the hill. I recalled from history lessons that the Catherine wheel firework commemorated her torture and execution. Or was it *celebrated?* According to Christian tradition she was evangelist and martyr, though there is no convincing evidence of any single historical figure of her description, and the Catholic Church has for years had her in and out of its good books, playing the Hokey Cokey with her existence.[148]

Until the last century, women of Abbotsbury visited the chapel to ask for her help. Perhaps they still do; behind me, a stocky woman approached from St Catherine's. She carried nothing with her and wore handmade clothes like someone from an earlier age. As I reached a field of tall crops, she moved quickly past, saying nothing.

The woman took a muddy descent, which I followed though when I reached the road she had vanished. Instead I was being watched by what appeared to be bouncers. Horses passed with red-jacketed riders and a horn sounded. It was a hunt. I kept eye contact with the two men atop their quad bikes, their suspicious gaze following me as I climbed onto the road and crossed.

'Hello there,' a well-dressed man with a quiff and plaid jacket addressed me from a four-wheel drive.

I nodded to him and said, 'If I were a hunt saboteur I'd probably carry less luggage.' His smile dropped and one of the apes rose slightly from his seat. *Tally ho!*

From the next hill I could see the hunt passing below me, first the hounds then the horn-blowing hunters on horseback closely behind, all jumping a fence onto the muddy track. *The Hunting Act, 2004* prohibits hunting wild animals with dogs, but there are ways around the law. One of the reasons I find group hunting particularly offensive is the willingness of some people to be lackeys to their 'masters' (the two on the quad bikes), threatening violence to anyone who challenges the hunt (me). Understanding it might give a clue as to why one class would vote back into power a government that had actively eroded a country's health and social care services.

In the wake of the hunt I walked through the field only to find that everything from the middle, where I stood, to the gate and beyond was under more than half a metre of water. It occurred to me that those flunkeys knew I was destined for this and were probably watching me through binoculars. Annoying. Rather than risk the edges of the field, which may have concealed barbed wire, concrete or machinery, I took the central, deeper section. In for a penny, in for a pound. From that point onwards my boots developed an irritating flatulent squelch.

The lagoon of West Fleet is separated from the sea by Chesil Beach, a natural shingle barrier beach which curves from the mainland towards the Isle of Portland's causeway. The rest of the Path followed West and East Fleet. As I traced their shores there was rapid gunfire close by. I instinctively ducked as the firing echoed around me. To the left three men appeared from a copse and walked towards me waving flags. Smoke hung in the air, the shooting stopped. Were they halting the shooting or surrendering? I hurried to the road where a sign read, tardily, 'PROCEED WITH CAUTION SHOOT IN PROGRESS'. Caution? A cautious person wouldn't enter a field full of shooters filled with sherry. What was it about farmers warning you only after the fact? Once over the next hill the firing resumed like the Somme.

'SUDDEN LOUD NOISE.' The poster, a head with fingers in its ears, was displayed on a sentry post. As though in further illustration, all the glass was shattered. No flags flew so I tentatively navigated round the firing range. The dark was impenetrable at Pirate's Cove and there was no sign of an onward Path. A dark figure carrying a lantern approached across the water. He held the hand of a small boy as he crossed the tiny beach. They would not have seen me, only heard the mysterious farting steps descend in the darkness. I followed the edge of the water past where they had come, and there was a continuation of the Path on the grass beyond the cove.

It was not the most obvious route and there were no signs, but I felt my way towards the lights of Weymouth, though technically Ferrybridge at Wyke Regis, one of Weymouth's sprawling suburbs.

The bed and breakfast charged a lower rate than many hostels. Its owner was friendly, asking what I was doing and then offering her own narrative of the homeless situation in the town. Refugee groups would huddle for warmth beside the sea in viewing shelters. While sympathetic to their plight, something in her choice of words suggested she would prefer that the objects of her sympathy were somewhere else, so they were not a daily reminder.

I had the benefit of an attic room for two nights while I circuited the Isle of Portland. Next door, a couple alternated between screaming at each other and hogging the shared bathroom, so I washed in the sink.

Armistice Day
Day 62. 10th November

Two soldiers were in Weymouth for the Remembrance Sunday service. The more talkative of the two asked me over breakfast what I was about, and I explained the walk and what I did for work.

'So, what do you think of the homeless then?' he asked. I wasn't entirely sure, but it seemed a question for which he had a prepared answer, and I had the sense of being lured into a trap. When I described the changes I had seen in London he nodded as though recalling something, but he simply replied: 'it's a problem.'

There then followed a volley of questions about Afghanistan, as he probed my thoughts. He stared into me, unblinking, as I gave my responses. Though I was careful not to make any judgments about our actions as a country, I was open about what I had seen and the lives of people I had met. More staring. He finally broke the silence.

'We made some mistakes,' he volunteered, perhaps sensing what was unspoken. 'I don't know why we got involved. So many dead, it's terrible.' This surprised me coming from a soldier. On reflection, who else would it come from? There weren't a great many local witnesses.

So many dead. Armistice Day was 101 years ago. There had been upwards of twenty million dead in that conflict, and more from the pandemic of influenza and encephalitis lethargica – 'sleepy sickness' – that followed it. Any statistic about that conflict is incomplete. It's hardly worth debating; an unimaginable number of people – civilians and military – died between July 1914 and December 1920.

'We'll be in the march from ten. Will you be back?' the soldier asked as I stood.

'I will. I'm walking around Portland then back tonight. I might
see the ceremony on the Portland side.'

The area of the guest house was Melcombe or Melcombe
Regis, and it held a special interest for me though it is a
coincidence that I found myself staying in this village suburb. This
had been the site of an historic event so calamitous that all events
since, revolutions, wars, natural disasters, are relatively
inconsequential.

Studying public health in the 1990s, I was fascinated by the
history of epidemics; my research was historical epidemiology. In
the 1890s Charles Creighton had documented all major
epidemics in Britain in two volumes. He had been sceptical about
the causes of communicable disease, but his documentation was
almost obsessively comprehensive. These volumes became the
definitive guides to pestilence, *A History of Epidemics in Britain*.
Melcombe was in there:

> It entered English soil at a port of Dorsetshire—said in
> the Eulogium *to have been Melcombe (Weymouth)—*
> *in the beginning of August, 1348. It is said to have*
> *spread rapidly through Dorset, Devon and Somerset,*
> *almost stripping those counties of their inhabitants,*
> *and to have reached Bristol by the 15th of August.*[149]

First Italy had fallen and then other countries in Europe. The
spread was rapid, from Weymouth at the beginning of the month
to Bristol two weeks later, and London by the end of the year.[150]
The urge to flee is understandable in those who had seen the
dead with their own eyes. However, with only horsepower
available to escape, and the infection having a very short
incubation period (one to three days), it's astonishing how quickly
it spread.

This period came to be known as *Magna Mortalitas*, or the
Great Death. Creighton wrote, 'The dead were expeditiously
buried in trenches; vacancies among the clergy were promptly
filled.'[151] We know it now as the Black Death, probably a
pneumonic plague or spread by lice; contemporary accounts
described the spread from person to person and on contact,

269

killing the priest giving the last rights so swiftly that both patient and confessor were interred in the same grave.[152] And it started metres from the spot I was standing, carried by ship.

Where did the wave of death originate? China, in retrospect, was blamed for the Black Death, and this blame continues. There were contemporary records of 'floods, droughts, earthquakes, famines and famine-fevers, but not by pestilence unconnected with these', yet the years from '1352, are marked in the Chinese Annals[153] by a succession of "great plagues".' [154] China was most likely the recipient of the Black Death, not its source. This hasn't prevented geneticists continuing to find its source there – and they *will*,[155] but it's circumstantial. So, if not China, where? The best evidence is that it originated somewhere in the 13,000 kilometres between Messina in Italy and the Bering Strait. Attempts to find a precise source are guesswork so long after events, and the motivation to do so is suspect.

Of the mortality, Creighton remarks on an important consequence: 'The effect of the mortality upon trade and industry was, momentarily, to paralyse them.'[156] An epidemic is one of many calamities that might lead to the failure of food supplies in a country so dependent – as it is now – on food imports. We have an economy based on ideas, cheap resources from poorer countries and market speculation rather than the production of the materials essential for survival. How would we cope if we thought we were approaching the end of our world?

The Isle was joined to the mainland by a thin causeway which ran as a tangent to the huge curve of Chesil Beach. At the top of the hill above the causeway, was Tout Quarry, now a statue 'garden'. Sculptors had carved the stone into infrastructure (like a tunnel or fireplace), faces, bodies and improbably difficult visual tricks such as Stephen Marsden's 'Fallen Fossil' (1985). This ornate flower-like shape lay in pieces on the ground beside a flat rock wall from which its impression, the negative to its positive, had been carved. It was as though it had fallen from the wall and broken, leaving its hollow. A bas relief of a person falling forever, hung high above me on the rock face. It was 'Still Falling' (1983) by Antony Gormley. Had it been a Banksy it would have stopped falling as commercial quarrying recommenced in Tout.

At eleven o'clock I paused in silence among the stones while above the quarry could be seen hundreds gathering at the war memorial. The two soldiers from the guest house would be in uniform at the Weymouth parade.

At the tip of the island three lighthouses were visible at one time. Most tourists gathered near the southernmost tower where there was a popular seafood restaurant. Its luminous yellow and pink signs revealed a petty management. 'Customer notice. Please remove excess mud from your boots/shoes before entering.' 'BEWARE! UNEVEN GROUND.' And, in case you were enjoying yourself too much, 'NO SWINGING ON THE RAILS!' They were the professional equivalent of notes left on taps and switches by an annoying housemate who was too parsimonious to rectify problems.

I moved beyond the screaming messages and through a mobile home camp, old quarries (a haven for rock climbers) and to the partly ruined Rufus Castle. This castle was used by several authors. Thomas Hardy called it Red William's Castle in *The Well-Beloved*,[157] a novel about a stone sculptor in a pagan land. Victor Hugo, in *The Man Who Laughed* (1869),[158] described it and this entire coastline. An American silent film version of the book starred Conrad Veidt ('Major Strasser has been shot, round up the usual suspects'[159]) as Gwynplaine, the man whose face was disfigured as a boy into a permanent grin. This portrayal was the model for the Batman comics' *Joker*. In the novel, Hugo described the land from Chesil Beach to Portland, including its railway (long since removed), the landscape disfigured by quarrying and storms, and a buoy that rang a melancholy bell out to sea only when you were on the lethal side of it.[160]

The bed of the former Portland branch railway mentioned by Hugo passed a working quarry before a cliff path took me up to the road. At the top was Verne Citadel, a Victorian fort where my childhood friend's father had worked. My family had stayed with them during 1976 in a desolate correctional facility estate while on holiday. The quarries and prison aren't the only sites of interest. There is also a youth offenders' institute.

Beyond a housing estate the Path rediscovered the coast and moved back along the old railway bed to Weymouth. Children on skateboards exuded the fragrance of marihuana. How quickly they grow up. One minute they're playing cops and robbers, the next they're extorting funds from their grandparents to fund their crack habit. In that heady atmosphere, in the dark approach to the headland of Nothe Fort, my phone rang.

'Hello?'

A North American drawl. 'Heeey, is thaaat Ahscaaar? We're having a great party here, margaritas and taaaacos. Will you be finished your waaaalk soon enough to join?' It was Vancouver Steve, not being entirely serious. I hoped.

'Where are you?'

'London, England. The second-best city in the world.'

'Well, no, I don't think I'll be available before ... let me check my watch ... late November.'

'That's too baaad. These margaritas are delicious. *No* salt. We'd even freeze the glass and give you a salty rim if you could make it.' Followed by a convoluted story of how he had inherited an ex-girlfriend's deceased partner's electric bicycle.

Now, Steve may sound like a west coast surfer on acid, but while he is from Vancouver, I can confirm that he cannot surf. Steve and I have a friendly competitiveness in collecting first editions and racing with heavy luggage but he's actually a psychology lecturer who specialises in perspective, memory and recall, three-dimensional perception and identification, and so on. Much of his work is relevant to police work, the validity of witness testimonies and two-dimensional recording (closed-circuit television). Steve's work might just keep you out of prison.

'Hey, Steve,' I said, starting to sound like him, 'I'm walking and I have to find my way back to town but it's too dark to read the Guide. Could you look up Nothe Fort in Weymouth? I've just passed it and am walking back along the shore towards town. Can you see if the Coast Path is along the water or further inland?'

'Let me check. Not *which* Fort?'

'Nothe. It's the name. N-o-t-h-e. Nothe Fort.' There was some delay while I passed along a wharf.

'Okay, if you're on the waterfront you need to move inland.' This is what I needed, an expert on spatial awareness, perception and memory to lead me through the darkness.

'Okay, I'm walking up steps and into a park. Does that look right?'

'Should be. Have you crossed Barrack Road?'

'I'm now on Barrack Road. Good, so I'm in the right place.'

'So you should be heading towards the water.'

'I've come *from* the water. If I keep going I'm back where I started. Should I stay on Barrack Road?' And so it went on until I was hopelessly lost. 'I need to find a streetlamp and look at the map. Thanks for your direction.'

'No proooblem, glad I could be of help. See you in December.'

In time I rediscovered the route and the old part of Weymouth, passing the King's Statue. A crowd huddled under a wooden viewing shelter on the promenade, their dress suggesting they were from other shores. Blankets covered the ground spotlights, trapping the warmth and up-lighting their dark faces. Sultan was each of them. It would soon be winter. *Where will you all go?*

The next day, the retired soldier wished me well as I left to start the walk to Lulworth Cove. Part of me wished we could have spent more time talking as there was something in his eyes that was troubled. His stare stayed with me as I edged along Weymouth Bay.

On Furzy Cliff the white modernist Riviera Hotel came into view, its arches and palm trees in a long crescent just below my horizon. Inexplicably it faced west north-west, away from the sea. Perhaps it was the only way to build something so large on those contours. To reach it, the Path moved through a sleepy holiday park and then took a rear view of the hotel that mooned towards the sea with air-conditioning ducts and downpipes.

Some areas of wet ground had boardwalks but there was enough water to ensure wet boots. Even on a blue-sky day the land was a large green sponge. At Osmington Mills the thatched

Smuggler's Inn displayed a cleverly improvised sign directing the Coast Path through the Inn's bar.

Beyond the Mills, Ringstead village was shown on the map in gothic script, indicating an ancient place. It is recorded in the Domesday Book (1086) as Ringestede with a population of fourteen households.[161] Ryngstede had a reducing population and two reasons are given on the internet for its depopulation: French pirates burning the village to the ground, and the Black Death.[162] As the plague arrived in Melcombe by boat, both Black Death or pirates amount to blaming the French.

According to research by the University of Hull, the population of this village largely fell between 1327 and 1334.[163] The plague arrived in 1348 and took leave in 1349,[164] after the decline began and long before taxpayers reduced to three households. This village's appeal had lost its mojo long before the plague. If marauding French pirates are to blame, then they burnt one house every ten years, showing a degree of restraint not commonly associated with piracy. Apply the principle of Occam's razor – that the simplest explanation is probably the the most likely – and villagers may simply have sought the bright torches of Osmington Mills after Ringstead's stupefying dullness.

Overwhelmed by the need to use a toilet, but ironically finding the present-day village too heavily populated, I hurried up the track to a church, St Catherine-by-the-Sea. It was a small wooden church where only those connected to the church, or who had died at sea and washed up here, could be buried. Tragic and poignant, yes, but no toilet. It would have made for a place to quietly contemplate had my kidneys not been screaming. I shuffled on to the area below Burning Cliff which had sufficient bushes to hide my purpose. It was so-called because oil shale had burst into flames in 1826, burning for three years following a landslip. I swear I could have extinguished the blaze with the volume I released.

Of the onward journey, Paddy Dillon had described: 'A monstrous roller-coaster route.' Never before had he applied the adjective *monstrous* to his favourite metaphor. Just beyond old coastguard cottages at White Nothe I was joined by a walker who set a good pace ahead of me. She provided me with the discipline to reach Lulworth.

The Path was a series of parallel bobsleigh runs, formed from years of temporary replacement trails after rains. My pace setter and I were moving in the raised grass between them but inevitably found ourselves stuck in their ruts, making balancing a challenge, at least for me. A tombstone-like Coast Path marker, common in Dorset, showed the distance to Lulworth Cove 3, Durdle Door 1½ and Scratchy Bottom 1¼.

Over the next hill was the distant giant limestone arch of Durdle Door. I challenge anyone to look at this and not see a dragon. As I reached the penultimate valley the woman ahead turned and took an inland route back. She squinted back at me and smiled in recognition of her disciple.

This valley felt like Scratchy Bottom. Scratchy Bottom came second only to Shitterton in a poll of Britain's most unfortunate place names, but polls are notoriously flawed. At least, so say the residents of Bell End in Worcestershire, Ugley in Hertfordshire and Twatt on Orkney.

Tourists thronged Durdle Door and its protected beach. A German couple stood aside as a man moved crablike up the steep steps from the beach, his back pressed against the rock, a look of abject fear in his eyes. Teutophobia – fear of Germans – is rare even in Dorset. I compensated with a Germanophile's welcome and took their photograph, which they reciprocated. The Germans looked fantastic in their matching Euro-apparel and perfect hair and teeth. I appeared badly dressed and untidy, like a wreck survivor after lying face up on a life raft for a month. To Europeans I simply looked British.

I had been here as a child, proof provided by a 1970s washed-out colour print. The seventies did look washed out. It showed a seven-year-old round-faced boy posing beside childhood friend Tim before the dragon. Tim had lived on the Isle of Portland near the Verne Citadel.

A Coast Path tombstone showed Lulworth Cove 1¼ with a carved mug. Where there is tea, there is hope. My rapid pace brought me to the Cove by two o'clock. Neither the South West Coast Path Association's website nor the gov.uk web page for army training in Lulworth showed any alternative routes around the firing ranges. Paddy Dillon made no mention of alternative routes in my Guide, despite the ranges having live firing for most of the year excluding the occasional weekend and public holiday. It seemed an odd oversight. It's all in the timing, he had written, yet almost all of October to November 2019 saw live firing.

Though I had successfully passed through before, that was on a summer weekend in 2005. Outside of summer the army liked to blow stuff up. Given that the coastal route can be summed up as 'walk with the sea to your right, and under no circumstances deviate as the area is littered with UXOs,' the absence of an alternative route is an oversight. Most walkers must simply leave out this section.

The official South West Coast Path website suggests a bus ride to Corfe Castle followed by a walk across a ridge towards Kimmeridge. It was a poor compromise, being discontinuous, but mainly because the sea would be on your left.

At Lulworth Cove red flags flew high on the ridge behind the YHA hostel. This reads as *proceed at own risk*. *Risk* meant *probable* death but *certain* arrest; I wasn't about to be man-handled by men in uniform again. I had expected a ceasefire, this being Armistice Day, November 11th. Where was their sense of history?

The drying room of the hostel was open, so I left my gear, took the day pack with my valuables and walked down to the Cove to seek advice. Lulworth Cove is poorly disguised as Lulwind Cove in Thomas Hardy's *Far from the Madding Crowd* (1874):

> *He undressed and plunged in. Inside the cove the water was uninteresting to a swimmer, being smooth as a pond, and to get a little of the ocean swell, Troy presently swam between the two projecting spurs of rock which formed the pillars of Hercules to this miniature Mediterranean. Unfortunately for Troy, a current unknown to him existed outside, which, unimportant to craft of any burden, was awkward for a swimmer who may be taken in it unawares.*[165]

Awkward is one word to describe swimming into the mountainous waves of the open sea. The Cove does resemble a miniature Mediterranean, a natural haven against the fierce sea beyond.

The former boat shed café on the Cove was perfect for research. 'I'm walking the Coast Path. Do you happen to know how I can find the route around the firing range?' I asked the woman behind the counter.

She passed me coffee and a brownie. 'Oh, I don't know, but I know who will.' I thanked her but secretly I didn't have much faith in information centres attached to gift shops. What I needed was a knowledgeable seafarer or smuggler. For a while I scanned the shore for men with grey beards or weather-beaten women knitting fishing nets. Having to improvise my route to Kimmeridge Bay didn't appeal. No local characters appeared so I trudged despondently up the hill to the information centre.

There, a man produced a folder and slowly withdrew a sheet of paper. He unfolded it to reveal a detailed map entitled 'Lulworth Cove to Kimmeridge Bay route around the MOD ranges. Distance 12.5 miles (20km). Terrain; mostly walking on tarmacked roads'. Also, like a conjuror, he pulled out a list of camp sites possibly still open, and suggested one closest to Kimmeridge Bay. I took back all I had said about heritage centres.

The campsite he mentioned was called Steeple Leaze Farm, which lay on the detour itself. We discussed the Path behind me and my accommodation choices, and I played down my various trespasses as benign occupations which I had left in a better state than they were found.

Back at the hostel I shared the enormous kitchen with a chatty family. The young girl and boy had clearly been told by their guardian to talk to strangers. It was difficult to stop them. All three had been to a talk by author Michael Rosen and had taken away the main message that you should not believe what your teacher tells you. Probably this message had been received through a filter. Michael Rosen's father was a secondary school teacher and his mother a primary school teacher. He also received an award from the National Union of Teachers and said he had the NUT 'running through [his] veins'.[166]

Don't believe all that your teachers say is a fair message, though why limit it to teachers? Why not ... parents? Sharee rapidly revealed that Hibernia and Horace were home schooled. Those aren't their names but we were already discussing pedagogical theory before being formally introduced.

'They can get all they need by learning at home,' Sharee said, crossing her arms then, immediately sensible of the significance, uncrossing them.

I'm unsure that home schooling is the correct term as I was fed on Ivan Illich, who was a favourite of Sydney anarchist collectives, and who had written *Deschooling Society.*[167] He argued that society would be better without our formal systems of education which are universally poor. I held him in high esteem, though he also suggested that child labour may not be all bad, and proposed a system of three-wheeled mechanical donkeys for transportation between villages in Peru, but nobody's perfect. If there was one thing we might benefit from, though, it was not more schools closer to home. He was as sure that parents needed guidance in support of their child's education as he was that we needed deschooling. I didn't say any of this, of course, but listened as I drank tea from my folding mug.

'And if she [Hibernia] wants, or needs, to learn about quantum mechanics?' I asked, provocatively.

'That's a common misconception about home schooling.'

'That parents can't teach quantum mechanics?'

'That it's the parent doing all the teaching. Much of it is self-directed learning.'

'They can self-learn quantum mechanics? It's not rocket science, but I wouldn't attempt it without a net,' I teased.

'I can ... we can find someone from outside to tutor them.'

'You mean, get a teacher in?'

'Um.'

Before Sharee could respond, Horace stood and said 'All of the other children at the talk were so baffled that we were home taught. They just follow each other like sheep. They can't think for themselves. They just accept what the teacher tells them.' This sounded suspiciously like something that had been ghost-written by a parent. I suppose much of our speech *is* ghost written by our parents.

Little Hibernia was trying to engage in the debate, and valiantly attempted, 'We're all individuals,' which was received with deafening silence. I filled the gap with some encouraging mutterings while wondering what the other children had made of these two curious individuals and their social graces. Certainly, I am endowed with sufficient self-confidence to recognise that a state school education hadn't harmed me. So spoke the middle-aged unemployed man living in a tent and going to the toilet in holes he dug with a small golden trowel.

As I retired, I couldn't help thinking that Sharee (or whatever she was called) looked and sounded familiar. We both seemed to be looking at one another curiously, a distant forgotten tune floating between us. I enjoyed the discussion with her and the two likeable and entertaining, though slightly precocious children. Nevertheless, there was something more just out of reach, that grew further away the more I tried to catch it, a dream dissolving in daylight.

In the morning I walked to the sea to watch the sunrise. The hostel was separated from the coast by a perfectly circular chalk hill. At the entrance to the Range Walk the high wooden gate was locked from the inside. The entrance displayed various warning notices: 'KEEP TO PATH AS INDICATED BY YELLOW MARKERS'; 'Military firing range keep out when gate is locked and flag is flying'; 'Danger Do not touch any military debris it may explode and kill you'; and the somewhat unnecessary 'No cycles'.

That was the South West Coast Path; in the war school of life, what doesn't kill you, maims you. A red flag flew above the Cove's pillars of Hercules as though a Maoist force had taken Dorset by storm during the night. It looked magnificent in the morning sun and I thought perhaps the worst was behind me, that the journey would end with sunshine, blue skies, a gently undulating ground and the wind at my back.

At the hostel I collected my bag, said goodbye to Sharee, little subdued Hibernia and outspoken Horace and headed off on my inland route. Today promised to be, if nothing else, diverting.

Minutes into the walk, in a field which had displayed a warning about sheep, I was set upon by a large untethered dog which took a dislike to my pack. 'Don't worry, he doesn't [something inaudible],' the owner shouted as assurance from a distance.

'Fungus-foraging dog-fancier,' I mumbled, pushing the beast from my chest, and receiving an expression that couldn't have been more indignant had I assaulted her child. Despite being a frequent disclaimer of responsibility on the Path, I had yet to register what it was that these hounds allegedly did not do. Without doubt she would throw her bag of gargantuan hound stool in a tree when nobody was watching.

This internal argument I carried with me as I marched down the tarred road and approached the junction to Lulworth Camp. The road to take was the one to East Lulworth.

'Sharee! Of course.' My Damascene moment came as I stared at the sign. Perhaps it was 'location updating effect' or else I am just getting old and my mind had emptied to make way for the new. Whatever the reason, I now had Sharee clearly in my focus through a powerful telescope.

We had known each other once, having collaborated on a suicide prevention working group in the north of England. Ours was a group with many problems and few solutions, which perhaps explained our amnesia the previous night. Possibly, in her case, it was polite avoidance. Since then (as the internet revealed to me) she had campaigned tirelessly for the inclusion of homelessness services in overstretched local authority budgets.

She is a good person. Perhaps her name was my one residual memory, though the more I thought about it, the more I suspected it of being a false memory.

There were stranger associated events to follow. I could not have predicted that within months Britain would be plunged reluctantly into compulsory home teaching as schools closed during a coronavirus epidemic. And writer Michael Rosen was to catch the infection and spend two months recovering in our local hospital.

An unlikely collection of subjects had gathered in the hostel that night, but less unrelated than they may first have appeared. My recollection, though, was disturbed by the sudden outbreak of live firing. From that point on there followed a continuous, ear-shattering cacophony. It was intolerable. The MoD may have been in collusion with the tourist office in directing this route down a shooting gallery. Hopefully the artillery pointed seaward or I risked being trepanned; I needed trepanning like I needed a hole in the head. Despite the firing, in the background there was the constant rhythmic squeaking of my boots. When there was a pause in the firing, the squeaking was intolerable, and I wished for the shooting to start anew.

Track five. The crash and silence forced my mind into escape. That escape was the song I had most frequently meditated on during this walk. Pink Floyd's *Wish You Were Here*[168] had particular relevance to the Path with its decaying landscape, military – both relic and active – and death. The most evocative image in the song described all those who have failed to escape from what is expected of them by society; the ones who have taken a major role, but not one they controlled. The many artists hiding on this coast, the watchers and rescuers were those who had spurned the city for a more fulfilling ... something. This being a quiet track, my singing was mercifully drowned out by the gunfire which, though dress-rehearsed, lent this film a more appropriate backing track.

A sign by the roadside on Lulworth Castle's wall warned me: 'Beware. Dangerous animal. Do not climb fence.' It was so faded I had to remove my sunglasses to read it. The vagueness in the choice of words was somehow more unsettling than a specific threat. Either they were saving on signage and there was a roster system of different animals, or else this one was so terrifying it could not be named.

Had there not been heavy artillery on the path south from the castle I could have strolled to Worbarrow Bay where, at one time, another vague warning had been directed at visitors. Montague Rhodes James, the ghost story writer, had taken a group of Eton scouts there in 1927 and had read aloud to them a story set in nearby fields. In *Wailing Well*,[169] a group of scouts were warned by a shepherd and their master not to enter a particular field marked on their maps by a red circle, much as danger areas might be shown today. However, one scout with a reckless disregard for authority entered the field. From a distance the others watched as a hideous female creature crawled towards him on all fours, dressed in ragged blackened clothing and a bonnet on her strangely thin neck. Three other similar creatures came from different directions meeting at the clump of trees where the well was hidden, and where the boy was to meet his terrible end, hanged and drained of all blood.

Casting wind to the caution I entered the castle grounds. It would have been a shame to miss it, and it offered some peace - despite an unspecified risk to life. I had no intention of waiting until opening time to pay the castle entrance fee, but the structure could be seen from St Andrew's Church which also displayed information on local author Thomas Hardy. The castle was described in one of his stories, 'in the midst of a park, surrounded by dusky elms, except to the southward; and when the moon shone out, the gleaming stone facade, backed by heavy boughs, was visible from the distant high road as a white spot on the surface of darkness.'[170] Seen from the church it was a grand house with the smoothness and symmetry of a white rook on a chess board. I lit a candle in the church, as was my habit, for our respective late parents and then strolled out to the village.

A traditional red telephone box had been adapted as a loyalty library, offering dog-eared paperbacks by Tom Clancy, David Baldacci and Wilbur Smith. There was a certain military flavour to the collection and to the place; it stood opposite a small stone pyramid dated exactly a year earlier on the centenary, 11-11-11

2018. When the guns fall silent we play at war, inventing another to fill the gap left by the last.

The shooting I had experienced while working abroad was usually from a rifle range near our compound, or else gunfire to send a message to the authorities, for illustrative purposes. Occasionally it was during a wedding celebration when revellers would shoot into the air and occasionally through our window. Weapon users never had any serious intentions for me, though I had near misses: guns pointed casually in my direction, a couple of bombed hotels, rioting and arson – always just after I had departed.

In later years, as things became more volatile and security was taken more seriously, we were required to provide *proof of life* questions in case of kidnap. There were only three questions. It was important that you didn't provide the answers, only the name of a person who could judge the validity of the response. If anyone involved in communicating an incident knew the responses, then it would no longer be hard proof of life. My own questions were silly and suitably obscure, and I've forgotten most. Obscurity is essential of course, but the stupidity was just me. One question I used involved an incident in the family in the 1970s, an incident which had an embarrassing outcome for me, and which still makes me laugh to think about.

It amused me to imagine myself chained in a basement in some grim outpost of a failed state and my sister, on one end of a phone, being asked to confirm the answer to that question. And then the HR person, hearing my sister giggling down the line, would wonder why she was being so flippant when her brother's life was on the line. That would mean I was alive. The giggling meant I was alive. If there was a puzzled silence it simply meant I was dead, and some confused captor had made a hurried attempt to guess the answer on the spot - like a dark game of *Who Wants to be a Millionaire?* This also made me smile - the thought of someone holding a gun and a piece of paper with the question, asking a friend dressed in black who, similarly, had no knowledge of British children's television nor my family's twisted sense of humour. That amused me.

It wasn't that I didn't take security seriously. I haven't told you the question. It's just that the thought of Julie giggling would give me some comfort. I'd hate to think of her crying because of something I'd stupidly gone and done.

What always worried me was there were only three questions, like the genie's three wishes. Once they ran out, you were on your own. Security advisors worked on the assumption that three were enough for a resolution. After that you were free - or something else. It's a lesson not to waste all your wishes prematurely.

The long, straight road led to West Holme through a wood where a fox crossed, running quickly into the safety of the danger area. It was my first fox, other than the suggestion of a soon-to-be-dead one in the hunt. I stopped in the open beside a sign reading 'Tanks crossing sudden gunfire' which wasted no punctuation, and ate lunch. Armoured vehicles passed, the occupants eyeing me suspiciously, so I moved on. Further up the road I was passed by military convoys whose drivers nodded in acknowledgment when I stepped from the road to give them space. Respect for heavily laden marching, not for picnicking. They were okay, I suppose; encountering Tom Clancy is inevitable in such an environment even if they secretly longed for Bridget Jones.

The next road led east through a shooting range to a bridleway and Bridewell Plantations where another fox – possibly the same one – crossed my path, scurrying across the carpet of leaves. Sun projected streamers between the birches. There were no signs that anyone had walked along the route recently. The only person I saw was a gardener on the estate who waved as I passed. The Path turned onto road and I was comforted when it finally moved back towards the coast.

At two o'clock the sky darkened with rain. Something ahead, a shop or pub, showed light. Grange Gallery was both a café and art gallery and offered escape from the icy rain. 'Hello?' Silence. I waved at a CCTV camera. Nothing. For the camera I dramatically mimed putting some of the art into my pockets. Still nothing. It had the air of being hurriedly deserted, most commonly felt after hostage-taking incidents.

'Oh hello, I just saw you on the camera. Gave me a fright,' came a voice from the spiral staircase. This, I assumed, was the artist responsible for the stylised purple fairy tale landscapes on the walls.

'I was considering shoplifting but as you can see, I'm already heavily laden. You have coffee?'

'We have smaller items for you to steal,' she said with a smile as she spooned some ground coffee.

'Oh, hello.' the other half of the partnership entered from the yard. An artist doesn't come along for hours, and then two arrive at the same time. They introduced themselves as Esme and Jason. 'So, you must be nearly at the end,' he calculated, smiling broadly.

'It feels that way.' I perched on a stool and rubbed my lower back.

We chatted about the Australian bushfires, then the main news item other than Brexit. The artists had considered moving there. They were reconsidering. The fires were declared a national state of emergency and my old school friend was in the thick of it.

'Where will you sleep tonight?' asked Esme.

'Somewhere called Sleaze Farm.'

They looked at me in puzzlement before Jason registered: 'Oh, he must mean Steeple Leaze. That will be Julian. They're okay there, they'll look after you.' I hoped so. Julian, if that was his name, had said he might be travelling north.

I finished my coffee, thanked them and then walked up onto a ridge, beyond which I could make out red tractors. There was a light drizzle and the air grew cold.

The farm advertised: 'NO MUSIC NO SKY LANTERNS NO UNAUTHORISED PARTIES'. I liked Steeple Leaze Farm, it was my sort of place. A young farm worker was parking a tractor, so I said hello and asked, 'which house deals with the camping?'

'That would be it.' He pointed to a small cottage and walked off. It was not the friendly farmer experience I had been expecting but I was not discouraged. Although greeted by an elderly, greying border collie who sniffed my crotch, the house was otherwise empty. I camped with the intention of seeking Julian in the morning. The working men on the farm paid me scant attention, perhaps even less than scant.

Distant, booming gunfire continued into the night. Controlled use of firearms didn't bother me.

A message came through from my brother. 'Have you started your long walk yet?' The gunfire fell silent, and although I could still hear the cicadas it was only tinnitus. An owl hooted as though with relief, and I fell to sleep.

'So shines a good deed in a naughty world'
Day 65. 13ᵗʰ November

Nine o'clock approached as I finished packing and walked to the farmhouse to pay my dues. This left just over seven hours before dark. There was no sign of Julian, so I left the money in a silver foil bag with a note. I rewrote the note several times. They were all variations on an elaborate and rambling missive, referencing Julian's trip to the north and the old sheepdog, and justifying my decision not to pay the farmhands directly on account of their demeanour. On reflection, I came across like a minor character from a Jane Austen novel, so I binned them. I was running out of post-it-notes. In the end I wrote simply '£10.50 as agreed, ta!', and hung it with the cash on a hook outside the cottage door.

I glanced at the shower building but the air was still icy, and I could see the state of the bridle path. *What's the point?* It began as a muddy track and ended as a deep quagmire of mud and faeces churned by hooves over successive storms. The incline and my cargo meant I had to penetrate deep into the chocolate brownie mix to gain purchase and avoid sliding backwards. With only one exit in the field's corner I climbed towards it. The distant booming lent the ridge the atmosphere of the Battle of Passchendaele. To avoid losing my boots in the extraordinary suction, I wriggled until free with every step. Once out of the first field the mud became shallower, and as I cleared the ridge the way was visible down towards flatter ground and the sea beyond. A tombstone-shaped marker, similar to those used at Lulworth and Durdle Door, showed the way to Kimmeridge and to the village of Steeple – the first sign that this might lead to the Coast Path.

The Path had been erased at a ploughed field, the footpath sign tossed into a bush. I crossed the rutted earth, adding to the mud already accumulated on my boots, and emerged on the road leading to Kimmeridge Bay.

To ensure I covered the full distance at the coast I approached the military barrier. There, a woman stared inland. 'Amazing isn't it?' she said.

It was something you wouldn't expect to see in the south of England. In a little fenced compound, its head nodded rhythmically and the tail spun as black treacle was secreted beneath its feet. A mechanical metal donkey. Ivan Illich would have felt vindicated. It was the nodding donkey pumpjack of an oil well, its gunmetal arm glinting in the sun, the air transmitting an eerie metallic hiss.

'Yes, I'd forgotten that it was this side of the fence. I thought I'd missed it.'

'You wouldn't believe it was here, a Dorset oil well. There are others, you know, around the countryside but not as accessible as this. This one has been pumping oil continuously since 1958. You're walking far?'

I briefly explained my quest, and then asked what her interest was in oil.

'I'm a geologist. It's a good place to bring students. So much to see – the rocks, cliffs, erosion.'

She wished me luck and wandered east. To the west lay the firing range, on this side of the fence the pump. Oil and war. You can choose your side, they're probably the same. The donkey nodded.

Two men climbed the path to Clavell Tower, one having some difficulty walking. I let them move ahead. On the beach lay relics of war – concrete tank defences and a cylindrical bunker subsiding in the shingle.

If anyone doubts the ferocity of the weather in the southwest, they should take heed from the experience of Antony Gormley. The sculptor was commissioned to produce four sculptures at compass points around the UK installed in early summer 2015 at Landmark Trust sites.[171] They are, or were, cubist human figures in deep red, staring at water from the land. The one near Clavell Tower in Kimmeridge Bay fell into the sea in a storm in September of the same year. Despite being made of steel and on a large, heavy stone base it was blown over by the wind and waves. Gormley explained that what he intended was to expose the sculptures to the elements. He was reported as saying that the destruction was proof of its 'dynamic relationship with ... nature'.[172] For a dynamic relationship with nature the council probably imagined a weather vane but Gormley was clearly thinking of the Hindenberg. Ignoring him, the council righted the statue. However, five days before the year was out, the sculpture was sheared from its base at the ankles. The sea would always win. As one resident commented, *it proved fatal.* Nothing lasts forever. Clavell Tower itself, a nineteenth century folly, had been at risk of destruction too. Crumbling when last I was here, a year later it was relocated back from the cliff leaving its cross-section in the foundations. Beyond the tower two men I didn't recognise stopped me and one spoke. 'You're doing a good thing, Oscar. I hope the end treats you well.' This came as something of a surprise. I didn't recall either of the two but I'd met so many people, perhaps they'd slipped my mind.

'I'm sorry ... I ...?'

They were both smiling. 'We met a woman, a geologist. She told us what you're doing. You're the only one who matched her description so it was a small gamble.' They laughed and slapped me on the shoulder as they passed.

'You're close to Kimmeridge,' I told them. 'There's a toilet,' I said pointlessly, still a little in shock.

'Welcome news,' one generously shouted back.

I soon caught up with the two men I had seen earlier. The younger was struggling to move his legs in the mud so the older man assisted. 'Where are you hoping to get?' I asked.

'Chapman's Pool,' the older responded.

'Do you know how far it is?'

'About an hour,' the younger said with confidence.

They let me squeeze past. As it was so close, I decided to stop at the Pool too.

One hour was a serious underestimation; the ascents and descents were relentless and by Houns-tout Cliff I was exhausted. The two showed no sign of following so I assumed they had turned back. Even at my pace I was still walking three hours later with no sign of the Pool. On the last hill a wooden shooting tower stood amid a field of crops – as though in watch for Washington Irving's headless Hessian. His company might have taken the edge off the pain.

A convoluted route inland past houses led to St Aldhem's, a massive headland. The whole of Chapman's Pool was visible as a perfect circle, but somehow more barren than I remembered, with black scars from landslides. An unimaginably long and steep flight of steps entered and left a valley before arriving at St Aldhem's Chapel, built around the time of Cambodia's Angkor Wat. While I rested in the vaulted chapel the rain started. It was difficult to believe that I had walked all the way to Lulworth Cove in a single day in 2005, but of course the days were longer, my pack lighter and my body had lower mileage.

Wind and rain, with neither trees nor buildings for shelter, made for a pleasant afternoon stroll. The Path became a narrow channel, a bobsleigh run, and I either walked astride the gap or balanced inside it, one foot in front of the other. Being tired I combined both methods and slid. I fell headlong into gorse bushes, my head over the edge of the cliff, just laying there, too exhausted to get up. Rolling onto my knees, I push down on the poles and continued to enjoy my walk.

Beyond the strange concrete structures of Winspit Quarry two women headed back towards the cliff edge so I advised them to turn back as they would likely die. They caught up with me at Seacombe Cliff while I rested on a wooden platform having run out of water.

'Are you walking the whole thing?'

'I am.'

'Why?' And so, for the last time I explained, with speech slurred by dehydration my blurred reasons for being here. And something I said seemed to have triggered a memory in the other as she held a far-off look.

'In the book they mention walking this route over Dancing Ledge ...'

'I'm afraid I haven't read the book.'

'No?'

'The story of the couple who lose their house and walk the Coast Path, right?'

'I haven't read it either,' she said, with a puzzled expression. *Then we must be the only ones.* 'I only meant the guidebook. It mentions that there are a few more miles from Dancing Ledge to Swanage – we're doing a loop. It will be dark soon. We better get a move on, you too.' They wished me well and hurried on towards the lighthouse.

Trailing behind, I sucked on water from my sodden sleeves as I passed daymark pylons and crumbling Dancing Ledge, keeping the two just in sight. At the lighthouse a road looped up to Durlston Castle by which time my thirst was suffocating. I pushed at the glass door but it didn't move and the interior was dark. Deep inside, staff rushed across a lit area holding trays. There was no response when I knocked. I tapped the door with my flask and the staff looked but continued on their way. So, I kept knocking rhythmically until eventually a woman came.

'It was open,' she said. 'It just sticks.'

'Scuse me, gud I drubble y'forsome warder? Ahv juswarged alongway.'

'There *is* a tap outside.'

I peered behind me into the blackness. 'Seruzzly?'

'Sure, I'll get you some.' She came back a minute later with my flask and looked me up and down.

'Fangs, I preshade it.' She nodded and closed the door. Though cold, my thirst was greater; my sleeves were all out of rainwater. I drank most of the flask there.

From the castle a woodland walk led to the suburbs of Swanage. On arrival in town I searched up and down the street for the hostel, in the end counting shop numbers until at last I came to number 45. A tiny name plate read *Swanage Auberge.* I pressed a silent doorbell then, in my delirium, panicked, thinking I would have to speak French. The thought was replaced by the possibility that there was nobody home, and I looked down at my state. My clothes were covered in mud up to my hips, my boots were cracked like the feet of an elephant, and my body stooped from the pack. The house was in complete darkness.

After a minute there was movement behind the glass then a fumbling of locks and I was greeted by Pete, white haired and bearded. He was the local advisor I had sought so earnestly in Lulworth Cove.

'Bonjoir,' I involuntarily slurred, immediately regretting it.

I was worried about bringing my residue into the hostel which was decorated in country cottage style. I bent to remove my boots.

'Get your pack off first', he said and, for the first time on the trip a stranger took the backpack from my shoulders and set it gently on the floor with the respect given by a museum curator to a precious relic. 'Don't worry about your boots. Would you like tea or coffee?' I was choked so I let him go ahead while I undressed in the porch and composed myself. In the end I stood in my swimming shorts and St Mungo's t-shirt.

Pete put the heating on in the dorm, made me tea and gave me one of Pam's (his partner) chocolate brownies. He then sat down at the farmhouse table to ask me about the trip, though his manner was more counsellor than landlord. It felt like a psychological debriefing following a field trip. I was the only guest, he explained, and he asked if I was doing the walk for charity.

'Does it show?' I said, looking down at my dayglow orange t-shirt.

'Well, I thought it might be the case'. He smiled.

'The weather has been pretty bad today,' I said, as though it was the exception. 'You wouldn't believe what I've had to walk through.'

'Oh, I know it. I've been there,' he said, and it dawned on me that he had done the same himself at some point. Of course, why else run a hostel here, so close to the end? He helped me dry my clothes and sat for a while with me – I think to ensure I was okay – before leaving me to shower. I stood under the warm water in a daze. Later, I briefly saw Pam who kindly asked me if there was anything I needed.

Sleep came as though it were the first sleep after giving birth. I was exhilarated and exhausted, I just wasn't allowed to see the baby.

In the morning I hunted for Pete but when I found him, he refused to take payment for the night. I'd never met this man and so was surprised that he was being so kind. 'You must get a lot of people doing the Path,' I said.

'Oh, yes. But the whole thing? About five, perhaps six, people.'

'That's not so many, one every couple of months.'

'No, five or six in all the years we've been here.'

'How long is that?'

'Since 2003'. I shook his hand and promised to put the cost towards the charity, and he wished me well. 'Walk along the promenade, not through the town unless you want to see housing estates.' I said I would.

On the waterfront the sea seemed to sigh; there were no waves, just the whole body of water moving in and out rhythmically. A sign read 'ENJOY THIS PRIVATE BEACH' and beneath that, 'at your own risk'. I walked as far as I could but found I was trapped by the sea and had to retrace my steps, precariously hugging an outcrop. My pack, a giant turtle shell home on my back, pulled me incrementally backwards seeking the open sea. I scrabbled at the column of earth for purchase, clods of earth plopping into the water below. In my mind I saw the inevitability of the disaster slowly unfolding, the wet humiliation and needless loss of all my photographs and notes on this, the driest of days. Then, something shifted in the balance and I felt my centre of gravity edge forward enough for me to lean and hasten my fall towards the safety of the concrete platform. For a moment I clung to the storm barrier as to a life raft and then, with relief, followed the steps slowly up the cliff to the road.

A footbridge separated the suburbs from the gentle grassed climb of Ballard Down. Only once inside the landscape did I recognise it. I had seen these chalk stacks many times but had never been able to place them. It was a landscape of white, green and blue. White pinnacles came into view, blinding in the sun. At the grassy headland was the most famous. Old Harry Rocks sounded more like graffiti at a music venue; in reality, chalk arches.

I sat for a while on my pack near Harry Rocks and drank tea. A message from Kenny in Glasgow: 'Where will you be in the next week? Or, have you finished already? In any case, the weather sounded shite. I'll see you at your birthday. I've organised a way of seeing the Cup Final. I'll bring Simone.'

Mags was in Ireland with her mother who was unwell. Kim and Andy had offered me their beach hut beyond Poole but the thought of Mags coming back to England to an empty flat unsettled me so I sent her a message: 'I'll be coming straight home.' I wasn't sure how I would do this, but surely there would be a coach in Poole.

There was no reply to my suggestion from Mags, yet a response to all other messages, which suggested evasion. I became resentful; she clearly didn't want me to come straight back.

Perhaps I would just go to the beach hut and stay there for a week. I now knew I would be finishing this on my own. One walker Kristiina and I met on his final day of the Path spoke of being underwhelmed with the anti-climax. I knew that wasn't what I would feel, but I knew I would miss this. If not the worst of conditions, I would miss the place, the freedom and the people; I would miss the kindness of strangers.

Track Six. The Echo & the Bunnymen song *Nothing Lasts Forever*[173] tells us to live for today, that the adage 'all things come to those who wait' will leave you with nothing, so you should act. In the end, though, the song is completely consumed by regret and pain. Ian McCulloch repeats a foreboding of doom seven times for good measure like a curse at the song's fade-out. *Do everything as I say and it will all work out,* but it's all a lie. As commentary on self-deception, it is a darker musical equivalent of Frost's *The Road Not Taken* (1916)[174] – America's most loved and misread poem, a misunderstanding which might explain its popularity. The Echo song is an optimistically dark lullaby.

I could see the finish of the Path across the bay from where I sat. While I can't say I was in the hopeless space of the song, the thought of limping towards the finish line alone gave the ending a tinge of melancholy. The failure of my musical technology had made these songs part of my mental soundtrack; if you counted my cow sedative, *Misty,* it comprised a mix tape of seven.

I walked around Headfast Point and located the Path towards Studland through a tunnel of trees. You might recognise that moment when you catch sight of a face in a crowd or a context other than that with which you associate it; your mind cannot make sense of it, however familiar.

Between the trees was such a face. It smiled a holiday snapshot in monochrome, a birthday party, a message from the staff of a home for the elderly, a face at a funeral, someone on the other end of the phone listening to a proof of life response and giggling.

From behind it emerged another face, equally familiar and unfamiliar.

'How did you know where I was?'

'We called the Swanage hostel and spoke to Pete,' my sister Julie squealed, eyes wide in mock surprise.

'How did you know I was there?' My mind was racing, Wile E Coyote had just walked over the edge of a chalk cliff and was frozen in mid-air.

'Mags told us,' her partner Annette smiled. I struggled to think. They led me back like an elderly resident to where I had sat, by the white cliffs. I wasn't crying. It was still beautiful sunshine.

'Look at that view,' my sister squealed.

'The weather has been just like this for the last few months. Beautiful sunshine.'

'We've seen this somewhere.'

'Don't get too close to the edge, Julia. This was in the photo in our hotel room.' Annette always called her Julia, which made me feel guilty for calling her just plain Julie. But then, do you remember just plain Julie Christie? They had come all the way from Northumberland to meet me.

I had thought, at first, it was a miracle that they had found me but of course they had. There is only one Path; it was inevitable, only the timing was variable. It's only that everyone sees the Path differently. Some see cliffs and seabirds, saltwater and castles. Some see miles and signs, cafés and alternate routes (okay, maybe those people would have missed their sister). I didn't see these things. I saw wrecks, crashes, abandonment, refugees from the city, tragic writers, pandemics, monuments to the dead and a storm that was never, ever, going to finish until the end of the world. Well, it *was* off-season. Like a near-death experience, you see what you expect to see. There was little genuine risk that I could have inspired anyone with my version of the South West Coast Path.

'We couldn't have you finishing on your tod,' Julie said.

'Can we carry something for you, Oscar?' Annette asked. I knew she meant it. She would have carried my pack or tried to. I kept it where it was. It had broken me in.

We found a café still operating and talked about their conspiracy to intercept me. They had called the hostel at eight o'clock that morning, while I was still there, Pete advising them to head for Old Harry.

During a lull in the conversation I fixed on the darkening clouds outside the café windows. Throughout autumn I had pointlessly followed the coastline, time that could have been better spent looking for work. A couple leaned across our table and asked if we were starting or finishing. They were enthusiastic, and they momentarily shook me out of my melancholy. There would be time for work later.

Julie and Annette walked while I limped across the dunes to the final signpost: '630 Minehead' and 'Poole via Ferry.' To Minehead it was only 118 kilometres as the crow flies. The official end was a blue steel sculpture with images from the route: a lighthouse; a ship beside a pinnacle; Clavell Tower; St Michael's Mount; porpoises; and walkers by an engine house.

I had frequently imagined this moment as either shared with a crowd of old friends or completely alone. Instead, there were the three of us and this seemed about right. The ferry operator shouted to us that they were about to leave. He was poised to raise the ramp. 'Run, and you'll make it.' We had taken the requisite pictures - and so I hobbled to the boat behind my two companions.

Annette, thinking I was out of earshot, whispered to Julie, 'What's with the fancy plastic sword on his pack?'

On the top deck the wind blew in our faces as we looked back at South Haven Point. They asked in stereo, 'How do you feel?'

The ferryman closed the steel gate on the Path with a clang.

ADDENDUM

Pandemonium
Day 67 15th November

*He began to cough - a dangerous cough, it sounded
to Fairfax, of the sort he had heard in many a death
chamber. He fumbled for his handkerchief and
turned away from his audience until he had
recovered. 'Amen! How evil must have been their
world to bring down upon its towers and steeples such
a shattering punishment!'*[175]
Robert Harris, *The Second Sleep* (2019)

How do you feel? Alone now, the bus pulled into Victoria Coach Station and I slalomed my way around indecisive tourists and striding phone-hypnotised Londoners, towards Buckingham Palace Road. Mags was waiting. It felt like returning to her from a long visit to another country; in a sense, that was what it had been.

At the flat I opened my mail, one parcel being that book by Robert Harris, the image of the red hands cave painting on its endpapers. The fires still raged in the Blue Mountains and Fossil was sure that this was the worst of it. I hoped the sacred cave survived. I read Harris's book and was disturbed by what it described, but it was only fiction.

Months passed and I could still not feel the ground. Nerve damage, from spinal compression. I had lost two centimetres in height. St Mungo's, The Rolling Stones' *Gimme Shelter* and I turned fifty. The year 2019 had tied with 1969 as the fourth most active Atlantic hurricane season on record. Camborne weather station recorded 538mm of rain for September to November 2019, the highest since it began recording in 1978.

When I was stronger, Kim asked me to join her on the last section of another long-distance path.

She made a confession that day. 'I never told you at the time, but that week we met in Dawlish I had just come back from my father's funeral. The walking was part of getting over it.'

'I'm sorry, I didn't realise.' I recalled the conversations we'd had about how the Path represented so much death, and I realised what a clumsy oaf I had been.

'You couldn't have known. Remember what you said about the cows?' she asked. I must have looked bewildered, so she went on. 'That you sang to keep them calm. The song your mum liked.'

'Oh, yes.'

At my dad's funeral the song that was chosen for my father was Johnny Mathis singing *Misty*.'

I could have hugged her, but I didn't. It seemed so unlikely. Improbable. Yet, improbable events are perhaps too infrequent. There are all those many connections that are never made, that lie floating, unspoken in the space between us, because we are so absorbed in our own world when we should be talking to strangers. Just as our parents told us not to. Coincidence. It's not magic, but sometimes it feels like it.

While I was hunting for work in 2020, something happened; people had started to die. The cause was a novel coronavirus, an aggressive distant relative of the common cold, which had originated in China soon after I finished the walk. Contagion spread to Italy and Iran and soon most countries had reported cases. Work became increasingly unlikely. COVID-19, as it came to be known, arrived on our shores, and there was panic buying of baked beans and toilet rolls, and fear in the streets. We had been living in a make-believe world for so long, convinced that what has been always will be. We had taken a sleepwalk into disaster. The city lights started to go out. People were confined to their homes, and for Mags and I our little flat became a temporary cell. Briefly, the homeless were helped off the streets and housed in hotels and hostels at Her Majesty's pleasure.

Amid this calamity, my efforts around homelessness felt hopelessly insignificant. Mine had been a Quixotic adventure, tilting at engine houses, driven on by reading too many romances inspired by the landscape and people on the Path. I had been so determined not to be seen to fail and here I was jobless, physically trapped, and nothing had materially changed. Yet, despite all that, there was something about the walk that lingered – about what we value as essential in possessions and status, and who we are. What will imprison us? What will set us free? So much of what had gone before no longer mattered.

During this recovery period and as brief release from the flat, I took to sitting on a bench in Waterlow Park, adjacent to Highgate Cemetery. From there could be seen the enormous Goldhammer Sepulchre, a recent addition to the West Cemetery. It was constructed of buff Indiana limestone, the same stone used in the Empire State Building. In a city where countless are without homes, the dead get a house to rest in. The bench I sat on, a recent discovery, gave me some comfort. It was dedicated to Hugh Carless, Eric Newby's diplomatic and adventuring companion in *A Short Walk in the Hindu Kush*,[176] his Afghan journey. One day, while I was sitting there, my phone rang; it was David. Dissatisfied with his short contribution to the Coast Path with an invalid, he had completed another section of the Camino de Santiago to the point where I had begun it years before. I had meant to join him, but in my state I would have been a burden.

'I've been stuck in Santander – the town not the bank,' he clarified unnecessarily. 'All the flights are being cancelled.'

He sounded troubled. Society, I wanted to tell him, would come through the other side stronger and the planet might even have a rest from our industry. But instead, all I said was, 'Can you get back?'

'I've got a chance of one of the last flights tomorrow, but we have to talk.' There was a pause. 'Oscar, I think we need to convene the Club. And Oscar?'

'Yes, David?'

'You need to work out how to make Nutella® from scratch.'

When David stopped speaking there was a sound, barely perceptible but familiar. I couldn't be sure, because the line was poor, but I swore I could hear the sound of the sea.

Acknowledgments

Friends have asked me if this story was non-fiction. To paraphrase Douglas Adams' Marvin the paranoid android, life is bad enough without wanting to make up more of it.

Thanks to all those who rescued me and my friends: my wife, Mags Cahill; Tony Jones and Sue Farrow-Jones; Barbara Main; Paul Boddington and friend Pete; L; Laura Willis, Olivia Clifton and Daniel Petkoff. My father Bob, brother Barry and sisters Aileen, Julie, and partner (sister-outlaw) Annette, who religiously kept in touch throughout my journey, even though I may have given the impression they simply popped up at random.

Thanks to the 150 or more strangers, friends and colleagues who sponsored the journey and in so doing, assisted people who are without shelter in these increasingly difficult times.

Thank you of course to the good friends who joined me - David Dalgado, Kristiina Kangas and Simone Santabarbara. I include among these Kim and Andy Priddis, and Freya Cohen who walked with me for a while and distracted me from the pain with their great company. Thanks to Dan Sanger who helped me practice the walk over an icy weekend in Wales in early 2019 when his own sleeping bag exploded. They all made the greatest sacrifice by having to spend time with me, enduring moderately bad weather. Thankfully, they were spared the worst of both.

I am grateful to the RNLI lifeguards and National Coastwatch Institution watchkeepers who were very kind to me, shared their wisdom about the sea, and more than once saved me from hypothermia. And to the fascinating people along the way who helped me find shelter, a safe place to pitch or just took an interest in what I thought I was trying to do.

Thanks to writer, editor and friend Sarah Kilby for giving thoughtful and intelligent advice on the labyrinthine irrelevant meanderings in my writing.

Finally, to Paddy Dillon, an inspiration and great remote walking companion without whose detailed advice I would never have finished. Then again, he must take some of the blame as I probably wouldn't have started it either.

The Path ends in Poole, birthplace of John le Carré. I was saddened to hear of his death shortly after I completed the draft manuscript in 2020. He was my moral compass. Mags and I had stayed in the hotel in Torquay, filling the empty booking left by his Ed Shannon in that final novel.

About the writer

Oscar Burton was born in England in 1969 and educated in Australia, Scotland and the USA. He is a public health specialist who has worked for many UK and international agencies, most recently focused on epidemic control. For years he planned to walk the South West Coast Path, not in fragments – but to cover the whole distance at one time. He raised funds for the homelessness charity St Mungo's throughout the walk, believing homelessness and poverty were a shameful stain on a country with so much apparent wealth.

Endnotes

[1] Dillon, Paddy. *The South West Coast Path from Minehead to South Haven Point*. Milnthorpe: Cicerone. 2003. Short references and quotations throughout this book are from this edition.

[2] *MEM15551 - Second World War Halifax crash site in Yearnor Wood (Monument)*. Historic Environment Record for Exmoor National Park. [https://www.exmoorher.co.uk/Monument/MEM15551 retrieved 28th November 2019].

[3] Ada Lovelace had lived here in the previous century. Her description of an algorithm, to be used with Charles Babbage's Analytical Engine, is considered to be a forerunner to computer programmes.

[4] Definitions in *Oxford Languages*. Oxford University Press. [https://languages.oup.com/ retrieved 19th Feb 2021].

[5] Ondaatje, Michael. *The English Patient*. London: Bloomsbury. 1992, p189.

[6] Bellah, James Warner, Goldbeck, Willis. *The Man Who Shot Liberty Valance*. [Screenplay]. Los Angeles: Paramount.

[7] The phone also had a compass though I was not to discover this.

[8] Irving, Washington. 'The Legend of Sleepy Hollow' in *The Sketch Book of Geoffrey Crayon, Gent*. New York: C.S. Van Winkle. 1819.

[9] Lonsdale, John [Series Producer]. 'North Devon.' *Grand Designs*. Channel 4 and Fremantle Media. October 2019.

[10] Williamson, Henry. *Tarka the Otter: His joyful water life and death in the country of the two rivers*. London: GP Putnam's Sons. 1927.

[11] Coincidentally, Mike had also worked in the former East Yelland power station nearby the shelter I had met the friend of Gary Crewe.

[12] This is not imaginary. ONS data show that only 10 per cent of homeless and rough sleepers were black in 2003-04, half of the current proportion. Office of National Statistics: UK Census 2001 and Office of the Deputy Prime Minister: Statutory Homelessness Statistics: homeless households in priority need accepted by local authorities under the 1985 and 1996 Housing Acts (April 2003 – March 2004).

[13] There is no religious connection to a saint in the charity (the association was to discourage police harassment during food distributions), but the actual St Mungo was the patron saint of Glasgow, against bullies and of those accused of infidelity.

[14] Robert Harris. *The Second Sleep*. London: Hutchinson. 2019.

[15] Kipling, Rudyard. *Stalky & Co*. London: Macmillan. 1899.

[16] Kipling, Rudyard. *Rewards and Fairies*. London: Macmillan. 1910, p176.

[17] Fielding, Helen. *Bridget Jones: The Edge of Reason.* London: Picador. 2000. p308.

[18] Leslie Noble died aged 30; Ernest Blair was 28; Frederick Le Bon 26; Charles Daniel 26; and Hamar Russ was 21 years old.

[19] The cast included Lily James who had been in the film adaptation of *The Guernsey Literary and Potato Peel Pie Society* (2018), which had decided that Clovelly to Hartland Quay were more like Guernsey than Guernsey.

[20] The screenplay to the film *Shadowlands*, the life of C.S. Lewis.

[21] Duncan, Ronald. *How to Make Enemies.* London: Rupert Hart Davies. 1968, p15.

[22] Trussler, Anna Claire. *The Importance of Being: The Autobiographical Subject in the Drama and Memoirs of Ronald Duncan.* Thesis. University of Plymouth School of Humanities and Cultural Interpretation. 2001, p19.

[23] 'Wir werden nichts dagegen unternehmen, es wird sonst bloß Staub aufgewirbelt.' 'Ronald Duncan'. *Der Spiegel.* 29th April 1964.

[24] Baring-Gould S. *The Vicar of Morwenstow Being a Life of Robert Stephen Hawker, M.A.* New and Revised Edition. London: Methuen & Co. 1899, p241.

[25] Ibid.

[26] MacAskill E, Borger J, Hopkins N, Davies N and Ball J. 'GCHQ taps fibre-optic cables for secret access to world's communications'. *The Guardian.* Fri 21 Jun 2013.

[27] Government Communications Headquarters, the state intelligence and security agency.

[28] Giono, Jean. 1953. *The Man Who Planted Trees.* Translation: Peter Doyle. Online.

[29] Aeolian sound is generated by air moving across a solid cylindrical shape like a ship's rigging or wire fences. Trailing vortices are formed that oscillate, and these create the sound. Sound varies with the thickness of the object, but it is independent of the tension, the material and its length. As the wind increases in velocity the sound also increases in pitch; doubling the speed increases the sound by an octave as it builds to a shriek.

[30] Dyserth (Cornish). Very steep.

[31] Du Maurier, Daphne. *Not After Midnight: five long stories.* London: Gollancz. 1971.

[32] Cervantes Saavedra, Miguel de [translation Ormsby, John]. *The Ingenious Gentleman Don Quixote of La Mancha.* London: Smith, Elder & Co. 1885.

[33] Geoffrey of Monmouth. *History of the Kings of Britain.* Translated by Aaron Thompson. Revisions G.A.Giles. In parentheses Publications. Cambridge Ontario. 1999.

[34] He revealed to me that he worked occasionally with St Martin-in-the-Fields Church in London which supports the homeless.

[35] Dominey, Hilary. Sample Menu Padstow. Rick Stein's Restaurant. [Retrieved 17 March 2020].

[36] Maeterlinck, Maurice. *The Life of the Bee.* Translated from French by Sutro, Alfred. London: George Allen. 1901. p317-318.

[37] Harris, Robert and Jeremy Paxman, Jeremy. *A Higher Form of Killing: The Secret Story of Gas and Germ Warfare.* London: Chatto & Windus. 1982, p.179.

[38] Graham, Winston. *Marnie.* London: Hodder and Stoughton. 1961.

[39] Woolf, Virginia. *To the Lighthouse.* London: The Hogarth Press. 1927.

[40] Steel, Mark. 'The comic quirks of British towns - from curse stones to peacock plagues'. *The Daily Mirror.* 18 February 2018.

[41] Hepworth, Barbara. 'Approach to Sculpture'. *The Studio.* London. Vol 132, no.643, October 1946.

[42] Orwell, George. 'Politics and the English Language'. *Horizon: A review of literature and art.* 1946. Vol 13, issue 76, pp252-265.

[43] Cooke, William & Turner, Joseph Mallord William. *Picturesque Views on the Southern Coast of England.* London: John and Arthur Arch. 1826.

[44] The list is (spellings as shown): Minehead; Porlock; Linmouth; Comb Martin; Ilfracomb; Clovelly Bay; Boscastle; Tintagel Castle; Land's End; Logan Stone (rocking stone near Treen); St Michael's Mount; Pendennis Castle; Falmouth; St Mawes; East and West Looe; Edystone lighthouse; Plymouth, with Mount Batten; Mew Stone; Salcomb; Dartmouth ; Dartmouth Castle; Torbay, from Brixham; Teignmouth; Dawlish; Sidmouth; Lyme; Bridport (West Bay); Weymouth; Weymouth Castle; Portland, Bow and Arrow Castle (Rufus Castle); Lulworth Cove; Lulworth Cliffs; Lulworth Castle; Poole.

[45] Finn, Neil Mullane. *Don't Dream It's Over.* Roundhead Music/EMI Music Publishing, Limited. 1986.

[46] Thiaminase is an enzyme contained in many seafoods which reduces the function of thiamine, assuming your diet had any in, which in his case it didn't.

[47] Wallinger, Karl Edmond De Vere. *Ship of Fools.* Universal Music Publishing Group. 1987.

[48] The Mexican Ambassador to the United Kingdom and, I discovered later, lawyer affiliated with Institutional Revolutionary Party. The miners who went to Real del Monte left more than their picks. Apparently Real del Monte has its own version of the Cornish Pasty.

[49] Pearce, Cathryn Jean. *'So Barbarous a Practice': Cornish Wrecking, ca. 1700-1860, and its survival as popular myth.* Maritime History PhD Thesis March 2007.

[50] Alfred Hitchcock [Dir]. *Rebecca.* London. 1940.

[51] Spielberg, Steven [Dir]. *Jaws.* LA 1975.

[52] Ibid.

[53] It came from a buoy that marks the Runnel Stone, which has claimed many ships. The daymarks were referenced in an early Hammond Innes thriller as 'the cones of Runnel', a clue which the protagonist solves by consulting the Ordnance Survey map makers. Innes, Hammond. *The Trojan Horse.* London: Fontana. 1940.

[54] Spielberg, Steven [Dir]. *Jaws.* LA 1975. Screenplay by Carl Gottlieb and Peter Benchley.

[55] Le Carré, John. *The Honourable Schoolboy.* London: Hodder and Stoughton, 1977, p74.

[56] Cornish. Tre-, a place or tribe. Gwithyas (also gwithyor), a guardian, from gwithya, to keep. It is the name given to a burial chamber, *Hirvedh Treguhyon* or passage grave of Tregiffian.

[57] Le Carré, John. *Tinker Tailor Soldier Spy.* London: Hodder and Stoughton, 1974.

[58] Le Carré, John. *The Spy Who Came in From the Cold.* Gollancz. 1963.

[59] Tangye, Derek. *The Way to Minack.* London: Michael Joseph. 1968.

[60] Ibid.

[61] Nicol, Jean *Meet Me at the Savoy.* London: Hamish Hamilton, London. 1952.

[62] Tangye, Derek. Op cit.

[63] Trevelyan, Raleigh. 'Obituary: Derek Tangye'. *The Independent.* Wednesday 6 November 1996 01:02

[64] Ibid.

[65] Sisman, Adam. John Le Carré. London: Bloomsbury. 2015, Pp325-6.

[66] 'A fatal fall.' *The Times.* 20th March 1873. A detailed investigation by Elizabeth Dale in *The Cornish Bird* is found at 'The celtic cross at Lamorna Cove': [https://cornishbirdblog.com/2018/09/23/the-celtic-cross-at-lamorna-cove/ retrieved 10th March 2020].

[67] 'Fishery Riots in Cornwall'. Commons Sitting Questions. Question from Mr Harry Foster, Lowestoft. *Hansard 1803–2005.* vol 41 cc1557-9. HC Deb 22 June 1896.

[68] 'The Cornish Fishermen.' *Sunderland Echo.* Wednesday May 20, 1896.

[69] Curiously, though, the line I made heads south-east, passing directly through Axum, legendary home of the Ark of Covenant - if you believe Graham Hancock's version of history.

[70] Gerardus Mercator was born in 1569, whereas St Michael's Mount had associations with Mont St Michel as early as the 11th century.

[71] Operation Chastise was a British morale booster. It cost many lives in civilians and those drowned in a forced labour camp, with short-term inconvenience to Germany.

[72] Tennyson, Alfred Lord. *Idylls of the Kings.* London: Edward Moxon & Co. 1859.

[73] Talmud: Bavli Sanhedrin 44[a]. Did not Rabbi Johanan say 'One may not greet his fellow at night for fear that he may be a demon'?

[74] Atwood, Margaret. *The Tent.* Toronto: McClelland & Stewart. 2006.

[75] Atwood, Margaret. 2006. Op cit., p142.

[76] Jung, C. Synchronicity: An acausal connecting principle. London: Routledge & Kegan Paul 1972.

[77] Waters, George Roger. *Eclipse.* From the album Dark Side of the Moon. ©BMG Rights Management 1973.

[78] In Memoriam. *The Art Newspaper.* 30th April 2017.

[79] Leogue, Joe. 'Gardaí confirm probe into death of homeless man in Cork is now a murder inquiry'. *Irish Examiner.* Sunday, October 13, 2019.

[80] Riegel, Ralph. 'Gardai arrest woman as part of five month probe into death of homeless chef Timmy Hourihane.' *Independent.ie.* February 5th 2020.

[81] Roads or a roadstead, is a body of water in which boats can shelter from ocean swell and rip tides, and lie safely at anchor without dragging.

[82] News. South West Coast Path Association. Nov 28th, 2013. [https://www.southwestcoastpath.org.uk/newsapp/article/118/ retrieved 15th December 2019].

[83] Du Maurier, Daphne. *The House on the Strand.* London: Virago. 2003. P145.

[84] Simmons, Jack. 'Obituary: A. L. Rowse'. *The Independent.* Monday 6 October 1997.

[85] Smith, Anthony. 'Review of Ollard, Richard [Ed]. The Diaries of AL Rowse. Allen Lane The Penguin Press.' *The Guardian.* Sunday 13 Apr 2003.

[86] Ibid.

[87] Slattery-Christy, David. *Other People's Fu**ing. The Story of A.L.Rowse and Adam von Trott.* A play in two acts. 2017.

[88] Austin, Richard. *Invisible Sleeper.* Sculpture for St Petroc's Society. 2015.

[89] Trumbull, Douglas Huntley. *Silent Running.* LA: Universal. 1972.

[90] Du Maurier, Daphne. *The House on the Strand.* London: Gollancz. 1969.

[91] Ibid.

[92] Du Maurier, Daphne. *Rule Britannia.* London: Victor Gollancz. 1972.

[93] Forster, Margaret, Daphne du Maurier. London: Chatto & Windus. 1993. p178.

[94] Du Maurier, Daphne. *Rebecca.* London: Gollancz. 1938.

[95] Johns, JR (Ed). *The wreck of the Albermarle.* Based on research by James Derriman. Polperro Heritage Museum.

[96] Mörttinen, Valtteri. 'Antti Mikkola takes Stephen King's torment from the Tampere Theater to get what he gets - and a little more.' *kulttuuritoimitus.fi.* 4th October 2019. [Retrieved 23rd May, 2020].

[97] Myöhänen, Ulriikka. 'Horror on stage: Kuopio City Theater will see Stephen King's "Torment" in the autumn' *YLE.fi.* 9th January 2019. [Retrieved 23rd May 2020].

[98] Christie, Agatha. *And Then There Were None.* New York: Dodd Mead and Company. 1940.

[99] Christie, Agatha. Evil Under the Sun. London: The Crime Club. 1941.

[100] Darwin, Charles. *On the Origin of Species by Means of Natural Selection.* London: John Murray. 1859.

[101] Doyle used the name Cullingworth, which he had also used in his earlier fictional account: Doyle, Arthur Conan. *The Stark Munro Letters Being series of twelve letters written by J. Stark Munro, M.B., to his friend and former fellow-student, Herbert Swanborough, of Lowell, Massachusetts, during the years 1881-1884.* London: Longmans, Green & Co. 1895.

[102] Ibid.

[103] Ibid.

[104] Ibid.

[105] Ibid.

[106] Ibid.

[107] If you ignore the role played by Alfred Russel Wallace and those who preceded him. The theory itself evolved.

[108] Ecclesiastes 3:19-21, King James Bible.

[109] Edwardes, Charlotte. 'Lawrence of Arabia wrote letter considering suicide.' *The Telegraph.* 18 Nov 2001.

[110] National Gallery of Ireland catalogue entry *A Ship against the Mewstone, at the Entrance to Plymouth Sound.* [https://www.nationalgallery.ie/art-and-artists/highlights-collection/ship-against-mewstone-entrance-plymouth-sound-jmw-turner-1775 retrieved 2nd May 2020].

[111] Cooke, William & Turner, Joseph Mallord William. 1826. Op. cit. A charnel ground is a place, above ground, for the decay of human remains.

[112] Lennon, John. *Across the Universe.* Liverpool: Northern songs. 1968.

[113] Sheff, David. *All We Are Saying: The Last Major Interview with John Lennon and Yoko Ono.* New York: St Martins Griffin. 2000. p191. [originally published in *Playboy*, 1981].

[114] Morris, Jonathan. 'Salcombe lifeboat disaster: How sand bar claimed 13 lives in 1916'. *BBC News Online.* 26 October 2016 [https://www.bbc.co.uk/news/uk-england-devon-37707203 retrieved 30th October 2020]

[115] Keith Richards Recalls Making the Rolling Stones' 'Gimme Shelter' Jeff Giles. *Ultimate Classic Rock.* October 27, 2017.

[116] The Rolling Stones. *Let it Bleed.* London: Decca. 1969.

[117] Jackson, Mick. *Five Boys.* London: Faber and Faber. 2003. The novel covers the experience of a group of children during the period of Operation Tiger, their education in the ways of bees and an encounter with

a deserter hiding in the woods. Jackson captures the mood of a rural England temporarily changed by military occupation, farmers giving up land and later having it returned to them. Jackson also used the pseudonym Kirkham Jackson under which he wrote the screenplay to Roman Road (2004), a television film about two friends who walk the Roman road from Chichester to London.

[118] Jones, Claire. The D-Day rehearsal that cost 800 lives. *BBC News Devon online.* 30 May 2014. [https://www.bbc.co.uk/news/uk-england-devon-27185893 retrieved 6th March 2020].

[119] Exercise Tiger: Bootprints mark D-Day disaster 75th anniversary. BBC News. 28 April 2019. [https://www.bbc.co.uk/news/uk-england-devon-48082397 retrieved 26th September 2020].

[120] Townsend, Mark. 'Did Allies kill GIs in D-Day training horror?' *The Observer.* Sunday 16 May 2004.

[121] National Public Radio. *Operation Tiger: D-Day's Disastrous Rehearsal. NPR* April 28, 2012. [https://www.npr.org/2012/04/28/151590212/operation-tiger-d-days-disastrous-rehearsal?t=1601075968579 retrieved 26th September 2020]. Paul Gerolstein was Gunners Mate 2nd Class in the US Navy.

[122] According to Professor Nick Haslam of Melbourne this revulsion extends to psychology with defaecation, aptly, scattered in obscure corners of the literature. Haslam, Nick. 'Toilet Psychology'. *The Psychologist.* Vol.25 pp.430-433. June 2012.

[123] 'English freedom restored by Orange'.

[124] Christie, Agatha. *The A.B.C. Murders.* London & Glasgow: Collins Crime Club. 1936.

[125] Le Carré, John. *Agent Running in the Field.* London: Viking 2019.

[126] Christie, Agatha. *Peril at End House.* New York: Dodd, Mead and Co. 1932.

[127] Christie, Agatha. *The Body in the Library.* New York: Dodd, Mead and Co. 1942.

[128] Christie, Agatha. *Sleeping Murder: Miss Marple's Last Case.* London: Collins Crime Club. 1976. [written in 1940 during the Blitz and published posthumously]

[129] Christie, Agatha. *Five Little Pigs.* New York: Dodd, Mead and Company. 1942.

[130] The original version had been written in 2014 by Christie to help raise funds for the Churston Ferrers church, though it was never published until adapted as *Dead Man's Folly.* It was later published as Christie, Agatha. *Hercule Poirot and the Greenshore Folly.* London: HarperCollins. 2014.

[131] Christie, Agatha. *Ordeal by Innocence.* London: Collins Crime Club. 1958.

[132] Naturally, pronounced like Letitia rather than lettuce.

[133] Ibid.

[134] Op.cit, p47.

[135] Sears, Neil. 'Peer used house he didn't own to pocket £200,000 expenses.' *Daily Mail.* 6th November, 2009. [online, retrieved 13 March 2020].

[136] Ibid.

[137] Keats, John. *Letter to Benjamin Bailey.* Teignmouth, Friday March 13th, 1818. Two years later Keats received medical advice to leave the dampness of England. He died in 1821 in Rome, from tuberculosis.

[138] Le Carré, John. *A Perfect Spy.* London: Hodder and Stoughton. 1986.

[139] Ibid.

[140] The Romans, appreciating its consistency compared to stone, were using concrete in bridges and domes, much of which still survive. 'Mass concrete does not employ the metal rods of reinforced or prestressed concrete and, when used for bridges, relies on radial compression, the weight being distributed outwards to the piers and abutments.' There were two other solely concrete bridges but now destroyed. Historic England. *Axmouth Bridge.* 19th December 1977. [https://historicengland.org.uk/listing/the-list/list-entry/1020419 retrieved 29th May 2020]

[141] Reisz, Karel [Director]. *The French Lieutenant's Woman.* London: United Artists.

[142] Near Glenbrook in the Blue Mountains, it is one of the best early examples of indigenous Australian art, a sacred place.

[143] 'I have seen similar designs in a book describing primitive peoples who dwelt in caves – ten thousand years before the ancients.' – Robert Harris. *The Second Sleep.* London: Hutchinson. 2019. Possibly Cuevas de las manos, Argentina.

[144] Fowles, John. *The Collector.* London: Jonathan Cape. 1963.

[145] Nobbs, David. *The Death of Reginald Perrin.* London: Victor Gollancz. 1975.

[146] Nye, Simon and Nobbs, David. *The Fall and Rise of Reginald Perrin* [adapted screenplay]. BBC 1976. It was a comedy but it also exposed discontent with the futility of much of modern life.

[147] His middle name was because his mother missed appearing in a local performance of the Gilbert and Sullivan opera of the fairy queen *Iolanthe*, when she was pregnant with him.

[148] By coincidence, it was claimed by some Catholics and MPs that the Hokey Cokey song itself was a parody of the Latin mass (*hoc est enim corpus meum*). But, it seems this was made up too. It was written by Jewish band leader Al Tabor in 1940 as a catchy dance tune and it mimicked the cry of ice cream vendors of the day. Kasriel, Alex. 'Do the Hokey Cokey? So that's what it's all about.' *The Jewish Chronical.* January 29, 2009.

[149] Creighton, Charles. A *History of Epidemics in Britain.* Cambridge: At the University Press. 1891. p116.

[150] Creighton, Charles. 1891. Op.cit. p116-7.
[151] Creighton, Charles. 1891. Op.cit. p140.
[152] Creighton, Charles. 1891. Op.cit. p121-2.
[153] As summarized in the *Imperial Encyclopædia of Peking*, 1726.
[154] Creighton, Charles. 1891. Op.cit. p150-3.
[155] Worobey, Michael; Cox, Jim; Gill, Douglas. 'The origins of the great pandemic.' *Evolution, Medicine, and Public Health*. Vol 2019 Iss 1. 2019, Pp18-25.
[156] Creighton, Charles. 1891. Op.cit. p193.
[157] Hardy, Thomas. *The Well-Beloved*. London: Osgood, McIlvaine and Co. 1897.
[158] Hugo, Victor. *L'Homme qui rit*. Paris: A. Lacroix, Verboeckhoven & Ce. 1869.
[159] Epstein, Julius J; Epstein, Philip G; Koch, Howard [Screenplay]. *Casablanca*. Los Angeles: Warner Bros 1ˢᵗ International. 1942.
[160] Hugo, Victor. 1869. Op.cit.
[161] Domesday Dorset Folio 16, 17, 19.
[162] Ringstead Bay. Why visit here? *eOceanic.com*. [https://eoceanic.com/sailing/harbours/490/ retrieved 18th February 2021].
[163] *Beresford's Lost Villages*. University of Hull [https://dmv.hull.ac.uk/dmvDetail.cfm?dbkey=5414&county=true retrieved 18th March 2020].
[164] Creighton, Charles. 1891. Op.cit. p174.
[165] Hardy, Thomas. 1874. *Far From the Madding Crowd*. London: Smith Elder. Chapter 47.
[166] *Michael Rosen is awarded the Fred & Anne Jarvis Award at NUT conference - press release*. National Union of Teachers News Centre 2010.
[167] Illich, Ivan. *Deschooling Society*. London: Calder. 1971.
[168] Waters, Roger and Gilmour, David Jon. *Wish You Were Here*. 1975. Rogers Waters Music Overseas Ltd and Pink Floyd Music Publishers Ltd. Warner/Chappell Artemic Ltd, London W6 8BS and Pink Floyd Music Publishers Ltd, London W1F 8GS.
[169] James, Montague Rhodes. *Wailing Well*. Stanford Dingley, The Mill House Press. 1928.
[170] Hardy, Thomas. 1891. *A Group of Noble Dames*. Chapter 9. London: Osgood.
[171] Lowsonford in Warwickshire, Lundy in the Bristol Channel, Saddell Bay in Scotland, the Martello Tower in Aldeburgh, Suffolk, and Clavell Tower here in Kimmeridge Bay, Dorset.
[172] BBC. 'Sir Antony Gormley sculpture downed by storms for second time.' *BBC News*. 28 December 2015. [https://www.bbc.co.uk/news/uk-england-dorset-35189458 retrieved 18th September 2020].

[173] Pattinson, Leslie and McCulloch, Ian. *Nothing Lasts Forever.* 1997. BMG Rights Management, Kobalt Music Publishing Ltd, Warner Chappell Music, Inc.

[174] Frost, Robert. *Mountain Interval.* New York: Henry Holt & Co. 1916.

[175] Harris, Robert. 2019. Op.cit., p156.

[176] Newby, Eric. *A Short Walk in the Hindu Kush.* London: Secker and Warburg. 1958. Coincidentally, Newby had been born exactly 50 years before the author.